CENSORSHIP IN AMERICA

A Reference Handbook

Other Titles in ABC-CLIO's
**CONTEMPORARY
WORLD ISSUES**
Series

Abortion, Second Edition, Marie Costa
Affirmative Action, Lynne Eisaguirre
AIDS Crisis in America, Second Edition, Eric K. Lerner and Mary Ellen Hombs
Cults in America, James R. Lewis
Feminism, Judith Harlan
Genetic Engineering, Harry LeVine III
Hate Crimes, Donald Altschiller
Human Rights, Second Edition, Nina Redman and Lucille Whalen
Intellectual Freedom, John B. Harer
Prisons in America, Nicole Hahn Rafter and Debra L. Stanley
Religion in the Schools, James John Jurinski
The Religious Right, Glenn H. Utter and John W. Storey
Violence and the Media, David E. Newton

Books in the Contemporary World Issues series address vital issues in today's society such as terrorism, sexual harassment, homelessness, AIDS, gambling, animal rights, and air pollution. Written by professional writers, scholars, and nonacademic experts, these books are authoritative, clearly written, up-to-date, and objective. They provide a good starting point for research by high school and college students, scholars, and general readers, as well as by legislators, businesspeople, activists, and others.

Each book, carefully organized and easy to use, contains an overview of the subject; a detailed chronology; biographical sketches; facts and data and/or documents and other primary-source material; a directory of organizations and agencies; annotated lists of print and nonprint resources; a glossary; and an index.

Readers of books in the Contemporary World Issues series will find the information they need in order to better understand the social, political, environmental, and economic issues facing the world today.

CENSORSHIP IN AMERICA

A Reference Handbook

Mary E. Hull

CONTEMPORARY WORLD ISSUES

Santa Barbara, California
Denver, Colorado
Oxford, England

Copyright © 1999 by Mary E. Hull

All rights reserved. No part of this publication may be reproduced, stored in a retrieval system, or transmitted, in any form or by any means, electronic, mechanical, photocopying, recording, or otherwise, except for the inclusion of brief quotations in a review, without prior permission in writing from the publishers.

Library of Congress Cataloging-in-Publication Data

Hull, Mary.
    Censorship in America : a reference handbook / Mary E. Hull.
      p. cm.—(Contemporary world issues)
    Includes bibliographical references and index.
    ISBN 1-57607-057-3 (alk. paper)
    1. Censorship—United States I. Title. II. Series.
Z658.U5H84   1999
363.3'1—dc21   99-26819
                                                                                       CIP

05 04 03 02 01 00 99   10 9 8 7 6 5 4 3 2 1

ABC-CLIO, Inc.
130 Cremona Drive, P.O. Box 1911
Santa Barbara, California 93116–1911

This book is printed on acid-free paper ∞.

Manufactured in the United States of America

Contents

Preface, xi

1 Introduction, 1
  Censorship in America, 2
  Censorship in Public
    Education, 4
      Why Are Books and Other
        Printed Materials
        Challenged? 6
      Textbook Controversies, 10
      Who Is Accused of Censorship?
        12
      Hate Speech, 15
  Censorship in the Arts, 17
      The Music Lyrics Controversy,
        17
      Censorship and Rap Music, 18
      Artistic Freedom, 20
      Should Publicly Funded Art Be
        Censored? 24
  Censorship in the News
    Media, 27
  Censorship and the
    Internet, 30
      Reno v. ACLU: Challenging the
        Communications Decency
        Act of 1996, 32

A V-Chip for the Net? 33
To Block or Not to Block: Libraries Confront Internet Access, 35
Encryption: Should the Government Have a Set of Keys? 37
Conclusion, 38
Notes, 39

2 Chronology, 43

3 Biographical Sketches, 57

4 Facts and Statistics, 77
Supreme Court Decisions, 78
Abrams v. United States, 250 U.S. 616 (1919), 78
Hannegan v. Esquire, 327 U.S. 146 (1946), 79
Joseph Burstyn, Inc. v. Wilson, 343 U.S. 495 (1952), 81
Butler v. Michigan, 352 U.S. 380 (1957), 81
Roth v. United States, 354 U.S. 476 (1957), 82
Engel v. Vitale, 370 U.S. 421 (1962), 84
Jacobellis v. Ohio, 378 U.S. 184 (1964), 86
Griswold v. Connecticut, 381 U.S. 479 (1965), 87
Epperson v. Arkansas, 393 U.S. 97 (1968), 88
Tinker v. Des Moines School District, 393 U.S. 503 (1969), 89
New York Times v. United States, 403 U.S. 713 (1971), 90
Miller v. California, 413 U.S. 15 (1973), 91
FCC v. Pacifica Foundation, 438 U.S. 726 (1978), 92
Smith v. Collin, 439 U.S. 916 (1978), 94
Board of Education v. Pico, 457 U.S. 853 (1982), 95
New York v. Ferber, 458 U.S. 747 (1982), 97
Wallace v. Jaffree, 466 U.S. 924 (1984), 98
Hazelwood School District v. Kuhlmeier, 484 U.S. 260 (1988), 99
United States v. Eichman, et al., 496 U.S. 310 (1990), 100
Wisconsin v. Mitchell, 508 U.S. 476 (1993), 101
Reno, Attorney General of the United States, et al., v. American Civil Liberties Union, et al. (appeal, 1997), 103
Graphs and Tables, 104

Documents, 112
　American Library Association's *Library Bill of Rights*, 112
　American Library Association's *Diversity in Collection Development*, 113
　Family Friendly Library's *Charter for a Family Friendly Library System*, 114
　American Library Association's *Freedom to Read*, 118
　American Civil Liberties Union's *Briefing Paper Number 14*, 123
　The Motion Picture Production Code of 1930, 129
　The Communications Decency Act of 1996, 140
　Electronic Privacy Information Center's *Faulty Filters: How Content Filters Block Access to Kid-Friendly Information on the Internet*, 149
　Excerpt from the Freedom of Information Act, 158

Selected Quotations, 166
　Censorship and Humanity, 166
　Censorship and Literature, 168
　The Public Funding of Art, 168
　Censorship and the Internet, 169
　Censorship and the Library, 169

5 Directory of Organizations, 171

6 Selected Print Resources, 189

Books, 189
　General Books on Censorship and Free Expression, 189
　Censorship in Art, 193
　Censorship in Cyberspace, 194
　Censorship in Film, 195
　Censorship in Literature, 197
　Censorship in Public Schools and Libraries, 198
　Censorship in the News Media, 200
　Books on Censorship for Young Adults, 201
　Books on Protecting Children from Violent or Explicit Media, 203
　Books on Obscenity and Pornography, 204
Periodicals, 205

7 Selected Nonprint Resources, 207
 Electronic Journals, Magazines, and
   Newsletters, 207
 Web Sites with Links to Censorship Topics, 209
 Electronic Texts, 212
 Videotapes, 213
  Videos for Purchase, 213
  Videos Available in Public Libraries, 218

Glossary, 221

Index, 225

About the Author, 235

Preface

This book provides a starting point for research on censorship and related issues of freedom of expression, obscenity, pornography, standards of decency, and liberty and democracy in the United States. Whether readers are students, concerned citizens, activists, teachers, or legislators interested in learning more about censorship, this book offers objective information on censorship's vital issues as well as an introduction to the many publications, organizations, and resources that are available for further research.

Chapter 1 is an introduction to the subject of censorship in the United States. It takes a brief look at the history of censorship in America, then explores current issues including the censorship of textbooks and other educational materials, children's literature, adult literature, music, art, theater, film, television, the news media, and the Internet. The rationale behind the censorship of materials or ideas is discussed, along with the ways in which Americans have tried to combat censorship.

Chapter 2 is a chronology of important events in the history of censorship. The chronology is designed to familiarize readers with the ways in which censorship has been used by different people at different times. It also explores the motivations and methods of those who have opposed censorship. Chapter 3 discusses key individuals who have made significant contributions to the public debate on censorship. Chapter 4 provides data on censorship in the United States. Supreme Court decisions, graphs, tables, and interesting quotations are included for the reader's reference. Chapter 5 is a directory of organizations and associations that can provide the reader with information helpful for developing a greater understanding of the issue of censorship. Chapters 6 and 7 include annotated bibliographical references for print and nonprint resources covering the topics addressed in this book, including censorship in schools and libraries, the censorship of various media, intellectual freedom, violence in the media, the proliferation of online pornography, and the issues of democracy and liberty in news media. Finally, the glossary at the back of the book contains helpful definitions for some of the terms used in this book, and the index guides the reader to specific pages on which to find topics of interest.

Mary E. Hull

Introduction

The dictionary defines *censorship* as the practice of supervising conduct or morals and a *censor* as someone who examines materials and prohibits what he or she considers morally, politically, or aesthetically objectionable. There is considerable disagreement, however, over what behavior actually constitutes censorship. Sometimes the term is used solely in reference to actions taken by a government or other official agency, and other times it is used to describe the actions of citizens or other nonofficial parties. Differing interpretations of censorship make it difficult to agree on when censorship has taken place. When parents object to the presence of a particular book in a school library or question the appropriateness of a textbook, are they acting as censors, or merely participating in their child's education? Does anything less than the removal of a book constitute censorship? Although parental and community concerns may, for example, indirectly influence the selection of books or movies used in classrooms, censorship is generally not considered to have taken place until a governing body, such as a school or library board, makes an official action to restrict access to information. Clouding this issue is the fact that not all organizations that compile databases on censorship distinguish between *official acts of censorship* and grassroots attacks from parents or local communities on books, curriculums, or other materials. Some anticensorship organizations consider widespread attacks on particular books or authors to be a form of censorship tantamount to the removal of books.

Though there is disagreement over the definition of censorship, it is understood that by prohibiting certain materials, a censor imposes a moral code of his or her own design. Censorship takes many forms: any kind of expression can be censored, from speech to art and literature, film, and electronic communication. Censors usually act out of a concern for protecting others from harmful material; they fear what will happen to an individual or to a society if people are exposed to too much violent, profane, or pornographic material. They may be especially concerned about protecting children from exposure to age-inappropriate material. Censors attempt to protect society by removing the objectionable material. Censors subscribe to a certain moral standard they wish to uphold; on these grounds, they oppose the circulation of any material that does not meet their standard of decency. In this way, censorship opens up a Pandora's box that brings all books, movies, and other works of art under scrutiny. What is indecent in one person's mind may be decent in another's; thus, regardless of the censor's motive, the result of censoring is the denial of another's freedom to choose.

Censorship is a practice dating back thousands of years. Governments and rulers censored writings they feared might cause people to rise up against the status quo. The writings of Confucius, the ancient Chinese philosopher, were censored after the installation of a new emperor who considered his ideas dangerous. Socrates, pressured by the Greek government to censor his teachings, committed suicide. For much of its history, the Catholic Church banned all literature it considered hostile to Catholicism. In fifteenth-century England, when printing presses made it possible to distribute pamphlets and tracts to the common people, monarchs in Great Britain passed licensing acts designed to silence unorthodox writers and thinkers.

Censorship in America

The United States has wrestled with issues of censorship since its beginnings. In one of the earliest cases of censorship of the press in colonial America, *New York Weekly Journal* publisher John Peter Zenger was accused of sedition for printing satirical commentaries on New York's colonial governor in 1734. Zenger was imprisoned, but a jury later acquitted him. The First Amendment, which protects the freedoms of speech, religion, and the press as well as the rights to assembly and to petition the government, was added to the Constitution in 1791. Yet, seven years later, in 1798, Congress passed the Sedition Act, which prohibited people from criticizing the government. The Sedition Act was designed by Federalists to suppress opposing political parties. The act clearly violated the First Amendment, and though it was later repealed, it illustrates a trend in U.S. history.

There has always been a tension between freedom of expression and the desire to protect society or promote a cause. Despite an emphasis on freedom and individualism within the United States, censors have continually tried—with some measure of success—to prohibit types of behavior and speech. During World War I, for example, the Wilson administration passed the Sedition and Espionage Acts. These acts banned "treasonous" material from the mail and made it illegal for anyone to speak against the U.S. government, flag, or military uniform. Two thousand people, primarily war protesters, were prosecuted under these acts. In 1919, however, the Sedition Act was overturned by the courts.

Like speech, obscenity has also been the target of censorship in the United States. Books containing sexual references, whether works of literature like James Joyce's *Ulysses* or manuals on reproduction, were banned under an 1873 federal anti-obscenity law. Birth-control advocate Margaret Sanger, who had sent articles on contraception through the mail, was forced to flee the country in 1914 after being indicted under this law. Sexually explicit books have long created controversy in the United States. In the 1960s, some of the most censored titles included *Lady Chatterley's Lover, Tropic of Cancer,* and *Lolita*—all of which contain sexually explicit material. In the 1980s, the most frequent objections to books and other printed materials were based on the claim that their content was sexually explicit, profane, or obscene.

With the passage of time, anti-obscenity laws in the United States evolved to the point where books like *Ulysses* could no longer be deemed obscene based on a few passages; instead, to be ruled obscene, a book had to be proven to have absolutely no redeeming artistic or literary merit. Obscenity is not protected by the First Amendment, but the courts have struggled to define obscenity and to distinguish it from constitutionally protected forms of speech. In 1996 obscenity law was given a boost when

Congress adopted the Communications Decency Act (CDA), which outlawed the distribution of pornography on the Internet. One year later, however, the Supreme Court declared the CDA unconstitutional. Though attempts at censorship occur frequently in U.S. history, they tend to be reversed with comparable frequency.

Censorship in Public Education

The issue of censorship is debated in many arenas, but few of them have been more controversial than the nation's public school system. Children have long been taught the basics of reading, spelling, math, and composition, but in colonial times and after, moral and religious teachings were an integral part of the curriculum. The first thing many children learned to read was Bible verses. However, as the country expanded and its population became more diverse, the question of what to teach children became harder to answer. As early as 1830, Catholic immigrants, who came in great numbers to the United States from Ireland and Italy, objected to the inclusion of mandatory Protestant prayers in many public schools. Historically, the debate on what to teach in schools has focused on the inclusion or exclusion of religion and science in the curriculum. In 1791, Congress adopted the First Amendment, which stipulated that "Congress shall make no law respecting an establishment of religion." This separation of church and state was intended to promote religious liberty by preventing any one religion from receiving official sanction from the state to the detriment of other religions. It also ensured that support for religion would be voluntary, not forced. The framers of the Constitution were religious men; they did not intend hostility toward religion, rather they believed that the best way to protect religion was to protect it from governmental interference. However, since its adoption, the separation of church and state clause in the Bill of Rights has been tested many times in the nation's courts by those seeking to defend their faith or impose their religion on others.

The landmark Scopes "monkey" trial of 1925, in which a high school biology teacher was put on trial for teaching evolution theory, ushered in an era of controversy in public education. Lawyers Clarence Darrow and William Jennings Bryan eloquently debated the extent to which religion and science should be taught in school. But the debate did not stop with them. Despite the mandated separation of church and state, the fight to teach creationism in public schools continued. Creationists have attempted to enact "equal-time" laws, which would give creationist thinking the same teaching time as evolution theory, in twenty-one states. In 1981 Arkansas passed an equal-time law—creating so much controversy the subsequent lawsuit came to be known as "Scopes II"—but one year later, the law was overturned. Now, with the growth of public education, the specialization of the school curriculum, and the subsequent boom in textbook publishing, ever increasing emphasis has been placed on what information children are taught and the way in which it is presented.

What should be taught to school children? Which material is right for each age group? Who should decide what is appropriate? In the 1995–1996 school year, there were 475 attempts to remove or restrict educational materials and school programs in the United States. This figure, which represents a record high, comes from People for the American Way (PAW), an organization that keeps an annual record of challenges to public education. There were more censorship incidents in 1995–1996 than in any other year in the 14-year history of the PAW study. This phenomenon is especially significant according to the American Library Association (ALA), which estimates that for every reported instance of censorship, four or five cases go unreported.

However, there is disagreement over what constitutes censorship. Conservative groups like Focus on the Family disagree with the figures quoted by the PAW study. They maintain that what are often counted as censorship incidents are actually instances of parental interaction and involvement in their children's education. For example, Focus on the Family maintains that when parents object to a book being placed in a school library, they risk being labeled censors, even if the book in question is never removed. Focus on the Family fears that the PAW studies are counting parental objections or challenges as incidents of censorship. The American Library Association, however, defines a challenge as "an attempt to remove or restrict materials based upon the objections of a person or group."[1] According to the ALA, a person simply expressing a point of view does not constitute a challenge. A challenge only takes place when an objector attempts to prevent someone else from having access to the material in question, usually by removing the material from the school curriculum or library. A parent may object to a specific book and ask that their child receive an alternate assignment. However, when a parent objects to a book and attempts to remove that book from the school, denying all other children access to the work, censorship is taking place, the ALA argues. Thus there is disagreement over what is being reported as censorship and whether statistics regarding censorship are truly accurate.

According to People for the American Way, challenges to public education in 1995–1996 occurred in 44 states and the District of Columbia. California, Pennsylvania, and Florida led the nation with the highest number of challenges. Of the 475 incidents of censorship documented by PAW in 1995 and 1996, 300 of the incidents were attempts to remove specific books from the school curriculum or library. For example, Maya Angelou's *I Know Why the Caged Bird Sings* was challenged by eight different school systems during 1995–1996 by complainants who felt the book was pornographic and sexually explicit. The remaining 175 incidents of censorship in 1995–1996 were broader challenges to the public school system itself, such as the questioning of specific books and materials, attempts to institute religious education in schools, and efforts to incorporate the teaching of creationism in biology classes. Although classroom and library books, school films and plays, field trips, student newspapers, school counseling, and health and sex education programs continue to be challenged in American schools each year, the success of such challenges seems to be decreasing. In the 1980s, 52 percent of censorship challenges were, on average, successful.[2] By the 1995–1996 school year, however, only 41 percent of challenges were successful in censoring the material in question.[3]

Why Are Books and Other Printed Materials Challenged?

Typically, materials are challenged because adults want to protect young people, and sometimes other adults, from exposure to what they believe are sexually explicit, violent, harmful, or troubling ideas or information. For example, groups that oppose pornography, such as the National Coalition to Protect Children and Families (NCPCF), do so because they believe pornography increases rape, child molestation, and crime rates. The NCPCF cites a study in which 86 percent of rapists interviewed admitted to regularly using pornography and 57 percent said they had imitated scenes from pornographic magazines while committing sex crimes.[4] The belief that violent and sexually explicit images can have harmful effects on audiences is behind many challenges to materials, particularly those used in schools.

Books and other materials are often challenged out of a concern that they are inappropriate for the age of their intended audience. Some parents do not want their children to learn about sex and sexual orientation until they are older, and they may challenge materials that they feel are too advanced for their child's age. Concerns for students' well-being have prompted the removal of books that touch on topics ranging from alcohol, rebellion, death, sex, witchcraft, and violence to cruelty to animals. Sometimes even seemingly innocuous classics of children's literature, like *Little Red Riding Hood* and *Black Beauty,* fall prey to the concerns of parents.

A huge percentage of challenges to public education involve objections to discussions of sex. During the 1995–1996 school year, 51 percent of challenges documented by People for the American Way involved objections to the discussion of sex and sexuality in schools.[5] Discussion of sexually transmitted diseases, contraception, and sexual orientation in classrooms was frequently challenged.

The issue of what level of sex and health education should be taught in schools is controversial and seems certain to ignite censors and anticensors for years to come. Although some parents welcome schools to teach their children about subjects like sex, contraception, and sexually transmitted diseases, others believe these are subjects best tackled at home or through religious education. Some parents want abstinence-only programs taught in schools. Other parents want their children to be taught how to protect themselves against AIDS and other sexually-transmitted diseases. Classroom discussions on topics like pregnancy, abortion, and sexual orientation can be particularly troubling to people with fundamentalist Christian values. In 1996, there were 92 incidents where sex education materials were opposed by parents. The discussion of homosexuality in schools was one of the most frequently opposed topics. In 1997 a Maryland school decided not to air a student panel discussion on same-sex marriages over the school's cable channel, for fear the program might offend some in the community. In California, a federally funded AIDS education program was revoked from high school classrooms in 1995–1996 after a school board received complaints that the program answered students' questions about how to protect themselves from AIDS during oral sex.

Accusations that its content was inappropriate and sexually explicit made author Maya Angelou's *I Know Why the Caged Bird Sings* the number-one target of censorship in high schools in the

1995, 1996, and 1997 school years, according to *Attacks on the Freedom to Learn* and the American Library Association. Because the book recounts the author's painful childhood, including her rape at age seven, *I Know Why the Caged Bird Sings* was challenged eight times in 1995–1996 by parents who claimed that its troubling content, particularly the sexually explicit rape scene, was too disturbing.[6]

Complaints that certain books are sexually offensive or obscene have long been leveled at literature in the United States. Some of the most-censored titles of the 1960s were accused of being sexually explicit. Among those titles challenged in the 1960s and 1970s for sexually explicit language were James Dickey's *Deliverance* and Joseph Heller's *Catch–22*. Again, the primary basis for book censorship in the 1980s was the claim that the material was sexually offensive. During the 1980s, Judy Blume, author of books for young adults, came under attack for *Deenie* (possibly the most-censored book of the 1980s), along with two of her other young adult titles: *Forever* and *Then Again, Maybe I Won't*. Once again, in the 1990s, the most frequent complaints leading to the challenge of books and other educational materials were that the materials in question were sexually offensive, violent, or profane.

Of 300 documented attempts to censor books and educational materials in 1995–1996, 44 percent of these attempts arose from concerns that the material in question was sexually offensive.[7] Many books in this category happen to be written by African American women, such as Maya Angelou's *I Know Why the Caged Bird Sings*, Alice Walker's *The Color Purple*, and Toni Morrison's *Beloved*, *The Bluest Eye*, and *Song of Solomon*. Children's books have also been accused of being sexually offensive. *In the Night Kitchen*, a picture book by renowned illustrator Maurice Sendak, has been challenged in several states because it contains an anatomically correct picture of a little boy's genitals.

Concerns that materials contained profanity or other offensive language made up 24 percent of censorship cases in 1995–1996.[8] Books in this category included Mark Twain's *The Adventures of Huckleberry Finn*, maligned for its use of the term "nigger," and John Steinbeck's *Of Mice and Men*, which contains swear words. Titles that have been challenged in the past for their profanity include J. D. Salinger's *Catcher in the Rye,* one of the most-censored titles since the 1960s, and Kurt Vonnegut's *Slaughter House Five*, published in 1968.

Materials that encourage the acceptance or understanding of different cultures and religious traditions have been challenged by parents who do not want their children to learn about cultures, religions, or belief systems different from their own. Textbooks that feature the history of women, blacks, and Native Americans have been challenged by groups that complain the books place too much emphasis on historically marginalized groups. Biology texts and other materials that teach human evolution have been challenged by Christian groups, parents, and school board members who argue that evolution is inconsistent with their religious beliefs about human origins. Similarly, parents may object to sexual education classes if they do not correspond with family religious beliefs. Some parents may want their children to hear only about abstinence, whereas others may not want their children to have any sex education at all. Materials that discuss homosexuality and sexual orientation are frequently opposed. At a school in New Ipswich, New Hampshire, parents challenged E. M. Forster's *Maurice*, which deals with homosexuality, and an English teacher at the school was fired for refusing to remove the book from a course. The film *Philadelphia*, shown to a health class in a South Carolina school, was opposed by the school board for allegedly teaching students about homosexuality.

According to *Attacks on the Freedom to Learn*, in the 1995–1996 school year, 18 percent of all censorship attempts were based on the concern that educational materials were anti-Christian or reflected a religion other than Christianity. Christian political organizations frequently charged that schools were promoting a religion by using "New Age" materials. In Georgia, two seventh-grade classes, "Critical and Creative Thinking: Content Application," and "Self-Discovery," were challenged by school board members associated with the Christian Coalition. The challengers opposed the courses on the grounds that they were anti-Christian and not sufficiently academic.[9] In North Carolina, the primary-school counseling and self-esteem program *Pumsy in Pursuit of Excellence* was challenged by a parent affiliated with the Christian group Focus on the Family. The parent complained that the program was anti-Christian and that it "distorted reality."[10]

Another challenge to books in public schools comes from parents who feel that racially offensive language should not appear in a school classroom. Mark Twain's *The Adventures of Huckleberry Finn* is frequently challenged for this reason. In addition, challenges have been made to books that supposedly portray minorities in a stereotypical manner. *The Indian in the Cupboard*, a children's book about a boy who plays with a toy Indian that comes to life, was challenged for allegedly promoting stereotypes of Native Americans. Members of the African American community have contested the inclusion in schools of works by black writers such as Richard Wright, Langston Hughes, and Maya Angelou because, they allege, their writing contains stereotypes of African Americans. Six percent of all censorship attempts in 1995–1996 were based on the claim that the challenged material presented a racist and stereotypical view of minorities that in some cases was not in line with established district diversity goals. *Attacks on the Freedom to Learn* noted that this type of attack generally came from left-wing political organizations or minority parents' groups.

Books on a school's required reading lists are often challenged. However, a significant percentage of all censorship attempts are to books and other materials in school libraries that are not part of a required reading list. In other words, many censors wish to remove not only material they consider "inappropriate" that students are asked to read, but also material they have deemed "inappropriate" that a student might find on his or her own in the school library.

Textbook Controversies

At the same time that public schools, under pressure to conform to the constitutional separation of church and state and implement federally mandated curriculums, have taken pains to present a secular and multicultural education, Christian organizations and parents have clamored for more moral and value-oriented textbooks in public schools. With an emphasis on multicultural education that reflects our nation's diversity, liberal groups have long advocated that school textbooks should include information on different groups as well as images of minorities, people with disabilities, and nontraditional families. Conversely, conservative groups frequently stress that textbooks should seek to uphold and promote traditional images of the family as well as traditional values and standards. As a result, textbooks remain one of the more controversial aspects of public education.

Dr. Paul Vitz, an educational psychologist who conducted a National Institute of Education study on bias in textbooks, reports that "religion, traditional family values, and conservative political and economic positions have been reliably excluded from children's textbooks."[11] For example, whereas affirmative action was mentioned in social studies texts, arguments opposing affirmative action were not always presented. Nor were pro-life arguments given equal exposure with pro-choice arguments. Vitz's study also concluded that Christianity was given considerably less attention in social studies and history textbooks than other world religions, such as Islam. What Vitz did find in the textbooks was a concerted emphasis on minority rights, feminism, and environmentalism, leaving him to conclude that textbooks did have a distinct bias, one very different from the textbook bias of fifty years ago.

In an attempt to counter a perceived bias against Christianity and conservatism in public education, religious right groups like the Christian Action Network have tried to reestablish prayer in schools and make the school curriculum more church- and nuclear-family oriented. Concerned Christian groups have challenged federally mandated curriculums. They have encouraged parents to sit on school boards and to become involved in their children's school curriculum. Christian groups like Focus on the Family also support home schooling and school voucher programs as means of ensuring that children are taught traditional, pro-family, pro-church values. Many of the broader challenges to the public school curriculum come from conservative Christians who feel the public school curriculum does not reflect their value system.

One of the nation's most significant textbook controversies occurred in West Virginia's Kanawha County High School in 1974, when parents initiated a prolonged protest over the content of state-approved English textbooks and supplementary reading material. Parents complained that the contents of the textbooks and materials, which included writings from poets Gwendolyn Brooks and Allen Ginsberg as well as works by Eldridge Cleaver and Malcolm X, were "disrespectful of authority and religion, destructive of social and cultural values, obscene, pornographic, unpatriotic, or in violation of individual and familial rights to privacy."[12]

Thousands of parents kept their children home for the first weeks of the fall semester to protest the materials, which were pulled from classrooms and placed under restricted access in school libraries. Responding to parents' concerns, the Kanawha County School Board adopted new guidelines for textbook selection, which stated that, among other things, textbooks must emphasize loyalty to the United States and must not ask personal questions about the feelings of students. In 1975, Kanawha County adopted new textbooks amenable to the community;

however, most of the contested materials eventually found their way back into the classroom.

Although courts have traditionally ruled against attempts to remove books from the curriculum, textbook publishers often accommodate those who take offense at their material. Anxious to please residents in Texas and California, the two states that purchase the largest numbers of textbooks, publishers have readily altered the contents of textbooks to suit the tastes of parents and school officials living in these states. Because textbooks are often distributed nationally, schools in other states may receive textbooks whose contents have been influenced by the concerns of residents in Texas and California.

Who Is Accused of Censorship?

As we have seen, censorship attacks in schools come from those of both right-wing and left-wing political orientation, whether they are parents, administrators, school board members, or community activists. All of these individuals and organizations are involved in the debate over what should be taught in the nation's public schools, and they are found in every state and region. From 1966 to 1975, Washington D.C., Rhode Island, and Vermont experienced the highest number of school and library-related censorship incidents; from 1981 to 1990, Washington D.C., Wyoming, and Nebraska were in the top three. In the 1990s, the three states with the highest number of censorship challenges were California, Pennsylvania, and Florida.[13]

During the 1995–1996 school year, 16 percent of the challenges to the curriculum came from local, state, and national political organizations allied with the religious right, which believes religion should be an important part of education. According to People for the American Way, another 16 percent of challenges in 1995–1996 were indirectly linked to or coordinated by these same religious groups.

The Family Research Council, a Judeo-Christian organization committed to the preservation of the family unit, supports voluntary student-initiated prayer in public schools and the teaching of abstinence-only sexual education. Focus on the Family, a national Christian organization headed by Dr. James Dobson, encourages parents to regain control over their local school systems, but it also advocates home schooling as a means of avoiding federally mandated curriculums and ensuring that children are taught traditional values. In addition, Focus on the Family lobbies for school voucher programs that would enable parents' tax dollars to fund a religious education for their children. The cities of Milwaukee, Wisconsin; Cleveland, Ohio; and San Antonio, Texas, are among those who have instituted voucher systems that refund the annual tax money parents have contributed to the cost of public education. Voucher programs allow parents to use their money toward the cost of a private or religious school for their children, if they so choose. Critics of voucher programs contend that they will lead to the abandonment of the public schools, while supporters argue that introducing a choice of schools will benefit education by forcing public schools to improve the quality of education in order to stay competitive. Where school voucher systems are not available to provide an alternative education for their children, many parents will undoubtedly continue to challenge what children are taught in the public school curriculum.

The Christian Action Network (CAN), a grassroots lobbying organization, opposes the discussion of homosexuality and sexual education in schools and seeks to abolish the Department of Education so that control of the public schools can be returned to the local level. CAN also seeks to eliminate the office of the Surgeon General, which it views as antifamily, pro-abortion, and pro–sex education, and advocates abolishing the National Endowment for the Arts and the Humanities, which it believes uses taxpayer money to subsidize obscene and antireligious art and revisionist history.

These and other groups, including the American Family Association, Family Friendly Libraries (FFL), and Citizens for Excellence in Education (CEE), have been involved in discussions of what is appropriate in school libraries and classrooms. Conservative in focus, these organizations encourage libraries and schools to seek out materials that support traditional family values and conform to local community standards. When FFL believes inappropriate material is being made available to students, the organization encourages parents and local citizens' groups to challenge that material or have it placed in a restricted-access zone that requires parental permission. FFL advocates returning the control of libraries to citizens and wants parents to have access to their children's library records. In the 1990s, Family Friendly Libraries and Focus on the Family accused the staunchly anticensorship American Library Association (ALA) of granting children access to age-inappropriate and sexually explicit material. The ALA, however, maintained that it was wrong for a library to restrict access to materials. "Our basic policy," said Judith Krug, director of the ALA's Office for Intellectual Freedom, "is that it is the responsibility of parents and only parents or guardians to guide their children and only their children in selecting appropriate reading material."[14] To celebrate the freedom to read, each year the ALA holds "Banned Books Week" and publishes a case-by-case report of all the book censorship incidents of the previous year. In response to "Banned Books Week," Family Friendly Libraries started "Family Library Libraries Week" to recognize and praise library materials that affirm traditional values. FFL has also launched a campaign to encourage libraries to replace the ALA's *Library Bill of Rights,* which champions the freedom to read, with its own *Charter for a Family-Friendly Library System,* which upholds traditional family values, parental library rights, and respect for community standards and laws.

Citizens for Excellence in Education is a coalition of Christian conservative parents and teachers working to restore traditional moral values to the nation's public schools. Toward that end, CEE has promoted the involvement of parents on school boards and on local chapters of the organization. CEE also has devised opt-out policies for sex education programs to help parents who do not want their children exposed to these programs.

In contrast to the religious right, groups associated with left-wing or liberal politics, such as the National Association for the Advancement of Colored People (NAACP) and coalitions of minority parents, represented 6 percent of all challenges to educational materials in 1995–1996.[15] The primary objections of these groups were that educational materials promoted racist views or stereotypes or that they failed to take into account the sensitivities of minority students. Organizations like the Council on Interracial Books for Children (CIBC) have worked to eliminate from libraries all books they consider to be racist or sexist. Among the children's books targeted by the CIBC are *Little Black Sambo*, which contains stereotypes of black people, *Little Red Riding Hood*, *Cinderella*, and other fairy tales alleged to promote culturally biased views or gender stereotypes.

Outside of the nation's public schools, affiliates of both the political and cultural left and right have been accused of supporting censorship in the United States. Among them are secular groups, like Morality in Media, and religious groups, like the Christian Action Network; both oppose pornography as well as the proliferation of violent and sexually explicit images in the media and, as discussed later in this chapter, in federally funded arts programs. Among their allies in the antipornography crusade is a faction within the feminist movement, represented by liberal feminists such as legal scholar Catharine MacKinnon and writer Andrea Dworkin, who have outspokenly sought to ban pornography, which they believe is a form of sexual harassment. In the 1980s MacKinnon and Dworkin worked together to help draft new antipornography legislation that would allow the victims of pornography to seek legal redress from those who create, distribute, and sell pornography. Though the Pornography Victims Compensation Act failed to pass in Congress, it drew attention to the concerns of those who oppose pornography's influence on society. Another area of censorship in which liberals have been active is the development of codes and laws to ban hate speech.

Hate Speech

In the late 1980s and 1990s a consciousness-raising movement known as *political correctness* swept American academia. Designed to remedy past wrongs and assure that discriminatory and exclusionary speech and practices no longer had a place in universities and colleges, the politically correct movement popularized speech codes, or rules regarding acceptable speech on campus. Many schools decided that "hate speech," language considered harmful because it is racist or sexist in nature, was not acceptable. Leading the way were some of the nation's most liberal institutions of higher learning. In 1991 a male student at Brown University was expelled for harassing several students with comments that were racist, homophobic, and anti-Semitic in nature. His verbal harassment violated the school's Code of Student Conduct, which then defined harassment as "the subjection of another person or group to abusive, threatening, or demeaning actions, based on race, religion, gender, handicap, ethnicity, national origin, or sexual orientation." The student's expulsion was the first of its kind in the country, and it touched off a national debate over speech codes on college campuses. Should the need for maintaining tolerance and standards of community behavior come before an individual's right to free speech? Where does one draw the line between action and speech? Some administrators and students argued that hate speech could inflict terrible harm and that sexist or racist language did not deserve a place at universities. Others believed that there was a difference between speech and action, and that outlawing certain speech would only create a climate of fear in which students would not dare discuss their differences of opinion.

Administrators at colleges and universities began experimenting with bans on "hate speech" in the late 1980s and early 1990s. Some of them implemented speech codes that were intended to promote tolerance on campus so that all groups, particularly minorities and homosexuals, would feel welcome and comfortable. But by the late 1990s, many schools had abandoned their speech codes after a backlash against political correctness surfaced. In 1993, a University of Pennsylvania student became a cause célèbre for those who opposed speech codes. The student was threatened with suspension after yelling "Shut up, you water buffalo!"[16] to five black women who were walking past his dorm window. The university deemed his comments racially offensive and insensitive, but the student, an orthodox Jew, maintained that "water buffalo" was simply a translation of the Hebrew word, "behemah," meaning fool. The incident created a media spectacle, and the University of Pennsylvania later abandoned its speech code.

Some members of the predominantly white student body at the University of Wisconsin's Madison campus staged racially offensive events during the late 1980s. Embarrassed university officials felt a speech code might protect minority students from future harassment. But in 1991 the university's speech code was ruled unconstitutional in the courts, which claimed it violated students' First Amendment rights. Proponents of the speech codes on the Madison campus were unsatisfied with this decision. They complained that the law was inconsistent—that it upheld certain types of speech while outlawing others. Whether or not certain speech is legal depends on the situation. It is against the law, for example, to yell "fire" in a crowded theater without just cause. This ban on free speech is designed to protect others. The University of Wisconsin speech code was also designed to protect people, but it was declared unconstitutional because the harm it incurred on free speech was ruled to be greater than any benefit it could supply. The American Association of University Professors agreed with the courts. Their official statement on freedom of expression and campus speech codes reads: "On a campus that is free and open, no idea can be banned or forbidden. No viewpoint or message may be deemed so hateful or disturbing that it may not be expressed."[17]

Censorship in the Arts

The Music Lyrics Controversy

The education of the nation's youth has been marked by disagreement, and the media to which young people are constantly exposed—music, television, movies—also generates debate. What kind of influence does popular music have on children and teenagers? Can music have harmful effects? Since the dawn of the rock and roll era, song lyrics and the habits of musicians have been called into question for suggestive, violent, profane, and sexual content. Elvis Presley's gyrating hips once provoked the *Ed Sullivan Show* to broadcast the singer to television audiences only from the waist up. The words to the Kingsmen's "Louie Louie," tame by today's standards, were sometimes censored by radio stations that did not want to offend listeners. The Everly Brothers' rendition of "Wake Up, Little Susie" was considered shocking when first released. But today, controversial music lyrics often contain frank descriptions of sex, rape, violence, and drug use.

Although record companies often defend the First Amendment rights of their artists and balk at the suggestion of regulating their industry, concerned individuals contend that violent and explicit lyrics can make a damaging impression on youthful minds. The Parents Music Resource Center (PMRC) has long advocated "responsible" music lyrics. Founded in 1985 by Tipper Gore, who became angry after she discovered the Prince tape she had bought for her daughter contained explicit lyrics, the PMRC is devoted to informing parents about music. In 1990, using the argument that violent and sexually explicit lyrics may be detrimental to some children, the PMRC persuaded the music industry to place parental advisory stickers on certain albums, warning buyers about their lyrics. The labels, which read "Parental Advisory—Explicit Lyrics," continue to be applied voluntarily by participating record companies, but they are not required by law. The warning stickers created an anticensorship backlash against the PMRC by the arts and civil liberties community. After a 1994 U.S. Senate hearing on explicit lyrics, anticensorship groups such as Rock Out Censorship and the National Campaign for Freedom of Expression expressed concern over what would happen if the government took a role in censoring or restricting access to certain forms of music. Solange Bitol of the American Civil Liberties Union (ACLU) has been an outspoken critic of government attempts to censor music. Bitol maintains, "Efforts to censor music often unfairly target certain groups. Congress's 1994 hearings on violent and misogynist lyrics focused primarily on African American artists. What about sexism or violence reflected in country music lyrics? Inevitably, government censorship is used politically, and will unfairly target certain groups."[18]

Despite criticism from the arts community, Barbara Wyatt, current head of the PMRC, is concerned that music labels are not doing enough to protect parents and children. In an article by Eddie Dean in *The Roc*, a magazine that opposes music censorship, Wyatt was quoted, "Only very few companies put the labels on, that's one of the problems . . . And even if there is a label on [a recording], any child can buy it, and the forbidden fruit is often the most appealing fruit."[19] Wyatt would prefer to restrict minors' access to explicit albums in much the same way as children are denied access to alcohol, tobacco, and other harmful substances. "Is it censorship that we say somebody under 18 cannot drink alcohol and buy drugs or a package of cigarettes? These things are detrimental to the growing body and the growing mind. There are many children that can listen to this music and it may not affect them, but there are many young people out there today kind of sitting on the edge."[20] In the 1990s, the PMRC was instrumental in pressuring the Time Warner Corporation, which had once backed the controversial Interscope record label, into abandoning its stake in the label. Recently, the PMRC has focused on convincing record company executives that they bear some of the responsibility for the impact songs from their labels have on children and teenagers.

Censorship and Rap Music

One of the most controversial and popular sounds in music today is rap. A relatively new musical genre, rap grew into a national phenomenon after beginning in the 1970s in cities like New York, Los Angeles, Oakland, and Miami—areas with large minority populations that have been hard hit by economic decline, unemployment, crime, and drugs. Rap evolved as disc jockeys, using two turntables and a sound mixer, started sampling—playing instrumental breaks from popular records and switching from one to another to create a never-ending dance mix. Using a microphone, a master of ceremonies (MC) could call to the crowd and create original rhymes. Rap's rhyming talk, which spoke of life in the inner city, began to express strong racial and political awareness. Despite its strong black nationalist flavor, rap has achieved crossover success into other segments of the population, as evidenced by record sales to nonblacks. In 1988, MTV debuted *Yo! MTV Raps,* featuring rap artists and hip-hop culture; it soon became one of the station's most popular programs. Today rap brings in over $600 million annually, and every major record company has made investments in rap music.

Though they have been commercially successful, some rap artists have been criticized for lyrics that are racist, misogynist, anti-Semitic, sexually explicit, and violent. Supporters of rap maintain that so-called gangsta rappers are simply expressing real-life experiences and exposing the conditions of life in the ghetto. Scholars who study rap music have likened rappers to urban storytellers—dispensing social commentary on the times and lives of youth in the city. Critics, however, charge that rappers exert enormous influence on young people and that they should use this power positively and act as role models. Critics also fear that rap music serves to glorify crime, violence, and drug use. In particular, sexually explicit rap lyrics that suggest violence toward women, or that treat women as sex objects, have aroused the fury of anti–gangsta rap activists like C. Delores Tucker. As the director of the National Political Congress of Black Women, Tucker launched a crusade against the Time Warner Corporation for backing music that she believed promoted the oppression of black women.

Though rap is well known for its controversial lyrics, female rappers like Queen Latifah, MC Lyte, and Salt-n-Pepa, together with coed groups like Arrested Development, have demonstrated that rap can also portray strong females and positive male-female relations. Other rap groups, like 2 Live Crew, have tested First Amendment rights with their music. In 1990, 2 Live Crew's album *Nasty as They Wanna Be,* which featured the song "Me So Horny," was the first album to be indicted for obscenity. The obscenity charges, which were later dropped, actually helped sell the album. Other rap artists, like Ice-T, have had their music censored. Following the acquittal of the Los Angeles police officers charged with beating Rodney King, Ice-T's song "Cop Killer," from his 1992 *Body Count* album, came under fire from police, who believed the song would encourage people to kill police officers. Ice-T's producer, Time Warner, was strongly criticized and police unions even threatened to stop investing their pension funds in Time Warner stock. Second Amendment activist

Charlton Heston spoke out against the song at a Time Warner shareholder meeting in New York and read the lyrics to "Cop Killer" aloud before a shocked audience. Bowing to pressure, Time Warner eventually removed the song from the album. Yet the removal of "Cop Killer" was criticized by some as setting a precedent for the censorship of rap.

Artistic Freedom

Film, theater, television, and fine art in the United States have also faced the conflict of free expression versus standards of decency. One of the earliest American motion pictures, released in 1915, was *Birth of a Nation*, a story of the Civil War and Reconstruction. The film's overt racism, glorification of the Ku Klux Klan (KKK), and portrayal of southern blacks as villains caused riots in some theaters, and the film was censored in many cities, including New York. The NAACP immediately reacted against the film, which continues to be controversial today, with some KKK groups using it to recruit new members. In 1930 the Motion Picture Producers and Distributors of America (MPPDA) adopted a production code that forbid the depiction of nudity, sex, childbirth, adultery, and homosexuality, among other topics. This code was known as the Hays Code, after Will Hays, the first director of the MPPDA. In the 1940s, anticommunist sentiment in the United States led to inquiries into the film industry, the blacklisting of screenwriters, and the censorship of pro-Soviet films. In 1966 the renamed Motion Picture Association of America (MPAA) updated the Hays Code for the first time to reflect the tastes of new film audiences, and in 1968 the MPAA replaced the code with a ratings board, which was given the responsibility of classifying films appropriate for different audiences. By the 1970s, a series of sexually explicit films had aroused controversy, including *Deep Throat* (1972) and *The Last Picture Show* (1973). Films perceived as antireligious, including *The Last Temptation of Christ* (1987), also generated tremendous controversy. Video store owners who stocked copies of *The Last Temptation of Christ* were boycotted by groups like the American Family Association and the Christian Coalition. In 1997, video store owners in Oklahoma became embroiled in a controversy surrounding the 1979 Academy Award–winning film *The Tin Drum*, which was brought to the attention of Oklahoma City police by a concerned citizen who thought the film violated a state child pornography statute. When an Oklahoma district judge declared one scene in the film to be obscene, police confiscated copies of the film from video stores, libraries, and even the home of a person who had rented the film.

At the close of the twentieth century, as movies continued to show more violence and nudity, parents challenged the increase in sex and violence by demanding a better movie ratings system. The MPAA responded by creating the PG-13 (parental guidance recommended for children under 13) rating in 1984, and the NC-17 (no children under 17 admitted) rating in 1990.

Theater has also been censored throughout its history in the United States, and plays that present themes not in keeping with the beliefs of conservative religious groups have been targeted. *The Children's Hour,* with its theme of lesbianism; *Inherit the Wind,* about the controversial Scopes trial; and Henrik Ibsen's feminist *The Doll's House* are among the plays that have been challenged by Christian religious groups. Plays perceived as mocking Christianity, however, have aroused the strongest response from religious groups. In a controversial 1998 decision, New York's Manhattan Theater Club initially canceled Terrence McNally's play *Corpus Christi,* about a Christ-like figure who has sexual relations with his disciples. The Catholic League for Religious and Civil Rights organized a letter-writing campaign condemning the production. After receiving numerous threats from anonymous callers—who threatened to burn down the theater, kill its staff, and execute McNally if the play were staged—management at the Manhattan Theater Club began to succumb to pressure. Some corporate sponsors of the theater also pledged to withdraw their financial support if *Corpus Christi* were staged. When the Manhattan Theater Club agreed to cancel the play in the name of safety, several prominent playwrights disagreed with the decision to yield to censors. They argued that art has no obligation to conform to religious beliefs. Tony Kushner, author of the award-winning play *Angels on Broadway,* which was attacked by the Christian Coalition in 1995 because of its homosexual themes, said, "It's shocking that in New York City, a major theater succumbs to pressure like this. . . . This is a medieval notion that the arts in the United States need to follow the Roman Catholic theological line."[21] Responding to criticism from those in the anti-censorship community, the Manhattan Theater Club eventually staged the play in October 1998.

Researchers from People for the American Way's Artsave project, one of the most comprehensive projects of its kind, compile information about censorship and the arts, which is then independently verified. Only those instances that call for the removal or restriction of the art in question are included in the project's report, *Artistic Freedom Under Attack*. This report records that in 1996 alone there were 137 reported challenges to artistic expression in the United States. These challenges took place in 41 states and the District of Columbia, and the censors were successful in 73 percent of the incidents. The common link between all incidents of art censorship is that they attempt to prevent a work of art from being displayed or funded because of a disagreement with its message or content. According to PAW, attempts to censor artistic expression fall under the following categories:

1. National challenges to federal arts programs, including the National Endowment for the Arts and the Corporation for Public Broadcasting
2. Local arts funding controversies
3. Calls for removal of individual works of art from galleries or spaces
4. Sponsor boycott campaigns designed to force television programs off of airwaves
5. Efforts to block access to artworks
6. Attempts to remove art from public schools
7. Legislative efforts to restrict artistic expression[22]

Challenged art ranges from fine art to television, movies, and photographs. As is the case with books, the majority of objections to art—some 38 percent in 1996—arise from the concern that the material is obscene or sexually explicit. Another 35 percent of challenged art in 1996 contained homosexual imagery. Fifteen percent of the challenged art works of 1996 were charged with being antireligious, blasphemous, or satanic. Finally, 7 percent of art censorship incidents were based on the complaint that the work promoted violence or showed too much violence. As with book censorship, many of these challenges to art—in this case 21 percent—come from organizations allied with the religious right.[23]

Censors frequently attack any suggestion of homosexuality in an artwork, calling it pornographic or obscene. They may act out of religious motivation, especially if they consider homosexuality to be immoral or destructive. In addition, conservative Christian organizations like the Family Research Council, the Christian Action Network, the American Family Association, and Focus on the Family encourage members to oppose the proliferation of homosexual images and literature. Thus the censorship of art reflects the broader picture of our society's attitudes about sexual orientation. As long as there are those who feel threatened by the presence of homosexuality, challenges will continue to be launched against art and other media that contain homosexual themes.

For example, when a television station in Huntsville, Alabama, censored a scene in a television drama about a woman discharged from the army because she was a lesbian, they were expressing the belief that other viewers would not appreciate the scene, which showed a brief kiss between two women, and the fear that viewers would be harmed by it. In the 1990s, Donald Wildmon, head of the American Family Association, launched a campaign to prevent the television program *Friends* from airing an episode about a marriage between two women. The campaign was not successful, but it illustrated the concern of those who feel homosexuality should not be allowed to appear on television.

Complaints about the appropriateness of some visual art may cause arts centers to tone down their programming in order to avoid funding cuts. If outraged groups organize a boycott of art galleries and centers that display controversial art, these venues may become less willing to showcase certain types of art. Similarly, when the sponsors of art centers are boycotted and picketed by those who disapprove of the kind of art being showcased, they may revoke their funding or pressure the center to drop a particular show or artist from its roster. Thus censors and their campaigns against particular works of art can make it very difficult for controversial artists to find a home for their art.

The trend toward the merger of art and media companies has also provided a powerful potential for more effective censorship. As broadcasting networks and film and television companies continue to merge, like the 1996 merger of Time Warner and Turner Broadcasting, for example, it becomes possible for censors to target a whole range of media and artistic outlets by focusing their boycotts and campaigns on a single corporation. To illustrate this potential, consider the fact that the Time Warner/Turner merger created one company behind fifty record labels, multiple television channels including CNN and HBO, the movie company Castle Rock Entertainment, the Warner Brothers retail store, the Six Flags theme parks, and magazines like *Time, People,* and *Money*.

Challenges to art can also foster self-censorship. If citizens consistently boycotted Disney movies about animals, for example, Disney might eventually be forced to stop making movies about animals. An example of this kind of self-censorship occurred in Chehalis, Washington, after a community member complained about a local high school's production of *South Pacific*, saying it was vulgar and profane. As a result of this criticism, the high school canceled an ongoing production of Shakespeare's *A Midsummer Night's Dream* for fear that its themes of desire and couples might spark another controversy in the community. Although some argue that art organizations should take the feelings of the local community into account before booking artists or plays, others maintain that self-censorship undermines some of the key functions of art, which are to inspire, to provoke, and to challenge existing assumptions.

Although an overwhelming number of challenges to art in recent years have come from the religious right, challenges to artistic freedom also come from the political left. In 1994, *Time* magazine received widespread condemnation from the NAACP and the *New York Times* for its June 27 cover artwork, which depicted O. J. Simpson. The photo-illustration, based on a Los Angeles Police Department mug shot of Simpson, was denounced because it projected a very black, ominous view of Simpson's face. Critics charged that the darkening of Simpson's face was meant to imply that he was guilty, and was therefore racist. (Simpson was then awaiting trial for the murder of his wife, Nicole, and her friend, Ron Goldman.) *Time* later apologized for the illustration. Another example of a left-wing challenge to artwork occurred in 1995 when parents in Oak Park, Illinois, complained that a 60-year-old mural at an elementary school presented minorities in a racist and stereotypical way. School officials removed the mural, called "People of the World," which featured a map of the world with the different peoples of the world superimposed on it.

Complicating the debate over freedom of artistic expression is the issue of government funding of the arts. Should taxpayers' money fund art that has been deemed objectionable by a portion of the population? Who gets to decide where the money should be spent and which artists are worthy of support? These questions have surrounded federal funding for the arts by the National Endowment for the Arts (NEA).

Should Publicly Funded Art Be Censored?

In 1989 U.S. Senator Jesse Helms attacked the National Endowment for the Arts for its funding of "obscene" art. At the core of this condemnation were controversial artists whose work had been funded in part by the NEA. One such artist was Andres Serrano, whose photograph "Piss Christ," depicting a crucifix submerged in urine, caused a national debate on the appropriateness of federal funding for the arts. Photographer Robert Mapplethorpe's works also drew strong criticism from religious groups, particularly his more graphic photos, which showed homosexuals engaging in sexual acts, such as Mapplethorpe himself being anally penetrated by a bull whip. When it was publicized that these works had been funded by the National Endowment for the Arts, many taxpayers were irate that their tax dollars had funded what they considered to be obscene works. Senator Helms's vocal campaign against controversial works of subsidized art eventually provoked Congress to reduce funding for the NEA.

The NEA was founded in 1965 to promote excellence in artistic endeavor among Americans. NEA grants are dispensed to artists whose work has been deemed worthy by select committees. But the selection of artists for grants has aroused controversy from those who feel the NEA should respect certain standards of decency in their selection process. The NEA, which uses a peer review system to judge all grant proposals, maintains that they select only the most promising talent, and that of over 100,000 grants it has awarded, only a small percentage has been controversial. In addition, the NEA defends its support of controversial artists, adding that one of the functions of art is to challenge and provoke.

The debate over artistic choices made by the NEA invokes the question of whether the government should be involved in funding art. Supporters of the NEA have long warned that the arts will suffer if the agency is abolished, but *Boston Globe* columnist Jeff Jacoby asserts, "Before anyone thought it was the government's business to subsidize art and entertainment . . . the Western world was incubating an artistic richness of unparalleled breadth and variety."[24] Indeed, private funding to the arts has always outstripped public funding, with American individuals, foundations, and corporations donating over $10 billion a year in philanthropy for the arts. "In 1994 alone," writes Jacoby, "private giving to the arts dwarfed the NEA budget by a ratio of 57 to 1."[25] By comparison with private funding, NEA funding for the arts is a relatively small sum, yet it has created a firestorm of controversy because the funds come from American taxpayers, who have no input in the grant-making process. Because the NEA supports numerous art centers around the country, each of these centers is subject to having their programs called into question by angry taxpayers. This was the case at Minneapolis's NEA-supported Walker Art Center, which hosted HIV-positive performance artist Ron Athey's "Four Scenes in a Harsh Life." In this presentation, Athey carved the back of another man with a knife, blotted the blood with paper towels, then strung the used towels up so they dangled over the heads of the audience members. The performance was added to Helms's growing list of inappropriate NEA-funded art.

Opponents of federal funding for the arts contend that since private-sector giving to the arts so outstrips the NEA's contributions, the NEA is an obsolete and unessential source of funding for the arts. In addition, they argue that federal funding has not helped improve the quality of art and in fact has only decreased the diversity of art. According to Dr. Laurence Jarvik of the Heritage Foundation, a conservative Washington think tank, "Government subsidies actually work to reduce choice and diversity in the artistic marketplace by encouraging artists to emulate each other in order to achieve success in the grants process."[26]

On the contrary, supporters of federal funding for the arts argue that the NEA fulfills a vital role in assisting arts organizations around the country. According to the American Arts Alliance (AAA), an advocate for nonprofit art organizations, public funding for the arts stimulates private giving because the NEA offers incentive matching programs, where the government matches a private sponsor, dollar for dollar, to increase their donation. The AAA denies that private funding for the arts provides enough assistance to warrant the abolition of the NEA. Without public support for the arts, the AAA argues, museums, symphonies, and theaters would have to charge more for admission, making it more difficult for Americans who are not well off to enjoy the arts. Supporters of the NEA argue that all the great nations of history have supported the arts, and that it is important to make a national commitment to the arts. They remind the NEA's detractors that public funding for the arts costs only 64 cents per person per year.

Censors and First Amendment advocates have battled over the nation's right to fund art that some people consider inappropriate. They have also battled over the issue of freedom of the press, and the extent to which the news media has an obligation to report sensitive information to the public.

Censorship in the News Media

In 1971 excerpts from the Pentagon Papers, controversial classified documents dealing with U.S. policy in Vietnam, were published by the *New York Times,* touching off a debate on national security versus the right of the people to know. Critics charged that the government resorted to excessive classification of documents in order to conceal activity from the public, whereas the government maintained that it was acting in the interests of national security. The Pentagon Papers issue began when a Defense Department staff member leaked the classified documents to several major newspapers. The Pentagon Papers showed that four different presidential administrations, from President Harry Truman through President Lyndon Johnson, had made major decisions about U.S. military and government policy in Asia without consulting Congress or the public. The U.S. Justice Department attempted to block further publication of the Pentagon Papers and filed suit against the newspapers that had begun to publish excerpts from them. Ultimately, a divided Supreme Court ruled in favor of the public's right to know, arguing that in this case, at least, the newspapers had the right to publish the information. The Pentagon Papers affair raised important issues such as government hostility toward the press, self-censorship of the press, and the limits of the public's right to know.

A nation-wide media research project known as Project Censored compiles a list each year of significant news stories that were not reported in the mainstream media. These stories, it maintains, were censored. Project Censored's goal is to monitor the extent of censorship in our society and publicize censored stories in order to encourage journalists to provide better news coverage and inspire the public to demand it. Dr. Carl Jensen, the director of Project Censored, acknowledges that censorship of the news is more subtle than censorship of books and movies. Rarely does someone actually come forward and say they are going to censor a story. Instead, newsroom policy or practice may lead reporters to kill stories they know will not receive approval. As a result, censorship of the news is difficult to allege. Yet each year, Project Censored publishes an impressive collection of censored news stories. For one reason or another, these stories failed to be published in the mainstream media. As a result, they have passed largely unnoticed and unheeded. When the media fails to report all the news accurately and fairly, people are not given the information they need to make appropriate decisions for themselves.

This is particularly important as people rely on the news to inform them on such issues as candidates for public office.

The United States prides itself on having a free press. Journalists are supposed to be able to write freely on topics, no matter how sensitive they might be. Yet media watchdog groups have established a number of factors that they believe contribute to the censorship of news in the United States. One of these factors is the corporate ownership of the press. The merger of media organizations in the United States has raised the concern of groups such as Fairness and Accuracy in Reporting (FAIR), who fear the influence a select few media managers may have on news reporting. Since corporations have an obligation to their stockholders to increase profits, media critics fear that corporate ownership of the press will stimulate a quest for profit that may affect the flow of information. For example, as news outlets compete against each other for ratings or subscriptions, they may strive for new and more sensational stories. They may be more concerned with getting the story first, rather than reporting it responsibly. However, some members of the media maintain that responsible journalism is economically sound journalism, and that it is cost-effective in the long run for the corporations that own media outlets to promote responsible journalism or else risk losing readers and viewers.

According to Project Censored, additional factors behind censored news stories are media bias and imbalance, the media's allegiance to official agendas, and media insensitivity to certain peoples based on ethnicity or geographic location. For example, American media coverage of an earthquake in Zambia is bound to generate less press coverage than an earthquake in France. This is because the American press is interested in covering stories that affect its readers. The average American feels more of a connection with the French than with the Zambians. However, the result of this bias is that tragedies in remote areas may go unheeded so long as Americans remain unaware. In a global society, journalists play a role in foreign policy. Photojournalists and news reporters have the power to turn the tide of public opinion and compel political action when they bring scenes and news from atrocities around the world into the living rooms of Americans. Without continuous coverage of Serbian atrocities against Bosnian Muslims, for example, the United States might not have authorized the intervention of NATO military forces. Thus, the censoring of news stories could seriously affect the course of events by preventing intervention. The media plays a powerful role in generating public support for intervention in conflicts, particularly foreign ones. If a story is not covered, nothing may be done.

One story that failed to make the news for most of the 1990s was that of slavery in the African nation of Sudan. A civil war still rages in Sudan, where a wealthy northern Islamic population is fighting for control of the oil-rich southern half of the nation, inhabited by Christian blacks. Throughout this war, the northern Sudanese have been ravaging and enslaving the southern Christian population. Northern soldiers have kidnapped children and forced them to serve as blood banks and human shields for their army. Girls and women have been kidnapped for use as concubines. The goal of the northern Sudanese is to conquer the southern population and their oil fields. For much of this conflict, the same media that focused on Bosnia, Rwanda, and Somalia appeared unconcerned with the enslavement and aggression that was occurring in Sudan. African American groups like the NAACP, the Congressional Black Caucus, and TransAfrica—all of which have been vocal about other forms of racial discrimination in Africa, such as apartheid—were perceived as being silent on the issue of slavery in Sudan. The American Anti-Slavery Group (AASG) worked to publicize slavery in Sudan and drum up support, but the lack of press coverage hindered them.

Finally, in 1996 the Baltimore *Sun* broke the story in a series of front-page articles, after sending two reporters to Sudan. Soon after, *Dateline NBC* aired a segment on the story. Then, in November 1997, after the situation in Sudan was publicized, the United States imposed economic sanctions on Sudan for its human rights violations. Why did the problems in Sudan remain untold in the U.S. press for so long? The American Anti-Slavery Group believes African American organizations were reluctant to take up this cause for fear of offending the perpetrators of the violence, the Islamic leaders of Sudan. In fact, Louis Farrakhan of the Nation of Islam denied the story of slavery in Sudan as mere propaganda intended to divide black Muslims from their Islamic counterparts abroad. When Mohammed Athie of the International Coalition Against Chattel Slavery asked to speak about the crisis of slavery in Africa at the 1996 Million Man March in Washington, D.C., Farrakhan refused the human rights worker's request.

In 1998, just months after imposing economic sanctions against Sudan, the Clinton administration allowed a Democratic party donor, the Occidental Petroleum Corporation, to negotiate an oil deal in Sudan. This time the press covered the story, and the power of the news media was demonstrated when, along with a letter-writing campaign sponsored by AASG, that coverage helped prompt Occidental Petroleum to withdraw from its deal.

According to a poll conducted by the PEW Research Center, a nonprofit media research group in Washington, D.C., Americans have become more and more cynical about the press's ability to cover issues fairly and accurately. In 1989, 34 percent of Americans felt that the press was fair in covering stories. By 1997, however, 67 percent of Americans felt that the press was favoring one side or another in its coverage of stories and issues.[27] Increased cynicism among readers and viewers raises the question of where people will turn to get the news. Although newspaper readership is predicted to fall in the coming years, the number of people who are now connected to an Internet service provider—like America On Line, for example—is greater than the total number of subscriptions held to both the *Wall Street Journal* and the *New York Times* combined. Increasingly, Americans are tuning in to the Internet at the same time that they are tuning out to more traditional forms of media. As a result, the Internet has become one of the most powerful new means of communication, and the most hotly contested new media for censorship.

Censorship and the Internet

In the 1990s, the proliferation of on-line communication, along with the level of information attainable on all subjects via the Internet, soon led to new challenges, such as how to curb children's access to pornography and other explicit material available on-line. With the click of a button, the Internet can provide cheap, anonymous access to an astonishing array of pornography, and the viewer need only click a box affirming that he or she is over eighteen years of age. Unlike drugstores and newsstands, where pornographic magazines are often covered with brown paper and kept behind the counter so that a clerk must access them for the customer, the Internet offers users of pornography a greater degree of privacy. As a result, many parents are concerned that their children might be able to access pornography on the Internet. At the same time, however, operators of sex sites do not want laws enacted that will affect their ability to do business over the Internet. Demand fuels supply, and the sheer volume of pornography on-line indicates that cyber pornography is a thriving industry.

The first legal measure designed to protect children from pornography on-line was the Communications Decency Act, part of the Telecommunications Reform Act of 1996. Despite intense opposition from cyber-liberties organizations, such as the Electronic Frontier Foundation, as well as Internet service providers and other business people anxious to explore the economic opportunities of the Internet without excessive government interference, the Communications Decency Act (CDA) passed overwhelmingly in the House and Senate and was signed by President Bill Clinton in February 1996. The CDA made it illegal to display any "indecent" material on a computer network unless efforts were made to restrict the network access of anyone under the age of eighteen. The CDA was an attempt to regulate pornography on the Internet and protect minors from being exposed to explicit material. However, many Internet groups were fearful of the broad censorship provisions contained in the CDA and the impact they would have on free speech on-line. The Communications Decency Act imposed broadcast-style content regulations on the Internet that were harsher than those enacted for other media, such as television and radio. Profanity, nudity, and explicit language and scenes were banned from the Internet under the CDA. Ironically, on-line versions of books and artwork were not guaranteed the same First Amendment rights they had in print form. For example, under the vague indecency law of the CDA, a person who posted a classic work of literature like *The Catcher in the Rye* on the Internet would potentially be liable for prosecution on obscenity charges, even though the same book in print form was protected under the First Amendment. Opponents of the CDA argued that broad restrictions like these were unnecessary, because unlike television or radio, the Internet was a medium that offered users tremendous control over the content they received. Parents concerned about protecting their children from pornography, for example, could use commercially available filtering software to block out objectionable material.

As soon as the CDA was passed, groups such as the Citizens Internet Empowerment Coalition mobilized to oppose it, charging that the law contained an overly broad definition of what constituted indecent speech on-line. Plaintiffs in the appeal against the CDA argued that it was wrong for all on-line content—from personal web pages and newsgroups to chat rooms—to be subject to interpretation under this vague indecency clause.

The Electronic Frontier Foundation (EFF), one of the most vocal opponents of the CDA, argued that the act also removed any incentive for the private sector to continue to develop filtering services that parents could use to oversee their children's on-line access. In its statement of opposition to the CDA, the EFF complained that the restrictions imposed on cyber communications were more severe than those already in place for radio or television, and that the restrictions were completely unnecessary for the Internet, since individuals could voluntarily exert a level of control over its content.

Opponents of the CDA agreed that protecting children from pornography was a laudable goal. However, they argued, the anti-obscenity laws already on the books, together with technical aids like NetNanny and SurfWatch, which allow parents to supervise their children's Internet access, were a better solution for protecting children from inappropriate material on-line. In addition, they argued, communication over the Internet deserved the same level of free-speech protection granted to the spoken word or to literature published in book form.

Reno v. ACLU: **Challenging the Communications Decency Act of 1996**

As soon as the CDA was passed, a wide range of civil liberties groups and concerned organizations, including the ACLU, the EFF, Microsoft Corporation, and Barnes and Noble, prepared to challenge the law. Their case was based on the CDA's vague and broad use of the term "indecent," which created uncertainty about what was or was not criminal. Opponents also charged that the CDA violated the First Amendment by hindering free speech on the Internet. More than a year after the CDA's passage, on June 26, 1997, the U.S. Supreme Court ruled unanimously in *Reno v. ACLU* that the Communications Decency Act did violate the First Amendment. The court also decided that the CDA's goal of protecting minors was better accomplished through the use of filtering technology, which could provide a less obtrusive solution to supervising Internet access. The Supreme Court's decision on the CDA was disappointing to those who supported censorship of the Internet, but it was hailed as a landmark victory by civil liberties groups. Executive Director of the EFF Lori Fena said, "What this means is that the responsibility for controlling our content lies on us—the citizens and the parents—and this is a call for all of us once again to demonstrate how we can be trusted to use this medium responsibly."[28]

The crusade to protect children from harmful material online versus the fight to preserve the right of free speech on-line is ongoing. Shortly after the Supreme Court struck down the Communications Decency Act, Congress passed a new law known as the Child Online Protection Act, which makes it a federal crime for commercial web sites to distribute material deemed harmful to minors. Because the Child Online Protection Act does not differentiate between those who operate pornography sites and those who provide educational or medical information, web sites such as the Sexual Health Network, which provides information on sex for disabled people and people with illnesses, worry that the new law will force them to shut down. As a result, the ACLU, the Electronic Privacy Information Center, and other plaintiffs challenged the constitutionality of the Child Online Protection Act in October 1998. In February 1999 a U.S. district judge entered a preliminary injunction against enforcement of the Child Online Protection Act.

A V-Chip for the Net?

In the summer of 1997, just after the Supreme Court struck down the Communications Decency Act, the White House held a summit on Internet censorship, discussing what methods could be used to prevent children from being exposed to sexually explicit and other inappropriate material on the Internet. Industry giants like Netscape and Microsoft spoke of software that could accompany a voluntary ratings system, similar to the "V-chip" technology already in place to limit television broadcasting. Such software could be used to screen out explicit sites, but it would require that all web-site operators rate their site, which would then be determined as either compatible or incompatible for use based on its rating. If operators failed to come up with a rating for their site, they could be screened out by the new software as an unrated site.

Ratings-based censoring was criticized by groups like the ALA and the ACLU, which labeled it censorship and felt that it was totally unnecessary and inappropriate, since filtering—a voluntary approach that would allow each individual to choose what level of blocking they desired—was available. Critics of a ratings-based censoring system also argued that web chat rooms would have a hard time coming up with a consistent rating because their content was always changing. According to Solveig Bernstein, author of *Beyond the Communications Decency Act: Constitutional Lessons of the Internet*, a Cato Institute study, asking web-site operators and content providers to label or rate their sites was not feasible. Bernstein said that rating computer speech, which is often spontaneous, would be like "requiring the labeling of conversations around a backyard barbecue."[29] In response to the White House summit on technological solutions for censoring the Internet, the ACLU said it feared the Clinton administration "was trying to achieve through technology what it could not achieve through the courts."[30] The ACLU favors the use of private-sector filtering systems that allow individuals to choose their own personal filtering program, rather than one giant ratings scheme. The difficulty of a ratings scheme would be in reaching a consensus on what is appropriate and what is not. This has been the bane of the movie ratings system in the United States, which has been criticized for failing to be consistent in its matching of content with ratings. Unlike a ratings-based V-chip system, where a few people would censor for many, personalized filtering software blocks only those elements a person chooses.

Commercially available filtering software, such as Net-Nanny, SurfWatch, Cyber Sitter, Cyber Patrol, and X-Stop, can limit access to the Internet. These programs allow parents to block a household user's access to pornography and other inappropriate material. Some of the software allows parents to choose what will be blocked, while other programs block information based on set criteria. In addition to filtering inappropriate material, some of these programs have a built-in surveillance that prevents computer users from searching with key words like "sex." Still more software offers parents the option to investigate what their child has accessed on-line. A program called Netsnitch records every site visited by a computer's user.

Although many advocates of freedom in cyberspace condone filtering because it is conducted privately at the discretion of parents, opponents of filtering software charge that it can inadvertently block access to a host of perfectly clean sites. According to Peacefire, an on-line organization that opposes blocking software, some filtering software blocks access to web sites like the National Organization for Women, the International Gay and Lesbian Human Rights Commission, and the Penal Lexicon—a site that promotes awareness of prison conditions. A blocking system that relies on key words is bound to make some mistakes. For example, it might block access to a site containing a reference to Middlesex County, Massachusetts, simply because the letters S, E, and X appear together in the county's name. Another problem with blocking programs, says Peacefire, is that many of them encrypt their list of censored sites, making it difficult for customers to know what is really being blocked from their computer.

Filtering Facts, a nonprofit organization dedicated to protecting children from Internet pornography, argues that filters have come a long way technologically since their inception and that they perform a crucial role in schools and libraries by blocking access to pornographic sites. In Utah, for example, a filtering program used in public schools blocked over 300,000 requests for on-line sex sites in the month of March, 1998.[31] Although many of these requests came from teachers or administrators checking the effectiveness of the system filter, others came from students seeking material inappropriate to the classroom. Organizations that advocate the use of Internet filtering software do not have the support of the ALA, which has taken a position against the use of filtering software in schools and libraries.

To Block or Not to Block: Libraries Confront Internet Access

The use of filtering programs in publicly funded libraries has angered anticensorship organizations, who object not only to filters but also to a private company choosing what will and will not be censored in a public space. In Loudon, Virginia, a citizens' group challenged Loudon County's decision to install X-Stop, one of the most effective blocking programs available, at the public library's computer terminals. X-Stop blocks sexually explicit material, but it has also been known to inadvertently block more innocuous content, such as the American Association of University Women and the AIDS quilt web sites. In 1997 *WIRED* magazine featured an article on the Loudon case, in which Dick Black, a Loudon library board member, explained the board's decision to restrict Internet access. His comments reflect the concerns of many librarians. "The stuff that is starting to travel on the Internet, it's sexual material that ordinary people would not even dream of in their wildest imaginations," said Black. "Let's face it: The reason for looking at porn is to become sexually aroused, and that shouldn't happen in libraries."[32] The Loudon board's decision to install a blocking program was supported by the National Law Center for Children and Families, a proponent of obscenity law. The center's president, Bruce Taylor, believes taxpayers should not have to pay for pornography and that the blocking system in the Loudon library is justified, even if it has not yet been technically perfected. Loudon's library policy allowed adults to override the blocking system with the permission of the librarian, and children could also access the Net uncensored, provided a parent gave permission and was present. In November 1998, however, a judge ruled that the Loudon library's filtering policy was unconstitutional.

Around the country, libraries have been dealing with the new issues created by the Internet. Most have adopted acceptable use policies that set guidelines for Internet users in public libraries. Acceptable use policies may ask Internet users to remember that they are in a public place and to be mindful of what they are displaying on the computer terminal, especially if it is likely to be offensive to someone else. In addition to acceptable use policies, some libraries have installed filters. The city of Boston installed filtering systems on computer terminals that were adjacent to children's sections. In Ohio, public libraries decided to leave the issue of whether to restrict Internet access up to individual communities. That way, each library can create its own policy, ensuring that local libraries will reflect the consensus of those who use them.

Whether local communities will continue to be able to set policy on Internet access in public institutions remains to be seen. Some supporters of restricted access are adamant that the government become involved in protecting children from harmful material on-line. In February 1998, U.S. Senator John McCain (R-AZ) proposed "The Internet School Filtering Act," a bill aimed at requiring public libraries and schools to install blocking programs that would protect children from sexually explicit and other inappropriate material on the Internet. At least one computer in each public library would have to be filtered for children's use. If public institutions failed to restrict Internet access, they would not qualify for federal funds to subsidize Internet access. Daniel Weitzner, deputy director of the Center for Democracy and Technology (CDT), opposed the new bill. According to Weitzner, the bill "attempts to impose a single national standard controlling what everyone on-line can see, think, and say. This approach is inconsistent with the decision of the U.S. Supreme Court, in overturning the CDA last year, that the Internet deserves the highest degree of First Amendment protections."[33] The bill garnered the support of other senators and some members of the on-line industry, but the ALA opposed the idea, maintaining that local communities, not the federal government, should make decisions about filtering.

Encryption: Should the Government Have a Set of Keys?

One of many issues of intellectual freedom to evolve since the boom in on-line communications and networked computer systems is that of encryption. Encryption is to electronic communication what a safety deposit box and a locked file drawer have traditionally been to printed communication. Encryption, or the enciphering of information into secret codes, is what makes it possible for computers to protect information that they store or transmit. Encryption is a highly effective means of making information secure, since access to the key that deciphers the code is limited. Encryption is particularly valuable as a means of ensuring privacy in medical and financial records, which are, increasingly, stored on and transferred between computers.

Prior to the advent of the communication revolution, encryption was a relatively small field, employed primarily by the military and by intelligence agencies, who needed to keep certain information confidential. But today, encryption is increasingly relied upon to facilitate commerce and communications on-line. The need for encryption in the private sector has grown tremendously. At the same time, the government's need to penetrate encryption has grown. An increase in terrorist activities being planned and assisted by the use of electronic communication has made it necessary, according to the Justice Department, for the Federal Bureau of Investigation (FBI) to access some encrypted information in order to protect national security. Technology has changed the way that criminals do business, and in order to track them, the Justice Department wants to be able to break their encoded information. The problem of nonrecoverable encryption has thwarted law enforcement efforts in the past. In January 1998, the Justice Department spoke before the Senate Select Committee on Intelligence to warn of the need for access to encryption-recovery information. Their statement included the example of Ramzi Yousef and eleven other international terrorists who were plotting to blow up U.S. commercial airliners in the Far East. Yousef's computer, which was seized by law enforcement officials, contained encrypted files describing the terrorist plot.

The Justice Department also warns that our society's reliance on computer networks and information technology has made us vulnerable to potential "cyberwarfare"—attacks on our infrastructure through the use of computers. Currently the FBI seeks access to encryption-recovery information that would give them the keys necessary to decode a wide range of information in the interests of national security. Industry, however, is reluctant to hand government the keys that would decode private information. To do so would be to restrict industry's privacy and its ability to guarantee the safety of encrypted information.

Advocates of electronic privacy don't believe the government should have access to private individuals' encoded information. They fear that government regulation of cryptographic security would endanger personal privacy and freedom by restricting an individual's ability to encode personal information.

Conclusion

At the dawn of the twenty-first century, the issue of censorship appears to be with us as much today as in the past. Censorship is still occurring in public education, where a great number of contemporary issues such as sex and health education and AIDS awareness have caused parents to worry about the message and content of their children's education. To protect their children, their belief systems, and way of life, parents have tried to prevent certain information and ideas from reaching their children, and sometimes other children as well. This has sparked a healthy debate about what is or is not appropriate for children at different ages. It has also provoked instances of censorship in schools and caused books to be removed from school classrooms and library shelves. School boards and parent groups have opposed state and federal curriculums, raising the question of whether control in the schools rests with the values of a community or with those of government. At the heart of these controversies are differing belief systems and attempts to promote those values that people feel will best serve students.

Artistic freedom is also being challenged: Citizens have demanded that art be deemed publicly acceptable before it is shown, theaters have received threats from those who disagree with the content of the plays they produce, videos have been confiscated from store shelves by angry protesters, and campaigns have been launched to boycott the sponsors of artistic venues. Taxpayers have protested the public funding of art that they consider obscene or pornographic, hence illegal, questioning the government's role and legitimacy in supporting the arts. In music, the debate over lyrics continues, with champions of artistic freedom debating those who fear the impact of violent lyrics on children.

Censorship in the form of political correctness has struck down art and speech that is supposedly not compatible with enlightened notions about race and diversity. And censorship has also occurred among news media not immune to bias and imbalance, which censor stories each year. Though the First Amendment provides a powerful counterweight to censorship with its protection for speech and beliefs, that protection continues to be tested. In recent years the challenges inherent in new media and technology—such as the Internet—have posed new problems. Censors and free speech advocates have tried to find a middle ground that would protect minors from some of the information the "information superhighway" has to offer, while allowing adults uncensored access to all on-line information. Different standards of decency, privacy, and personal freedom provide the basis for the ongoing battle between censors and their foes.

As citizens continue to negotiate the challenges presented by opposing viewpoints, those who feel the need to censor and those who will not tolerate censorship will time and again come together in debate.

Notes

1. People for the American Way, "Attacks on the Freedom to Learn 1995–1996," available Internet, http://www.pfaw.org.

2. Ibid.

3. Ibid.

4. National Coalition to Protect Children and Families, "This Is Harmless Fun?" available Internet, http://www2.nationalcoaltion.org/ncpcf.

5. People for the American Way, "Attacks on the Freedom to Learn 1995–1996."

6. Ibid.

7. Ibid.

8. Ibid.

9. Ibid.

10. Ibid.

11. Dr. K. Alan Snyder, "Who Is Censoring Whom in Schools?" *Chronicle-Tribune*, Marion, Ind., Sept. 5, 1993; available Internet, *http://www.regent.edu/acad/schgov/asnyder/writing/censor.html*.

12. Robert B. Downs and Ralph E. McCoy, *The First Freedom Today: Critical Issues Relating to Censorship and to Intellectual Freedom*, Chicago: American Library Association, 1984, p. 71.

13. People for the American Way, "Attacks on the Freedom to Learn 1995–1996."

14. Karen Diegmueller, "Library Group Seeks to Encourage a More 'Family Friendly' Focus," Teacher Magazine on the Web, December 6, 1995, http://www.teachermag.org.

15. People for the American Way, "Attacks on the Freedom to Learn 1995–1996."

16. Alt.culture "speech codes" entry, http://www.pathfinder.com/alt-culture/aentries/s/speechxcod.html.

17. *Academe: The Chronicle of Higher Education*, July/August 1992; available Internet, *http://www.lib.udel.freedom/aaup.html*.

18. ACLU press release, Nov. 6, 1997, "Increased Government Censorship Looms on the Horizon"; available Internet, http://www.aclu.org/news.

19. Eddie Dean, "Dirty War," *The Roc*, available Internet, http://www.theroc.org/roc-mag/textarch/roc–20/roc20–02.htm.

20. Ibid.

21. Jack Nichols, "Playwrights Protest Theatre's Cancellation of 'Corpus Christi,'" *Badpuppy's Gay Today*, http://www.badpuppy.com/gaytoday/garchive/events/052898ev.htm.

22. People for the American Way, *Artistic Freedom Under Attack*, 1996, Vol. 4, p. 6; available Internet, *http://www.pfaw.org/artsave/artsave.htm*.

23. Ibid.

24. Jeff Jacoby, "Art Without the NEA," *Boston Globe*, April 15, 1997; available Internet, *http://www.bigeye.com/jj041597.htm*.

25. Ibid.

26. Dr. Laurence Jarvik, "Ten Good Reasons to Eliminate Funding for the National Endowment for the Arts," April 29, 1997, The Heritage Foundation; available Internet, *http://www.frc.org/heritage/library/categories/budgettax/bg1110*.

27. Alexandra Marks, "News Media Seek Credibility, *Christian Science Monitor*, Aug. 27, 1997; available Internet, http://www.csmonitor.com/durable/1997/09/27/us/us.4.html.

28. EFF press release, June 26, 1997; available Internet, http://www.eff.org/pub/Legal/Cases/EFF_ACLU_v_DoJ/19970626_eff_cda.announce.

29. ACLU news, Nov. 26, 1996, http://www.aclu.org/news/w112696b.html.

30. ACLU news, July 16, 1997, http://www.aclu.org/news/n071697a.html.

31. Pamela Mendels, "Utah Filtering Figures Show Students Surf Sex Sites—But Not Many," *New York Times,* April 25, 1998; available Internet, *http:*//www.nytimes.com/library/tech/98/04/cyber/articles/25utah.html.

32. Rebecca Vesely, "Library Tries Critical Porn-Blocking Approach," *Wired,* July 28, 1997; available Internet, http://www.wired.com/news/politics/story/5559.html.

33. Center for Democracy and Technology, press release, Feb. 10, 1998, "McCain and Coats Bills Go Down Same Mistaken Path"; available Internet, http://www.cdt.org/speech/980210_mccain.html.

Chronology 2

This chapter presents a timeline of events relevant to a study of censorship. The entries are intended to provide the reader with a brief history of the ways in which censorship has been used at different times to promote varying points of view. The majority of entries pertain to the fight for and against censorship in the United States, although some examples from world history are given in order to provide greater background and perspective. Many of the entries denote the censorship of specific works of literature or art. Others address attempts to restrict or deny access to specific modes of communication, such as film, television, and the Internet. Also cited are more broad-based efforts to prevent the spread of certain teachings and theories. This chronology is intended to provide the reader with a greater understanding of the events that have fueled the ongoing debate about censorship.

443 B.C.   Ancient Rome establishes the office of censor to keep track of the population; eventually, the censor, a highly regarded individual, becomes the official

443 B.C. cont.	upholder of public morals and is in charge of prosecuting Roman senators accused of corruption.
circa 399 B.C.	The Greek philosopher Socrates chooses to die rather than censor his teachings.
212 B.C.	The ancient Chinese emperor Shih Huang-ti burns all the books he can find in his empire in an attempt to make history start over with him at the beginning. Among the books burned are Confucius's *Analects*.
A.D. 66	*Lysistrata*, by the Greek playwright Aristophanes, is banned by ancient Rome because it projects an antiwar stance.
1205	Saint Dominic, founder of the Dominican Order of Preaching Friars, travels among the Albigensian heretics and oversees the burning of their books.
1294	French aristocracy install codes of dress, mandating that only the upper classes may wear squirrel or ermine fur, jewels, gold, or crowns.
circa 1350	After conquering their enemies in Mexico, the Aztecs collect and destroy all histories so a new and favorable history of the Aztec conquest may be written.
1455	Johannes Gutenberg prints the first book made with movable type; printed material becomes available to more people than at any prior date in history.
1497	The ascetic leader Savonarola holds a bonfire, known as "the bonfire of the vanities," in Florence, Italy, to destroy all "indecent" books and works of art.
circa 1500	Attempting to convert the Meso-American Indians to Christianity, missionaries in the New World destroy almost all of their books, leaving future scholars with few written resources with which to study Meso-American civilization.
1501	Protesting its nudity, onlookers stone Michelangelo's statue *David* after its unveiling in Florence.

Chronology

1517	Pope Leo X condemns Martin Luther's *Ninety-Five Theses*.
1521	Holy Roman Emperor Charles V issues the *Edict of Worms*, which includes a law prohibiting the reading, printing, and copying of Luther's works.
1525	Earliest report of book burning occurs in England; William Tyndale's translation of the New Testament is destroyed.
1526	Fearing certain books would cause unrest in his kingdom, the English monarch Henry VIII issues a list of eighteen prohibited theology books, many of them by Reformation leader Martin Luther. In order to control the publication of religious works, Henry VIII and other Tudor monarchs begin requiring press operators to obtain licenses.
1564	The Catholic Church issues the *Index librorum prohibitorum* (Index of Forbidden Books) declaring which books may not be read or printed by Catholics.
1624	At the order of the Pope, officials burn Martin Luther's German translation of the Bible in Germany.
1635	Puritans banish Roger Williams from the Puritan Massachusetts Colony because he espouses religious toleration; Williams founds the Rhode Island colony as a haven for free thinkers.
1644	John Milton submits "Areopagitica," an argument against censorship, to Parliament. In the work Milton says, "Give me the liberty to know, to utter, and to argue freely according to conscience, above all other liberties." Parliament condemns the work.
1664–1669	Moliere's comedy *Tartuffe*, about religious hypocrisy, is banned from public stages in France.
1712	The first Stamp Act, or tax on paper, is passed in England with the hope of eliminating the growing

1712 cont.	number of radical newspapers and tracts being disseminated among the populace.
1734–1735	*New York Weekly Journal* publisher John Peter Zenger is tried for sedition because his paper printed satires of New York's colonial governor; Zenger is acquitted, and his case establishes an important precedent for the freedom of the press in the American colonies.
1764–1768	British thinker John Wilkes is tried for treason and sedition after criticizing King George III in a work called *North Briton;* Wilkes is jailed, but he becomes a celebrated figure in both Britain and the American colonies for having had the courage to express his views.
1791	The First Amendment, which protects the freedoms of religion, speech, and the press as well as the rights to assembly and petition, is approved and made a permanent part of the U.S. Constitution.
1798	Congress adopts the Sedition Act, which outlaws "false, scandalous, and malicious" statements against the U.S. government. The act, which is the first national attempt at political censorship, is allowed to expire during Thomas Jefferson's administration.
1807	Thomas Bowdler publishes *The Family Shakespeare,* a sanitized version of the original plays, giving rise to the term "bowdlerization," meaning "to expurgate vulgar parts."
1834	Abner Kneeland, editor of the *Boston Investigator,* is tried for blasphemy by a Massachusetts court because he publicized his lack of belief in prayer, miracles, and Christ. The Supreme Court of Massachusetts upholds the state's blasphemy law; Kneeland is convicted and jailed.
1837	Abolitionist newspaper publisher and editor Elijah Lovejoy is murdered in Alton, Illinois, by a mob of proslavery men who feared his publications would help end slavery in the United States.

1853	The armless classical statue known as the *Venus de Milo* is tried, convicted, and condemned for nudity in Mannheim, Germany.
1862	The U.S. House of Representatives Judiciary Committee publishes a report criticizing a system set up to censor sensitive news stories during the Civil War.
1868	The Fourteenth Amendment to the Constitution, which strengthens the protections offered by the First Amendment by guaranteeing that no state can make a law abridging the rights of citizens of the United States, is ratified.
1873	The "Comstock Law," or Federal Anti-Obscenity Act—inspired by censorship advocate Anthony Comstock—bans the sale of items "for the prevention of contraception" in the United States. The law also bans works of literature such as Aristophanes's *Lysistrata,* Chaucer's *Canterbury Tales,* Boccaccio's *Decameron,* Defoe's *Moll Flanders,* and certain editions of *The Arabian Nights* from traveling via U.S. mail.
1914	Margaret Sanger, leader of the birth-control movement, is indicted for sending articles on contraception (deemed "obscene literature") through the U.S. mail; Sanger is forced to flee the country.
	Journalists reporting from the frontlines of World War I send their reports through army censors, who adjust their news coverage to prevent sensitive information from reaching enemy hands. Military censors are also concerned that graphic photos and accounts of battles might demoralize the American public.
1915	*Birth of a Nation,* the controversial film about the Civil War and Reconstruction, is released, causing riots in some theaters; the film is censored in New York.
1918	The Sedition and Espionage Acts, passed during Woodrow Wilson's administration, make it illegal for Americans to use "disloyal" or "abusive" language

1918 cont.	against the United States government, the American flag, U.S. military uniforms, or the Constitution.
1919	In *Abrams v. United States* the Supreme Court upholds the Espionage Act, arguing that citizens do not always have the right to publicize their antigovernment beliefs. Justice Oliver Wendell Holmes, however, argues the dissenting opinion that people should be free to criticize their own government, both in times of war and times of peace.
1920s	Social worker, war protestor, and civil libertarian Roger Baldwin founds the American Civil Liberties Union (ACLU), an organization championing the First Amendment.

Attorney General Mitchell Palmer conducts raids on the meeting places of trade unionists, immigrant groups, and radical political organizations in 33 U.S. cities; over 4,000 people are put in jail and denied counsel. Hundreds of immigrants are deported for so-called "un-American" activities. |
1925	John T. Scopes, a high-school teacher in Dayton, Tennessee, is tried for violating state law by teaching the theory of evolution to a biology class. Tennessee's anti-evolution act of 1925 outlawed the teaching of Darwinian theory. An ACLU defense team headed by attorney Clarence Darrow defends Scopes against prosecuting attorney and three-time presidential candidate William Jennings Bryan in a famous case that becomes a major media event and inspires the play *Inherit the Wind*.
1929	U.S. Customs officials in Boston confiscate copies of Voltaire's *Candide* and deem it obscene; however, the book is on the assigned reading list at Harvard University.
1930	At the urging of the ACLU, an appeals court reverses obscenity charges against civil liberties advocate and educator Mary Ware Dennett. Dennet had been found guilty of disseminating educational information on sex and reproduction to adolescents.

The Motion Picture Producers and Distributors of America (MPPDA) voluntarily adopt the Motion Picture Production Code, or "Hays Code," a detailed description of what is and is not morally acceptable on the screen. The MPPDA opts to censor itself through this code rather than be subjected to government censorship.

The ACLU organizes the National Committee on Freedom from Censorship to oppose censorship in the discussion of sex, as well as censorship of any kind in literature, the media, radio, and cinema.

1933 Nazi officials in Germany conduct mass book-burnings in an attempt to destroy the work of Jewish and liberal thinkers and writers; the largest bonfire is held outside the University of Berlin, where the works of Albert Einstein, Ernest Hemingway, and Erich Maria Remarque, among others, are destroyed.

A U.S. Customs official impounds an art history book on the Sistine Chapel because it contains nude pictures.

After a protracted legal battle fought with the support of the ACLU, James Joyce's novel *Ulysses* is allowed past the U.S. Customs Service and into the country following a landmark anticensorship decision handed down by New York federal court Judge John M. Woolsey on December 6. Random House immediately publishes an American edition of Joyce's *Ulysses*.

1941–1945 Military censors during World War II purge reporters' accounts of shell shock and battle fatigue among the soldiers so this news will not reach the homefront.

1946 In *Hannegan v. Esquire,* the Supreme Court rules on whether *Esquire* magazine should be allowed to send its publication through the U.S. mail; the Court rules in favor of *Esquire* and severely limits the power of the U.S. Postmaster General to deem materials obscene.

1948	The Catholic Church issues its last *Index of Forbidden Books*; the index lists over 5,000 titles.
1950s	Senator Joseph McCarthy, chairman of the Senate Permanent Subcommittee on Investigations of the Committee on Government Operations, launches a crusade against communism in the United States government; books suspected of containing communist propaganda are burned in U.S. information libraries abroad, and many of these libraries are closed.
1952	The Supreme Court hands down a decision in *Joseph Burstyn, Inc. v. Wilson* that favors the film industry, deciding that the content of films cannot be censored by state laws because a state deems them sacrilegious.
1957	Producers of the *Ed Sullivan Show* instruct the camera crew to film singer Elvis Presley from the waist up so his gyrating pelvis will not be broadcast.
	Overturning a Michigan state law that banned indecent literature, the Supreme Court rules in *Butler v. Michigan* that such a law denies adults their First Amendment right to read what they choose.
	In *Roth v. United States*, the Supreme Court establishes the criteria for judging obscenity as "contemporary community standards," makes a distinction between indecency and obscenity, and upholds the notion that obscenity is not protected by the First Amendment. In order to be declared obscene, a book now has to go through three different tests: The book's descriptions of nudity or sex must go beyond the limits of taste established by community standards, it must not appeal to the interest of the average adult, and it must have no redeeming social or literary value whatsoever.
1958	In a decision hailed by many in the literary community, a federal district court in New York rules that the text of D. H. Lawrence's *Lady Chatterly's Lover* is not obscene.

1963	Comedian Lenny Bruce is tried for obscenity and for mocking religion in Philadelphia, Chicago, and Beverly Hills; in 1964, Bruce is deported from the United Kingdom on similar charges.
1965	In *Griswold v. Connecticut*, the Supreme Court invalidates an old state law that prohibited the use or dissemination of birth control.
1966	Believing the music of the Beatles was corrupting youth, some Christian groups in the United States burn Beatles records and try to prevent their music from being played on the radio.
	The Hays Code, or Motion Picture Production Code, adopted by the motion picture industry in 1930, is updated for the first time to suit new audiences and tastes.
1967	In *Epperson v. Arkansas*, the Supreme Court rules that a 1928 anti-evolution statute still on the books in Arkansas violates the freedom of speech guaranteed under the First Amendment.
	The Motion Picture Association of America (MPAA) establishes a ratings board to classify films as either G, M, R, or X.
1971	Excerpts from the Pentagon Papers, controversial classified documents dealing with U.S. policy in Vietnam, are published by the *New York Times*, touching off a debate on national security versus the right of the people to know.
1972	The Supreme Court rules in *Miller v. California* that obscenity must be defined by community, not national, standards.
1973	Parents in Kanawha County, West Virginia, protest the school board's selection of high school literature textbooks and readings because they include the writings of Gwendolyn Brooks, Allen Ginsburg, Malcolm X, and Eldridge Cleaver; parents remove

1973 cont.	their children from school for up to nine weeks and march on the state capital.
1978	In *Smith v. Collin*, the Supreme Court upholds the right of Nazi party members to march in Skokie, Illinois, home to many Holocaust survivors.
1979	Schools in Midland, Michigan, remove William Shakespeare's play *The Merchant of Venice* from classrooms because of concerns that the Jewish character Shylock, portrayed as a shrewd and heartless money lender, promotes Jewish stereotyping.
1980	U.S. District Judge William R. Overton rules that an Arkansas statute to teach scientific creationism in public schools is unconstitutional because creationism is a religion, not a science, and therefore cannot be mandated by state law.
1981	In *Board of Education v. Pico* the Supreme Court rules that students in an Island Trees, New York, school district have the right to read the books *Slaughterhouse Five, Black Boy, Soul on Ice,* and *A Hero Ain't Nothing But a Sandwich*, which the school board had removed from their classrooms because they were considered "anti-American."
1982	The Ethiopian famine makes headlines throughout the world but goes unreported within Ethiopia for two years due to censorship of the press.
1983	Henrik Ibsen's play *A Doll's House* is rejected by four members of the Alabama State Textbook Committee because it expounds feminist views.
1984	The Motion Picture Association of America introduces the PG-13 rating, urging parental guidance for children under 13, after parents' groups complained about a scene in the film *Indiana Jones and the Temple of Doom*, in which a man's still-beating heart is ripped from his chest.
	The Supreme Court rules in *Wallace v. Jaffree* that an

Alabama law requiring a moment of silence in public schools is unconstitutional under the First Amendment, which prohibits laws that establish religion.

1985   The Parents Music Resource Center (PMRC) is founded; Frank Zappa and other musicians attend hearings before the U.S. Senate on pornography in rock lyrics.

1988   In *Hazelwood v. Kuhlmeier,* the U.S. Supreme Court rules that student journalists may be censored by school officials if their material is considered inappropriate for the school newspaper.

The University of Michigan becomes one of the first higher education institutions in the country to adopt a speech code that punishes racist and sexist expression.

1989   Two California school districts remove *Little Red Riding Hood* from their libraries after parents objected to the mention of alcohol in the tale, in which Little Red Riding Hood brings her grandmother a basket of food and wine.

Salman Rushdie's novel *The Satanic Verses* is published. Statements within it offend Iranian leader Ayatollah Khomeini; he calls for Rushdie's execution, forcing the British author into hiding.

U.S. Senator Jesse Helms attacks the National Endowment for the Arts for its funding of obscene art.

1990   The Motion Picture Association of America establishes the NC-17 rating, barring children under the age of seventeen admittance to movies with this label. The NC-17 rating is intended to designate movies showing adult or explicit material without giving the film the stigma of an X rating.

The publisher Simon and Schuster cancels distribution of Bret Easton Ellis's controversial novel *American Psycho,* which contains many descriptions of violence against women; in 1991 Vintage Press, a division of

54 Chronology

1990 cont.
: Random House, publishes the novel, which critics accuse of glamorizing the life of a serial killer.

: The Parents Music Resource Center convinces major record companies to affix parental advisory warning stickers on albums containing explicit lyrics.

: The rap album *Nasty As They Wanna Be* by 2 Live Crew is indicted for obscenity charges in Florida.

: In *United States v. Eichman* the Supreme Court upholds the rights of demonstrators to burn the flag, overturning the Flag Protection Act passed by Congress in 1989.

1991
: A hate-speech code at the University of Wisconsin is declared unconstitutional in a federal district court.

1992
: Rap artist Ice T's song "Cop Killer" is removed from his *Body Count* album after his sponsor, Time Warner, is pressured to drop the song by police associations.

1993
: A University of Pennsylvania student is threatened with suspension after violating a campus ban on hate speech, touching off a national debate on political correctness that ultimately leads the University of Pennsylvania to abandon its speech code.

: In *Wisconsin v. Mitchell* the Supreme Court upholds a Wisconsin hate crime statute, arguing that it is constitutional because it only punishes those who commit crimes in the name of racism and does not apply to racist thoughts.

1994
: Congress holds hearings on the issue of violent, misogynist, and sexually explicit music lyrics.

1996
: Congress adopts the Communications Decency Act (CDA), which criminalizes the use of pornography or any "indecent" material on any computer network unless steps are taken to restrict anyone under the age of eighteen from having access to that information. The CDA meets a firestorm of criticism from groups advocating free speech in cyberspace.

Claiming it violated the school board's decision not to teach children about alternative lifestyles, schools in Merrimack, New Hampshire, remove Shakespeare's play *Twelfth Night* from the curriculum.

Congress passes the Child Pornography Prevention Act, which expands the existing definition of child pornography to include computer-generated images.

Congress passes the Military Honor and Decency Act, which prohibits the sale or rental of any magazine, recording, or video depicting "lascivious" nudity from a military facility.

1997   After one scene in the film *Tin Drum* is declared obscene by an Oklahoma judge, police in Oklahoma City, Oklahoma, confiscate copies of the film from video store owners, libraries, and a citizen's home.

On June 26, The Communications Decency Act is declared unconstitutional by the U.S. Supreme Court, which strikes down the censorship provisions of the act in *Reno v. ACLU*. Justice John Paul Stevens writes, "the interest in encouraging freedom of expression in a democratic society outweighs any theoretical but unproven benefit of censorship." (ACLU website press release, July 15, 1997, http://www.aclu.org/news/n071597a.html.)

In August, antipornography activists begin a national campaign to pressure booksellers not to sell photography books containing pictures of nude children. Among the activists are Randall Terry, former leader of the anti-abortion group Operation Rescue, and members of Focus on the Family.

1998   An Alabama grand jury charges the book chain Barnes and Noble with selling obscene material for stocking books by photographers Jock Sturges and David Hamilton, whose photographic collections contain nude pictures of children.

1998
cont.

The U.S. Justice Department speaks before the Senate Select Committee on Intelligence, warning of the need for law enforcement access to encryption recovery information.

U.S. Senator John McCain (R-AZ) proposes the Internet School Filtering Act, designed to prevent students from accessing inappropriate material while using the Internet at school; electronic privacy advocates oppose the measure, which sparks a national debate on the efficacy of filters and the impact of the Internet on children.

A Texas jury rules in favor of Oprah Winfrey's right to free speech in a lawsuit brought against her by Texas cattlemen, who claimed that her comments about beef during a talk show devoted to Mad Cow Disease had slowed beef sales.

New York's Manhattan Theater Club cancels production of Terrence McNally's play *Corpus Christi* after receiving death threats from angry callers who consider the play a perversion of Christianity; later, amid criticism that the club had bowed to pressure from censors, it stages the controversial play in October 1998.

In October, the Child Online Protection Act, which makes it a crime to distribute pornography and other material "harmful to minors" on-line without the use of an age-verification system, is passed by Congress and signed into law by President Clinton. Cyber-liberties groups immediately oppose the new law, calling it "CDA II" and filing suit against it.

On November 23, in *Loudon v. Board of Trustees of the Loudon County Library*, a federal judge in Virginia rules that the use of Internet filtering software on public library computers violates the First Amendment. The constitutionality of Internet filtering programs remains in dispute throughout the country.

Biographical Sketches 3

The following brief descriptions highlight some of the individuals, both historical and contemporary, whose lives and work have made significant contributions to the debate surrounding the issue of censorship in various media—including art, music, literature, the press, and the Internet. Some of these people have worked to protect others, especially minors, from harmful and violent images and ideas, and to ensure that the media and the national government are held accountable for the kind of images they present or foster. Others have worked to protect civil liberties and to eradicate censorship of any kind. With their different and often conflicting points of view, these artists, writers, activists, and business leaders have furthered the public discourse on the issues raised by censorship, obscenity, traditional values and standards of decency, and the First Amendment.

Roger Nash Baldwin (1884–1981)

Roger Nash Baldwin, born in Wellesley, Massachusetts, in 1884, was an American civil libertarian who crusaded for human rights and civil liberties and helped found the American Civil Liberties Union in 1920. As a young man, Baldwin became a social worker, and in 1913 he joined the American Union Against Militarism, which was composed of social reformers and radicals who opposed American involvement in World War I. As a social worker in St. Louis during World War I, Baldwin experienced the discrimination that city's foreign-born citizens were subject to, particularly if they held radical political beliefs. Adamant that all Americans should be able to express their beliefs freely, both during war and times of peace, Baldwin campaigned against government suppression of protestors' views.

In 1917, with fellow civil libertarians Crystal Eastman and Norman Thomas, Baldwin helped found the National Civil Liberties Bureau (NCLB). The NCLB's goal was to protect the liberties of all Americans as enumerated in the Bill of Rights in the U.S. Constitution. The NCLB opposed the Sedition Act of 1918, which outlawed speech or actions against the U.S. government. It fought against the deportation of Americans because of their political beliefs, defended the right of trade unions to organize, and negotiated the release of hundreds of wartime activists. In 1920, the NCLB became the American Civil Liberties Union, today the nation's foremost civil liberties organization. Baldwin served as director of the ACLU until 1950, when he became its advisor on international affairs. Baldwin also taught at the New School of Social Research from 1938 to 1942 and at the University of Puerto Rico from 1966 to 1974.

In 1989, the ACLU established the Roger Baldwin Medal of Liberty, which is awarded annually to the individuals or organizations in the world who have made outstanding contributions to the advancement of civil liberties and human rights.

Gary L. Bauer (b. 1946)

Nationally recognized speaker and commentator Gary Bauer is one of the country's foremost advocates of pro-family policy. Former president of the Family Research Council, a pro-family policy and lobbying group, Bauer took a leave of absence from that organization in 1999 in order to consider a run for the U.S. presidency in 2000.

An advocate of education reform, Bauer believes parents should have more say in their children's education and supports educational savings accounts and school voucher programs, which allow parents greater choice in education. Bauer also has lobbied Congress to eliminate the marriage tax penalty and to enact legislation that would encourage, rather than discourage, the family unit. While president of the Family Research Council, Bauer supported initiatives enhancing religious freedom, such as the Ten Commandments Defense Act, proposed in 1998, which would allow state, county, and town governments to display symbols of religious faith in the workplace. Concerned about the type of images television presents to children, Bauer has addressed the need for broadcasters to be more responsible with their programming. In 1998, as news of President Clinton's improprieties swamped the news media, Bauer urged the nation's broadcasters to "carefully balance the public's right to know and the requirement for broadcast of all details necessary for a reasoned public debate with the urgent need to protect children" (*Bauer to TV Networks: "Children at Risk: Use Restraint with Starr Report Coverage,"* Family Research Council press release, September 10, 1998; available Internet, http://www.frc.org/press/091098.html).

Bauer received his bachelor's degree from Georgetown College, Georgetown, Kentucky, in 1968 and his law degree from Georgetown Law School in Washington, D.C., in 1973. A former senior policy analyst for the Reagan/Bush campaign, in 1985 Bauer became the undersecretary of the U.S. Department of Education. Later, President Ronald Reagan appointed Bauer director of the White House's Office of Policy Development. In 1988 Bauer joined the Family Research Council, which merged with another pro-family group, James Dobson's Focus on the Family, that same year. Bauer served as senior vice president of Focus on the Family and later served as president of the Family Research Council when it again became a separate organization. In the late 1990s, Bauer became chairman of the Campaign for Working Families, a political action committee that supports free enterprise, family values, and the right-to-life movement.

Bauer is the author of several books, including *Children At Risk: The Battle for the Hearts and Minds of Our Kids*, which was coauthored with James Dobson, and *Our Hopes, Our Dreams: A Vision for America*. He lives in Virginia with his wife, Carol, and their three children.

Jerry Berman (b. 1939)

Jerry Berman is the executive director and cofounder of the Center for Democracy and Technology, which works to protect constitutional liberties in new communications media. He is also the chairman of the Advisory Committee to the Congressional Internet Caucus. A leading voice in the public policy debates that continue to affect the future of on-line commerce and communication, Berman has opposed government attempts to censor the Internet and supported technology and policy solutions that enhance individual rather than government control over Internet content, such as filtering. Berman coordinated the Citizens Internet Empowerment Coalition, a national grassroots campaign that challenged the Communications Decency Act of 1996. A strong advocate for encryption, Berman has also testified before the Senate Subcommittee on Science, Technology, and Space, attesting to his belief that the United States needs to encourage the development and sale of encryption technology in order to make secure software available to the average citizen.

Berman holds his bachelor's, master's, and law degrees from the University of California at Berkeley, where he graduated with honors and was elected to Phi Beta Kappa. Prior to co-founding the Center for Democracy and Technology in 1994, Berman was already actively lobbying Congress to enact policies that would protect privacy and freedom on-line, such as the Electronic Communications Privacy Act of 1986. He served as executive director of the Electronic Frontier Foundation, an organization working to safeguard freedom and privacy on the Internet. From 1978 to 1988 Berman served as chief legislative counsel at the American Civil Liberties Union, and he directed the ACLU projects on privacy and information technology.

Judy Blume (b.1938)

Judy Blume is an award-winning young-adult author whose books include *Are You There God? It's Me Margaret* (1970) and *Blubber* (1974). Over 65 million copies of Blume's books have been sold, making her one of the country's most popular middle-grade and young-adult book authors, and she has received over ninety awards for her fiction. Yet Blume's frank, honest language and her subject matter—puberty, obesity, adolescence, premarital sex, and divorce, to name a few—have been targeted by censors. Her novel *Deenie* (1973), about a teenage girl dealing with scoliosis, was one of the most censored young-adult books of the 1980s, and other novels, such as *Blubber* and *Then Again Maybe I Won't* (1971), are among the most frequently banned books of the 1990s. At her web site, http://www.judyblume.com, Blume addresses the censorship her books have faced, noting that when one of her books is challenged, the challenges, like hysteria, tend to multiply quickly. "I believe that censorship grows out of fear," Blume writes, "and because fear is contagious, some parents are easily swayed. Book banning satisfies their need to feel in control of their children's lives. They want to believe that if their children don't read about it, their children won't know about it" (http://www.judyblume.com/home-menu.html).

Blume was born in Elizabethtown, New Jersey, in 1938. She received her bachelor's degree in education from New York University in 1961. She has written 21 books, both children's and adult titles. Blume lives in New York City with her husband. She is the founder and trustee of Kids Fund, a charitable and educational foundation supported by royalties from her books. Blume also works with the National Coalition Against Censorship as a spokesperson on intellectual freedom issues, and she serves on the Council of the Author's Guild. Blume is a board member of the Society of Children's Book Writers and Illustrators, for whom she helps sponsor a grant to support and encourage other children's book writers working in the field of contemporary fiction.

David Burt (b. 1961)

David Burt is the president and founder of Filtering Facts, a nonprofit organization that promotes the use of software filters in order to protect minors from on-line pornography. Burt believes that minors' access to the Internet in public libraries should be filtered, and his organization recommends several types of filtering software. Burt also believes that each community should make its own decision about whether to filter adult access to the Internet in public libraries. Since libraries have not traditionally offered pornographic magazines to their patrons, Burt argues, preventing people from accessing this same pornography on-line is not inconsistent with library policy.

Burt is an American Library Association (ALA) member and a self-described liberal. He founded Filtering Facts in 1997 after the ALA took a stand against the use of filtering programs in libraries. Burt defends filtering as a safe and effective means of ensuring that children do not access inappropriate material while searching the Internet. He started Filtering Facts in order to counter the misconception that filtering programs were not effective and to raise awareness about the prevalence of pornography on the Internet. As demand for filtering software has increased, Burt notes, the technology has improved so that filters are now much more effective and can be programmed to block pornography alone.

Burt received his master's degree in library science from the University of Washington in 1992 and has worked for several branches of the New York Public Library. He is currently the information technology librarian at the Lake Oswego, Oregon, public library, where he provides technical support, maintains the library's computers and web site, teaches classes, and works the reference desk. An ALA member since 1991, Burt served on the ALA's Library Information Technology Association Research Committee from 1995 to 1996. His articles on libraries and the Internet have appeared in professional library publications, including *American Libraries* and *Public Libraries*. Burt also speaks regularly before professional library associations about policies for public access of the Internet and the efficacy of filtering software. For more information about Filtering Facts, view their web site at http://www.filteringfacts.org.

Anthony Comstock (1844–1915)

Anthony Comstock, an American crusader against obscenity, was born in Canaan, Connecticut, in 1844. A former dry goods clerk, Comstock dedicated his life to fighting obscenity and in 1873 helped found the New York Society for the Suppression of Vice. That same year, as secretary for the Committee for the Suppression of Vice, he was instrumental in lobbying Congress to pass the Federal Anti-Obscenity Act, or Comstock Law, as it became known. The Comstock Law banned obscenity from the U.S. mail.

The United States Post Office made Comstock a special agent, with powers of arrest, and he was able to travel the country at the expense of the taxpayers, searching for obscenity and its perpetrators. At the end of his life, Comstock boasted that he had caused the criminal conviction of enough people to fill a 61-coach passenger train.

Under the Comstock Law classic works of literature by authors like James Joyce, D. H. Lawrence, Theodore Dreiser, Leo Tolstoy, and Voltaire were censored in the United States for the next 60 years. People who sent or received these books in the mail could be arrested, fined, or jailed. In addition to banning works of literature, the Comstock Law made it a crime to send material on sex, birth control, or abortion through the mail. In

1914, Margaret Sanger, founder of the birth control movement, was indicted eight times under the Comstock Law for publishing articles on birth control in newspapers and sending information on birth control through the mail. Sanger was eventually forced to flee the United States. In 1915 her husband, William Sanger, was convicted under the Comstock Law for selling a pamphlet on family planning.

Anthony Comstock's personal crusade against what he considered to be obscenity created a climate where doctors, scientists, and pharmacists could be prosecuted for disseminating information on reproduction and contraception. Medical and scientific works were also vulnerable to attack, and their writers sometimes resorted to self-censorship in order to protect themselves. The Comstock Law had a chilling effect on free speech in the United States and prompted the British playwright George Bernard Shaw to coin the term "Comstockery," which today refers to any enthusiastic censoring of supposed immorality.

Robert Cormier (b. 1925)

Robert Cormier is an award-winning author of controversial young adult novels, including *The Chocolate War* (1974) and *I Am The Cheese* (1977). Heralded by the *School Library Journal,* the *New York Times,* and the American Library Association, his books are popular with young people, but they have aroused controversy among parents, teachers, and school boards. *The Chocolate War,* with its theme of students rebelling against authority, was one of the most frequently banned books of the 1990s. The book is about a male student who decides he is not going to participate in his Catholic school's annual chocolate sales fund-raiser. "I'm very much interested in intimidation and the way people manipulate other people," Cormier told an interviewer from the *School Library Journal* (Robert Cormier on-line biography, http://www.inergy.com/accounts.dean/www/cormier.htm).

Cormier is a native of Leominster, Massachusetts, and is father of three grown children. He began his writing career as a newspaper reporter and columnist for the *Worcester Telegram and Gazette* and the *Fitchburg Sentinel.* He has received several journalism awards and is the author of 15 novels and one work of nonfiction, a collection of his newspaper columns.

Because of his realistic portrayal of life, in which good guys don't always win, Cormier is accused of having an absence of hope and a darkness in his work. Critics of his work also charge that he presents disturbing subject matter and a lack of respect for authority. In 1986 Cormier's novel *I Am The Cheese* was successfully banned three times—twice in Cormier's home state of Massachusetts and once in Florida—by school administrators who felt it presented a lack of respect for government. The novel is about a boy whose parents are enrolled in a federal witness protection program.

Cormier believes those who want to censor his novels are upset that his books don't always have role models or happy endings. Committed to realism, he tries to portray characters and stories that are true to life. Says Cormier, "I can sympathize with a parent when they don't want their child to read a book. But I disagree when that parent wants no one else to read that book" (quoted in *Attacks on the Freedom to Learn*, Vol. 2 No. 1, http://www.pfaw.org/1997/aflo.2–3.html). He has tried to fight the censorship of his books, but he maintains that any time he is diverted from his writing, it is a victory for the censors. Christian Fundamentalists comprise the brunt of the opposition to his books, and Cormier feels that they are among the hardest people to fight because of their sense of self-righteousness and their conviction that what they are doing is necessary.

Some of Cormier's more recent books include *Tenderness* (1997), *In the Middle of the Night* (1995), and *We All Fall Down* (1991).

James C. Dobson (b. 1936)

James Dobson is the founder and president of Focus on the Family, a pro-family policy and support organization started in 1977. Today, Focus on the Family is an international organization that sponsors daily radio broadcasts heard around the world and publishes ten magazines received by over 2.3 million people each month.

Dobson earned a Ph.D. in child development from the University of Southern California (USC) in 1967. While working as a professor of pediatrics at the USC School of Medicine, Dobson became concerned with the fate of the American family, and this concern prompted him to start Focus on the Family. Among the initiatives Dobson supports are pro-family policies, religious liberty, and the pro-life movement. An evangelical Christian, Dobson believes homosexuality is immoral and opposes the movement for gay rights.

Dobson has been active in government efforts aimed at families. In the 1980s, under the Reagan administration, he served on the National Advisory Commission to the Office of Juvenile Justice and Delinquency Protection, the Commission on Pornography, the Advisory Board on Missing and Exploited Children, and the Panel on Teen Pregnancy Prevention. He was also chairman of the United States Army's Family Initiative. In the 1990s Dobson served on the Senate Commission on Child and Family Welfare and the National Gambling Impact Study Commission.

Perhaps best known for his parenting guides, Dobson supports disciplining through child spanking; his first guide for parents, *Dare to Discipline*, sold over three million copies. Dobson has since written numerous best-selling books on parenting, relationships, and children, including *Parenting Isn't for Cowards*. Dobson is married, has two grown children, and resides in Colorado.

Crystal Eastman (1881–1928)

Reformer, suffragist, labor activist, and civil libertarian, Crystal Eastman was one of the founders of the American Civil Liberties Union, today the foremost advocate for civil liberties in America. The daughter of two Congregational ministers, Eastman was born in Glenora, New York, in 1881 and was brought up to think independently at a time when most women were not encouraged to do so. Eastman graduated from Vassar College for women in 1903, earned her master's degree in sociology from Columbia University in New York, and went on to receive a degree from the New York University School of Law in 1907.

Eastman became a labor activist and was an investigating attorney for the U.S. Commission on Industrial Relations during the Wilson presidency. On the eve of World War I she founded the Women's International League for Peace and Freedom, still in existence today. Eastman also became the executive director of the American Union Against Militarism, which opposed U.S. involvement in World War I. In 1917 Eastman, together with her friends Roger Baldwin and Norman Thomas, founded the National Civil Liberties Bureau (NCLB), an organization devoted to protecting the Bill of Rights. Through the NCLB Eastman championed individual freedom and defended Americans who held radical political beliefs. Eastman's own socialist beliefs and her activism caused her to be blacklisted during the Red Scare of 1919–1921.

In 1920 the NCLB was renamed the American Civil Liberties Union. Eastman was involved in the women's suffrage movement, which finally gained all women the right to vote in 1920, and she helped author the Equal Rights Amendment, first proposed in 1923, which called for equal pay and equal opportunity for women in the work force. Eastman continued to campaign for civil liberties for all Americans until her death in 1928.

Tipper Gore (b. 1948)

Mary Elizabeth "Tipper" Gore, the wife of United States Vice-President Al Gore, has worked to increase parental awareness of music lyrics and to publicize the prevalence of violent and sexually explicit lyrics in rock and rap music. During 1978–1979 Tipper Gore chaired the Congressional Wives task force, which drew attention to the impact of media violence on children. In 1985, Gore cofounded the Parents Music Resource Center (PMRC), an organization that lobbies the music industry for greater responsibility and accountability in the proliferation of violent lyrics. The PMRC succeeded in brokering an agreement between the Recording Industry Association of America and the National Parent Teacher Organization to voluntarily engage in music labeling that warns customers about the contents of certain albums. The result was the creation of "parental advisory" warning labels on music that contains explicit lyrics.

Tipper Gore grew up in Arlington, Virginia, and received her undergraduate degree in psychology from Boston College in 1970. In 1975 she earned her master's in psychology from the George Peabody College at Vanderbilt University. A mother of four children, Mrs. Gore became an activist in the fight to warn parents about explicit music lyrics after she purchased Prince's *Purple Rain* album for her 11-year-old daughter, unaware that it contained adult lyrics. Though Gore has been criticized by freedom of expression advocates in the music industry, she maintains that warning people about the contents of a CD is not the same thing as censoring the material. In an address to the Parent Teachers Organization of America, Gore affirmed that she supports free speech. "I am for free speech, including my freedom of speech as a mother. I am free to call it as I see it," she said. "I can say trash is trash, violence is violence, and that treating women as objects to be exploited, humiliated, raped, murdered, and forgotten is degrading beyond all moral measure" (Tipper Gore, "Parenting in the Information Age," *Our Children,* March/April 1996; available Internet, http://www.pta.org/pta/ pubs/ tgore/ htm).

Gore is the author of *Raising PG Kids in an X-rated Society* (1987), which chronicles her attempts to bring the entertainment industry to accountability for the spread of media violence. Though no longer head of the PMRC, Gore continues to support the center's role as an active and vital resource for concerned parents and church and community groups.

Karen Jo Gounaud (b. 1947)

Karen Jo Gounaud is the president and founder of Family Friendly Libraries, a national organization that raises awareness about the need to protect children form harmful or age-inappropriate material in public libraries. Gounaud, who is married and has two grown children, holds a degree in education from the University of Nebraska. She is also a children's book author; in 1981 her book *A Very Mice Joke Book* won a New York "Children's Choice" award. Gounaud lives in Fairfax County, Virginia, where she first began lobbying for age-appropriate access policies in local libraries. These policies would require the placement of library books and other media that contain troubling or disturbing material on shelves where young children would not encounter them while browsing. Rather than removing such materials from the library, Gounaud believes they should be placed in areas where access is restricted without parental permission. Gounaud believes parents should be actively involved in their children's education and that libraries should encourage parental involvement and take parents' concerns into consideration when devising library policy. Rather than brushing off parents' suggestions as attempts to censor, Gounaud believes librarians have a responsibility to address those concerns.

Realizing that other people around the country share her beliefs, Gounaud founded Family Friendly Libraries in 1995. Since then, FFL has offered information and advice to concerned citizens' groups seeking access control over specific materials. Gounaud has spoken before groups such as the National Coalition for the Protection of Children and Families, and the Public Library Association. In 1996 she received the American Family Association's God and Country Award. In recent years Gounaud has made the problem of Internet pornography a top priority. Her organization now works to promote the use of filtering software in public libraries. For more information on Family Friendly Libraries, view their web site at http://www.fflibraries.org.

Nat Hentoff (b. 1925)

Writer and former ACLU board member Nat Hentoff has championed free speech throughout his journalistic career. Born in Boston in 1925, Hentoff studied at Northeastern University, where the campus newspaper was censored by university officials after it published some controversial exposés. Hentoff cites this early experience as one of the impetuses behind his interest in freedom of speech.

After doing graduate work at Harvard and attending the Sorbonne on a Fulbright Fellowship, Hentoff worked as an associate editor at *Down Beat* magazine. A staff writer for the *New Yorker* for over 25 years, Hentoff has consistently written about music, censorship, and First Amendment issues. Hentoff has built a reputation as a journalist committed to the protection of the First Amendment, and he is widely regarded as an authority on the Bill of Rights, the Supreme Court, and students' rights. In 1980 Hentoff received a Guggenheim Fellowship in education. In 1983 he addressed the censorship of classic books in the public school curriculum with his novel for children, *The Day They Came to Arrest the Book,* which tells the story of how Mark Twain's *Huckleberry Finn* is challenged at an American high school. In the late 1980s and early 1990s when colleges and universities began experimenting with speech codes to ban sexist and racist speech, Hentoff was a vocal opponent of laws against so-called hate speech, and he argued that they interfered with academic freedom and the ability to explore ideas and issues fully.

Hentoff writes a weekly column for the *Village Voice*. His writing has also appeared in the *Washington Post,* the *Wall Street Journal,* the *New York Times,* the *New Republic, Commonweal,* and the *Atlantic*. His books on censorship and the First Amendment include *Living the Bill of Rights: How to Be an Authentic American* (1998), *Speaking Freely: A Memoir* (1997), *The First Freedom: The Tumultuous History of Free Speech in America* (1988), *Free Speech for Me and Not for Thee: How the American Left and Right Relentlessly Censor Each Other* (1993), and the children's book *The Day They Came to Arrest the Book* (1983).

Judith Krug (b. 1940)

Judith Krug is the director of the American Library Association's Office for Intellectual Freedom, which is responsible for carrying out ALA policies on intellectual freedom. Through her work,

Krug has educated librarians and the general public about the importance of intellectual freedom in libraries. As editor of the *Newsletter on Intellectual Freedom*, the *Freedom to Read Foundation News*, and the *Intellectual Freedom Action News*, she keeps ALA members informed on current events and issues associated with libraries and the freedom to read.

Krug earned her bachelor's degree in political theory from the University of Pittsburgh and her master's at the Graduate Library School of the University of Chicago. She worked as a reference librarian and cataloguer before becoming a research analyst for the American Library Association, with whom she has now worked for over 30 years.

An active speaker on intellectual freedom issues, Krug was an outspoken opponent of the Communications Decency Act of 1996 and worked with the ALA to oppose it. Krug and the ALA have also been vocal opponents of the use of Internet filtering software in public libraries, because of the tendency of these programs to block out more than just pornographic sites. "I personally believe that very few [library] board members understand that they are blocking more than they realize," says Krug. "Over time, I hope that library boards will become more knowledgeable as to the realities of the software" (Rebecca Vesely, "Library Tries Critical Porn-Blocking Approach," *Wired*, July 28, 1997; available Internet, http:www.wired.com/news/politics/story/5559.html). Supporting her position against the use of filtering programs in public libraries, Krug has repeatedly stressed that "the librarian's role is to bring people together with information, not keep it from them" (ALA Intellectual Freedom Committee, "Libraries Tackle Issues of Internet Access," *Newsletter on Intellectual Freedom*, March 1997, Vol. 46, No. 2, p. 51).

Krug is also the executive director of the Freedom to Read Foundation, an independent organization that promotes First Amendment freedoms in libraries, and she has been a board member of the Illinois Division of the American Civil Liberties Union.

Sally Mann (b. 1951)

Internationally recognized artist Sally Mann is one of the most provocative woman photographers of the late twentieth century. Critics have accused her of creating child pornography with her nude black-and-white photos of children and adolescents, while fans praise her work as sincere reflections of childhood, family, and motherhood. In the 1990s, Randall Terry of Loyal Opposition, together with members from the conservative pro-family group Focus on the Family, deemed Mann's photographs pornographic and protested their presence in bookstores. Some of Mann's books were damaged in stores by her detractors.

Mann grew up in Lexington, Virginia, where her father was the town doctor. Mann credits her father with introducing her to photography. She attended the Putney School, Bennington College, and Friends World College, and received her bachelor's degree summa cum laude from Hollins College in 1974. Mann studied photography at the Praestegaard Film School, the Aegean School of Fine Arts, Apeiron, and the Ansel Adams Yosemite workshop. Her work focuses on her family, children, and friends in Virginia. Her 8 x 10 black-and-white photographs often depict nude children who show a real confidence and presence. In 1988 her series "At Twelve: Portraits of Young Women" was published by Aperture Press. This series featured intimate portraits of girls from Mann's Virginia neighborhood. At times sinister and seductive, these photographs of girls on the cusp of womanhood are among her most controversial works. However, Mann was also praised by many for her serious look at 12-year-old girls, who are otherwise largely ignored or unexplored in art. In 1992 Mann's series "Immediate Family," a photographic record of her own three children, focused on children and their relationships. Critics accused Mann of exploiting her own children with these often nude and provocative photographs. She was strongly criticized by many for including portraits of her children that showed them with injuries—swollen eyes or bloody skin—which they had received naturally, as the result of accidents. But Mann maintained that her goal was to record what happened, whether it was pretty or not.

Mann has received three National Endowment for the Arts individual artists fellowships, and her funding from the NEA has drawn strong criticism from conservative groups such as the Christian Action Network, which identifies Mann as an example of the ways in which it believes the NEA funds pornographic art. Mann has also received a Guggenheim fellowship, and she has been the recipient of fellowships from the Virginia Museum of Fine Arts and Artists in the Visual Arts. Her photographs have been displayed at the Museum of Modern Art in New York, the Metropolitan Museum of Art, the National Museum of American Art in New York, the San Francisco Museum of Modern Art, and the Whitney Museum of American Art, among others. In addition to her work with children, Mann has photographed the dying as part of her collaboration between the National Hospice Foundation and the Corcoran Gallery of Art.

Michael Powell (b. 1941)

Michael Powell is the president of Powell's Bookstore, the largest new and used bookstore in the United States, located in Portland, Oregon. Powell was born in Portland and attended the University of Chicago, where he began selling used books at the university's co-op bookstore. Powell's professors loaned him money to open his first bookstore in Chicago in 1970, and in 1979 he began working at his father's Portland bookstore. Since that time Powell has created a bookstore like no other. Powell's Bookstore in Portland is considered an anomaly in an era when superstore book chains such as Borders and Barnes and Noble have gobbled up independent stores, capturing nearly 50 percent of all bookstore sales. Powell's Bookstore also fulfills an important role as a successful independent store, since critics of chain bookstores have charged that the marketing strategies of chains pose a threat to diversity in literature. Outspoken freedom of expression advocate Nat Hentoff has called book chains one of the biggest threats to free expression today, since chain stores often fail to stock midlist authors who may lack commercial appeal. In contrast, independent bookstores play an important role in making emerging writers' voices heard. Independents have shown that they are also less likely to bow to pressure from interest groups. In 1989, when Salmon Rushdie's *Satanic Verses* was published amidst controversy, America's two largest book chains pulled the book from its stores. Independents like Powell's, however, continued to proudly display the *Satanic Verses*.

Michael Powell has long promoted his bookstore as a vehicle for free expression and a champion of diversity. When the Oregon Citizens Alliance put a measure on a 1992 state ballot declaring that homosexuality was wrong, Powell responded by placing signs throughout his store that publicized the proposal. The measure was defeated. In 1994 and 1996, when antipornography initiatives designed to ban obscene material threatened to impinge Oregon's free speech protections, Powell was concerned that the measures, if passed, would lead booksellers to censor their stock. So he placed orange tags throughout the store, below titles that have been censored in the past, such as *Huckleberry Finn* and *I Know Why the Caged Bird Sings*. He turned his store into an advertisement for free speech and free thought. In both 1994 and 1996, Oregon voters defeated the initiatives.

The mission statement of Powell's Bookstore reads: "We have a social responsibility to the community and to our industry to fight censorship, promote literary awareness, and encourage authors and their works." As an independent bookstore owner and free speech activist, Powell, together with his staff and customers, has proved to be a formidable obstacle to censorship.

Andres Serrano (b. 1950)

Andres Serrano's glossy color photographs achieved great notoriety in the late 1980s and early 1990s when they sparked a national debate on federal funding of the arts. Serrano is perhaps best known for his photograph *Piss Christ* (1987), which depicts a crucifix submerged in urine. It was this photograph that inspired the American Family Association and U.S. Senator Jesse Helms to launch a vocal campaign against federal funding for the arts through the National Endowment for the Arts.

Serrano was born in New York in 1950 to an African Cuban mother and Honduran father and was raised in a Roman Catholic household. At age 15 he dropped out of high school, later enrolling at the Brooklyn Museum Art School, where he studied from 1967 to 1969. In his early twenties Serrano developed drug addictions that distracted his focus from art. By his late twenties Serrano had stopped taking drugs and returned to his art. Preferring large color cibachrome photographs, Serrano began exploring photography as a conceptual rather than a representational art. Among his subjects were religious icons and Catholic clergy, whom he photographed in ways that questioned the authority of Catholic beliefs. Serrano also began using bodily fluids such as blood and urine instead of paint to create the colors he wanted to photograph. In 1988 Serrano received a grant for $15,000 from Awards in the Visual Arts, funded in part by the National Endowment for the Arts. After his "Fluid Abstractions" series—which included *Piss Christ*—created picket lines of religious protesters outside his exhibitions, Serrano gained national attention as a controversial and provocative artist. The debate over whether taxpayer money should fund controversial art eventually caused Congress to cut funding for the National Endowment for the Arts.

Serrano's photographs of taboo subjects have continued to arouse controversy and discussion, particularly his 1992 series

"The Morgue," which featured close-up portraits of corpses. Other subjects of interest to Serrano include Ku Klux Klan members and the homeless people of New York City, whom he documented in a critically acclaimed 1990 series entitled "Nomads." Serrano lives in New York City.

C. Delores Tucker

C. Delores Tucker is the chair of the National Political Congress of Black Women (NPCBW), a nonprofit, nonpartisan organization devoted to the economic and political empowerment of African American women and their families. Alarmed by the distribution of pornographic, violent "gangsta" rap music, which she believes is detrimental to black youth, Tucker and the NPCBW have crusaded against the rappers and the music companies that produce hard-core rap. Tucker's activism in the African American community dates to the Civil Rights movement; in 1965 she marched from Selma to Montgomery, Alabama, with Dr. Martin Luther King. For six years, Tucker also served as secretary of state in Pennsylvania. She is a past president of the National Federation of Democratic Women and a former chair of the Democratic National Committee Black Caucus. She attended Temple University and the University of Pennsylvania Wharton School.

The daughter of a minister, Tucker grew up in Philadelphia in a home where she listened to positive, empowering gospel music. Concerned about the social impact of music lyrics that glorify violence, especially violence toward women, Tucker has worked to change the kind of messages that popular music is sending children. Angry about the prevalence of gangster rap, Tucker pursued Time Warner Corporation's Interscope record label, which distributed the works of the well-known gangster rapper Snoop Doggy Dogg. After purchasing ten shares of Time Warner stock, Tucker attended the annual shareholder's meeting in New York, where she stood up and gave a speech that blamed the company for contributing to the destruction of the black community in America. Her speech was applauded by many in the room, and several months later, Time Warner agreed to abandon its stake in the Interscope label.

At a congressional hearing on the impact of music violence in 1997, Tucker urged Congress to clarify and strengthen existing laws designed to protect children from pornography, so that they might apply to music lyrics that "grossly malign black women . . . and pander pornography to our innocent young children"

(C. Delores Tucker, address to the Senate subcommittee, "The Social Impact of Music Violence," Nov. 6, 1997, http://www.senate.gov/~brownback/music/tucker.html). Tucker remarked on the devastation wreaked on black communities by the drug trade and added that gangster rap was driven by drugs, greed, violence and sex.

Tucker has also voiced the concern that record company executives encourage hard-core rap, leaving black musicians with positive messages no market for their form of expression. Tucker wants the music industry to respond to African Americans' concern about rap music, much the way they responded to Jewish community protests that the lyrics on a Michael Jackson album were anti-Semitic. In that instance, which took place in 1995, Jackson removed the offending lyrics from his album, and the music channel MTV immediately took the song off its play lists. Convinced that musical messages do make a difference in young people's lives, she and the National Political Congress of Black Women continue to lobby for changes in the music industry.

Donald Wildmon (b. 1938)

One of the country's best-known anti-obscenity and antipornography crusaders, the Reverend Donald Wildmon is the president of the American Family Association, a nonprofit organization devoted to preserving traditional Christian family values and curbing the influence that television and other media—particularly pornography—have on society. Rev. Wildmon, an ordained United Methodist minister, earned his master's degree in Divinity from Emory College in 1965 and served as a pastor until 1977, when he founded what is now the American Family Association (AFA).

Feeling bombarded by violent, sexually explicit images on television, Wildmon gained national recognition in 1977 when he organized a "Turn off TV" week for his church. The success of Turn off TV week prompted him to create an organization called the National Federation for Decency (which later became the American Family Association), in order to connect like-minded people around the United States.

As head of the American Family Association, Wildmon has accused the National Endowment for the Arts of abusing taxpayer money by supporting pornographic art. He has spearheaded boycotts against Disney/ABC and the advertisers who supported its show *Ellen*, which the AFA denounced for being pro-homosexual. He has also campaigned against the Howard Stern radio show because of its profanity and explicit content. In 1984, the AFA launched a successful boycott against the 7–11 chain of stores and succeeded in having the company remove pornographic magazines from their stores' shelves. The AFA also lobbied the federal prison system until pornographic magazines were removed from federal prison commissaries.

Through Wildmon's efforts, companies like Burger King, Clorox, and S. C. Johnson have altered their advertising policies so that they do not upset their customers by supporting violent or explicit television programming. Wildmon's AFA has worked to remind companies of the need for responsibility in their programming and products. For example, in 1989, the AFA convinced Matchbox Toys Ltd. to stop making its "Freddy Kruger" doll, which was based on the violent horror film series *Nightmare on Elm Street.*

Wildmon believes in holding companies accountable for their attacks on traditional family values and is committed to encouraging quality family programming and entertainment.

Facts and Statistics 4

This chapter provides data on censorship in the form of court decisions, graphs and tables, reprinted documents, and relevant quotations from prominent individuals. Supreme Court decisions that have had a significant impact on the censorship debate are summarized and excerpted. Graphs show the number of challenges to books and other materials over the course of the 1990s, the nature of these challenges, the initiators of these challenges, and the institutions where these challenges occur. The states where censorship attempts have occurred most frequently are also listed. A pie graph depicts the number of libraries that use filters to screen Internet access for minors, and a table depicts the percentage of public libraries that have acceptable-use policies to regulate public access to the Internet. Included in the documents section of the chapter are (1) the American Library Association's *Library Bill of Rights*, (2) the ALA's *Diversity in Collection Development* interpretation, (3) Family Friendly Libraries' *Charter for a Family-Friendly Library System*, (4) the ALA's *Freedom to Read* statement, (5) the ACLU's *Briefing Paper Number 14*, with its statement on artistic freedom, (6) the Motion Picture Production Code adopted by the Motion Picture Producers and Distributors of

America in 1934, (7) the text of the Communications Decency Act passed by Congress in 1996 but later declared unconstitutional by the Supreme Court, (8) the Electronic Privacy Information Center's 1997 report on Internet filtering programs, *Faulty Filters*, and (9) excerpts from the U.S. Freedom of Information Act. At the end of the chapter are a number of interesting quotations on censorship and freedom of expression.

Supreme Court Decisions

Abrams v. United States, 250 U.S. 616 (1919)

Five Russian-born men who disseminated thousands of anti-government pamphlets in the U.S. during WWI were charged with violating the Espionage Act of 1918, which outlawed the publication of "disloyal" language against the U.S. while the nation was at war. Although lawyers for the men argued that the Espionage Act was an unconstitutional violation of First Amendment rights, the Court affirmed the ruling. Only Justice Oliver Wendell Holmes offered a dissenting opinion, arguing that free speech was a right even in times of war. Justice Holmes wrote:

> Persecution for the expression of opinions seems to me perfectly logical. If you have no doubt of your premises or your power and want a certain result with all your heart you naturally express your wishes in law and sweep away all opposition. To allow opposition by speech seems to indicate that you think the speech impotent, as when a man says that he has squared the circle, or that you do not care wholeheartedly for the result, or that you doubt either your power or your premises. But when men have realized that time has upset many fighting faiths, they may come to believe even more than they believe the very foundations of their own conduct that the ultimate good desired is better reached by free trade in ideas—that the best test of truth is the power of the thought to get itself accepted in the competition of the market, and that truth is the only ground upon which their wishes safely can be carried out. That at any rate is the theory of our Constitution. It is an experiment, as all life is an experiment. Every year if not every day we

have to wager our salvation upon some prophecy based upon imperfect knowledge. While that experiment is part of our system I think that we should be eternally vigilant against attempts to check the expression of opinions that we loathe and believe to be fraught with death, unless they so imminently threaten immediate interference with the lawful and pressing purposes of the law that an immediate check is required to save the country.

I wholly disagree with the argument of the Government that the First Amendment left the common law as to seditious libel in force. History seems to me against the notion. I had conceived that the United States through many years had shown its repentance for the Sedition Act of 1798 (Act July 14, 1798, c. 73, 1 Stat. 596), by repaying fines that it imposed. Only the emergency that makes it immediately dangerous to leave the correction of evil counsels to time warrants [250 U.S. 616, 631] making any exception to the sweeping command, 'Congress shall make no law abridging the freedom of speech.' Of course I am speaking only of expressions of opinion and exhortations, which were all that were uttered here, but I regret that I cannot put into more impressive words my belief that in their conviction upon this indictment the defendants were deprived of their rights under the Constitution of the United States. [footnotes omitted]

Hannegan v. Esquire, 327 U.S. 146 (1946)

Esquire magazine's second-class postal privileges were revoked by the postmaster general on the grounds that the magazine violated a law banning the mailing of obscene material through the U.S. Post Office. The Court ruled in favor of *Esquire,* arguing that the postmaster general should not have the power to set the standard for taste in literature or art. This decision severely limited the power of the postmaster general to revoke mailing privileges. Justice William O. Douglas wrote:

> Under our system of government there is an accommodation for the widest varieties of tastes and ideas. What is good literature, what has educational value,

what is refined public information, what is good art, varies with individuals as it does from one generation to another. There doubtless would be a contrariety of views concerning Cervantes' *Don Quixote,* [327 U.S. 146, 158] Shakespeare's *Venus & Adonis,* or Zola's *Nana.* But a requirement that literature or art conform to some norm prescribed by an official smacks of an ideology foreign to our system. The basic values implicit in the requirements of the Fourth condition can be served only by uncensored distribution of literature. From the multitude of competing offerings the public will pick and choose. What seems to one to be trash may have for others fleeting or even enduring values. But to withdraw the second-class rate from this publication today because its contents seemed to one official not good for the public would sanction withdrawal of the second-class rate tomorrow from another periodical whose social or economic views seemed harmful to another official. The validity of the obscenity laws is recognition that the mails may not be used to satisfy all tastes, no matter how perverted. But Congress has left the Postmaster General with no power to prescribed standards for the literature or the art which a mailable periodical disseminates.

This is not to say that there is nothing left to the Postmaster General under the Fourth condition. It is his duty to 'execute all laws relative to the Postal Service' [Rev. Stat. 396, 5 U.S.C. 369, 5 U.S.C. A. 369]. For example, questions will arise . . . whether the publication which seeks the favorable second-class rate is a periodical as defined in the Fourth condition or a book or other type of publication. And it may appear that the information contained in a periodical may not be of a 'public character.' But the power to determine whether a periodical (which is mailable) contains information of a public character, literature or art does not include the further power [327 U.S. 146, 159] to determine whether the contents meet some standard of the public good or welfare. [footnotes omitted]

Joseph Burstyn, Inc. v. Wilson, 343 U.S. 495 (1952)

A film company seeking to license a film called *The Miracle* was prevented from doing so under a New York statute that allowed motion pictures to be banned if they appeared to be sacrilegious. The Court ruled that the New York state law was unconstitutional and that the movie's content was protected by the First Amendment and by the Due Process clause of the Fourteenth Amendment, which prevents states from interfering with federal law. Justice Tom C. Clark wrote:

> It is urged that motion pictures do not fall within the First Amendment's aegis because their production, distribution, and exhibition is a large-scale business conducted for private profit. We cannot agree. That books, newspapers, and magazines are published and sold for profit does not prevent them from being a form of expression whose liberty is safeguarded by the First Amendment [343 U.S. 495, 502]. We fail to see why operation for profit should have any different effect in the case of motion pictures.
>
> It is further urged that motion pictures possess a greater capacity for evil, particularly among the youth of a community, than other modes of expression. Even if one were to accept this hypothesis, it does not follow that motion pictures should be disqualified from First Amendment protection. If there be capacity for evil it may be relevant in determining the permissible scope of community control, but it does not authorize substantially unbridled censorship such as we have here.
>
> For the foregoing reasons, we conclude that expression by means of motion pictures is included within the free speech and free press guaranty of the First and Fourteenth Amendments. [footnotes omitted]

Butler v. Michigan, 352 U.S. 380 (1957)

A Michigan citizen who sold a book containing explicit material to an undercover police officer was charged with violating a Michigan state obscenity law designed to shield children from inappropriate material. The Court, arguing that the man had not endangered children by selling the book to an adult and that the Michigan law denied adults their First Amendment rights to read what they chose, overturned the Michigan law's ban on indecent literature. Explaining this reversal, Justice Felix Frankfurter wrote:

> It is clear on the record that appellant was convicted because Michigan, by 343, made it an offense for him to make available for the general reading public (and he in fact sold to a police officer) a book that the trial judge [352 U.S. 380, 383] found to have a potentially deleterious influence upon youth. The State insists that, by thus quarantining the general reading public against books not too rugged for grown men and women in order to shield juvenile innocence, it is exercising its power to promote the general welfare. Surely, this is to burn the house to roast the pig. Indeed, the Solicitor General of Michigan has, with characteristic candor, advised the Court that Michigan has a statute specifically designed to protect its children against obscene matter "tending to the corruption of the morals of youth." But the appellant was not convicted for violating this statute.
>
> We have before us legislation not reasonably restricted to the evil with which it is said to deal. The incidence of this enactment is to reduce the adult population of Michigan to reading only what is fit for children. It thereby [352 U.S. 380, 384] arbitrarily curtails one of those liberties of the individual, now enshrined in the Due Process Clause of the Fourteenth Amendment, that history has attested as the indispensable conditions for the maintenance and progress of a free society. [footnotes omitted]

Roth v. United States, 354 U.S. 476 (1957)

Booksellers in New York and Los Angeles were convicted on state and federal obscenity laws of mailing obscene fliers and advertisements through the U.S. mail. The Court upheld their convictions, ruling that obscenity was not protected by the First Amendment. The Court also determined that the criteria for judging obscenity should be "contemporary community standards." The following are excerpts from the opinion of the Court, delivered by Justice William J. Brennan Jr.:

The constitutionality of a criminal obscenity statute is the question in each of these cases. In Roth, the primary constitutional question is whether the federal obscenity statute violates the provision of the First Amendment that "Congress shall make no law . . . abridging the freedom of speech, or of the press. . . ."

Roth conducted a business in New York in the publication and sale of books, photographs and magazines. He used circulars and advertising matter to solicit sales. He was convicted by a jury in the District Court for the Southern District of New York upon 4 counts of a 26-count indictment charging him with mailing obscene circulars and advertising, and an obscene book, in violation of the federal obscenity statute. His conviction was affirmed by the Court of Appeals for the Second Circuit. We granted certiorari [354 U.S. 476, 481].

The dispositive question is whether obscenity is utterance within the area of protected speech and press. Although this is the first time the question has been squarely presented to this Court, either under the First Amendment or under the Fourteenth Amendment, expressions found in numerous opinions indicate that this Court has always assumed that obscenity is not protected by the freedoms of speech and press. Ex parte Jackson, 96 U.S. 727, 736–737; *United States v. Chase,* 135 U.S. 255, 261; *Robertson v. Baldwin,* 165 U.S. 275, 281; *Public Clearing House v. Coyne,* 194 U.S. 497, 508; *Hoke v. United States,* 227 U.S. 308, 322; *Near v. Minnesota,* 283 U.S. 697, 716; *Chaplinsky v. New Hampshire,* 315 U.S. 568, 571–572; *Hannegan v. Esquire, Inc.,* 327 U.S. 146, 158; *Winters v. New York,* 333 U.S. 507, 510; *Beauharnais v. Illinois,* 343 U.S. 250, 266.9 [354 U.S. 476, 482].

. . . The guaranties of freedom of expression in effect in 10 of the 14 States which by 1792 had ratified the Constitution, gave no absolute protection for every utterance. Thirteen of the 14 States provided for the prosecution of libel, and all of those States made either blasphemy or profanity, or both, statutory crimes. As early as [354 U.S. 476, 483] 1712, Massachusetts made it criminal to publish "any filthy, obscene, or profane song, pamphlet, libel or mock sermon" in imitation or mimicking of religious services. Acts and Laws of the Province of Mass. Bay, c. CV, 8 (1712), Mass. Bay Colony Charters & Laws 399 (1814). Thus, profanity and obscenity were related offenses.

In light of this history, it is apparent that the unconditional phrasing of the First Amendment was not intended to protect every utterance. This phrasing did not prevent this Court from concluding that libelous utterances are not within the area of constitutionally protected speech. *Beauharnais v. Illinois,* 343 U.S. 250, 266. At the time of the adoption of the First Amendment, obscenity law was not as fully developed as libel law, but there is sufficiently contemporaneous evidence to show that obscenity, too, was outside the protection intended for speech and press [354 U.S. 476, 484].

The protection given speech and press was fashioned to assure unfettered interchange of ideas for the bringing about of political and social changes desired by the people. . . . All ideas having even the slightest redeeming social importance—unorthodox ideas, controversial ideas, even ideas hateful to the prevailing climate of opinion—have the full protection of the guaranties, unless excludable because they encroach upon the limited area of more important interests. But implicit in the history of the First Amendment is the rejection of obscenity as utterly without redeeming social importance. This rejection for [354 U.S. 476, 485] that reason is mirrored in the universal judgment that obscenity should be restrained, reflected in the international agreement of over 50 nations, in the obscenity laws of all of the 48 States, and in the 20 obscenity laws enacted by the Congress from 1842 to 1956 . . . We hold that obscenity is not within the area of constitutionally protected speech or press. [footnotes omitted]

Engel v. Vitale, 370 U.S. 421 (1962)

Public school students in the state of New York were asked to recite a nondenominational prayer each morning. The Court decided that under the First Amendment's insistence that no law "respecting an establishment of religion" be passed, New York state officials could not impose an official state prayer on school children, even if was nondenominational or voluntary. Justice Hugo L. Black wrote:

> The history of governmentally established religion, both in England and in this country, showed that whenever government had allied itself with one particular form of religion, the inevitable result had been that it had incurred the hatred, disrespect and even contempt of those who held contrary beliefs. That same history showed that many people had lost their respect for any religion that had relied upon the support of government to spread its faith. The Establishment Clause [370 U.S. 421, 432] thus stands as an expression of principle on the part of the Founders of our Constitution that religion is too personal, too sacred, too holy, to permit its "unhallowed perversion" by a civil magistrate. Another purpose of the Establishment Clause rested upon an awareness of the historical fact that governmentally established religions and religious persecutions go hand in hand. The Founders knew that only a few years after the Book of Common Prayer became the only accepted form of religious services in the established Church of England, an Act of Uniformity was passed to compel all Englishmen to attend those services and to make it a criminal offense to conduct or attend religious gatherings of any other kind—a law [370 U.S. 421, 433] which was consistently flouted by dissenting religious groups in England and which contributed to widespread persecutions of people like John Bunyan who persisted in holding "unlawful [religious] meetings ... to the great disturbance and distraction of the good subjects of this kingdom. . . ." And they knew that similar persecutions had received the sanction of law in several of the colonies in this country soon after the establishment of official religions in those colonies. It was in large part to get completely away from this sort of systematic religious persecution that the Founders brought into being our Nation, our Constitution, and our Bill of Rights with its prohibition against any governmental establishment of religion. The New York

laws officially prescribing the Regents' prayer are inconsistent both with the purposes of the Establishment Clause and with the Establishment Clause itself. [footnotes omitted]

Jacobellis v. Ohio, 378 U.S. 184 (1964)

A movie theater manager was convicted under an Ohio state obscenity law for showing an allegedly obscene film, *The Lovers*, by filmmaker Louis Malle. The Ohio state supreme court upheld the conviction. However, the Supreme Court reversed the decision on the basis that the film, which was not hard-core pornography, did not meet the criteria for being declared obscene. Justice William J. Brennan Jr. wrote:

> We recognize the legitimate and indeed exigent interest of States and localities throughout the Nation in preventing the dissemination of material deemed harmful to children. But that interest does not justify a total suppression of such material, the effect of which would be to "reduce the adult population . . . to reading only what is fit for children." *Butler v. Michigan*, 352 U.S. 380, 383. State and local authorities might well consider whether their objectives in this area would be better served by laws aimed specifically at preventing distribution of objectionable material to children, rather than at totally prohibiting its dissemination. Since the present conviction is based upon exhibition of the film to the public at large and not upon its exhibition to children, the judgment must be reviewed under the strict standard applicable in determining the scope of the expression that is protected by the Constitution.
>
> We have applied that standard to the motion picture in question. "The Lovers" involves a woman bored with her life and marriage who abandons her husband and family for a young archaeologist with whom she has [378 U.S. 184, 196] suddenly fallen in love. There is an explicit love scene in the last reel of the film, and the State's objections are based almost entirely upon that scene. The film was favorably reviewed in a number of national publications, although disparaged in others, and was rated by at least two

critics of national stature among the best films of the year in which it was produced. It was shown in approximately 100 of the larger cities in the United States, including Columbus and Toledo, Ohio. We have viewed the film, in the light of the record made in the trial court, and we conclude that it is not obscene within the standards enunciated in *Roth v. United States* and *Alberts v. California,* which we reaffirm here. [footnotes omitted]

Griswold v. Connecticut, 381 U.S. 479 (1965)

The executive director of the Planned Parenthood League of Connecticut and its medical director were convicted of breaking a Connecticut anti-birth control law when they prescribed contraceptives for a married couple. The Court ruled that the Connecticut law violated the Fourteenth Amendment because it interfered with the guarantees supplied by the First Amendment. Justice William O. Douglas delivered the opinion of the Court:

> The present case, then, concerns a relationship lying within the zone of privacy created by several fundamental constitutional guarantees. And it concerns a law which, in forbidding the use of contraceptives rather than regulating their manufacture or sale, seeks to achieve its goals by means having a maximum destructive impact upon that relationship. Such a law cannot stand in light of the familiar principle, so often applied by this Court, that a "governmental purpose to control or prevent activities constitutionally subject to state regulation may not be achieved by means which sweep unnecessarily broadly and thereby invade the area of protected freedoms." *NAACP v. Alabama,* 377 U.S. 288, 307. Would we allow the police to search the sacred precincts of marital bedrooms for telltale signs of the use of contraceptives? The very idea is repulsive to the notions of privacy surrounding the marriage relationship.
>
> We deal with a right of privacy older than the Bill of Rights—older than our political parties, older than our school system. Marriage is a coming together for better or for worse, hopefully enduring, and intimate

to the degree of being sacred. It is an association that promotes a way of life, not causes; a harmony in living, not political faiths; a bilateral loyalty, not commercial or social projects. Yet it is an association for as noble a purpose as any involved in our prior decisions. [footnotes omitted]

Epperson v. Arkansas, 393 U.S. 97 (1968)

A high school biology teacher in Little Rock, Arkansas, challenged the constitutionality of a 1928 Arkansas statute forbidding the teaching of evolution. Reversing the decision of the supreme court of Arkansas, the Supreme Court of the United States ruled that the anti-evolution statute interfered with the freedom of speech guaranteed in the First Amendment and therefore violated the Fourteenth Amendment as well. Justice Abe Fortas delivered the opinion of the court:

> The antecedents of today's decision are many and unmistakable. They are rooted in the foundation soil of our Nation. They are fundamental to freedom. Government in our democracy, state and national, must be neutral in matters of religious theory, doctrine [393 U.S. 97, 104], and practice. It may not be hostile to any religion or to the advocacy of no-religion; and it may not aid, foster, or promote one religion or religious theory against another or even against the militant opposite. The First Amendment mandates governmental neutrality between religion and religion, and between religion and nonreligion.
>
> As early as 1872, this Court said: "The law knows no heresy, and is committed to the support of no dogma, the establishment of no sect." *Watson v. Jones*, 13 Wall. 679, 728. This has been the interpretation of the great First Amendment which this Court has applied in the many and subtle problems which the ferment of our national life has presented for decision within the Amendment's broad command.
>
> Judicial interposition in the operation of the public school system of the Nation raises problems requiring care and restraint. Our courts, however, have not failed to apply the First Amendment's mandate in our educational system where essential to safeguard the

fundamental values of freedom of speech and inquiry and of belief. By and large, public education in our Nation is committed to the control of state and local authorities. Courts do not and cannot intervene in the resolution of conflicts which arise in the daily operation of school systems and which do not directly and sharply implicate basic constitutional values. On the other hand, "[t]he vigilant protection of constitutional freedoms is nowhere more vital than in the community of American schools," *Shelton v. Tucker,* 364 U.S. 479, 487 (1960). As this [393 U.S. 97, 105] Court said in *Keyishian v. Board of Regents,* the First Amendment "does not tolerate laws that cast a pall of orthodoxy over the classroom." 385 U.S. 589, 603 (1967). [footnotes omitted]

Tinker v. Des Moines School District, 393 U.S. 503 (1969)

Three Des Moines, Iowa, public school students were suspended for wearing black arm bands to school to protest U.S. policy in Vietnam. The students argued that their suspension was unjustified. Because their conduct was passive and did not interfere with other people's right to expression, the Supreme Court ruled the students' behavior was protected by the First Amendment and the due process clause of the Fourteenth Amendment. Justice Abe Fortas delivered the opinion of the Court:

> First Amendment rights, applied in light of the special characteristics of the school environment, are available to teachers and students. It can hardly be argued that either students or teachers shed their constitutional rights to freedom of speech or expression at the schoolhouse gate. . . .
>
> In our system, state-operated schools may not be enclaves of totalitarianism. School officials do not possess absolute authority over their students. Students in school as well as out of school are "persons" under our Constitution. They are possessed of fundamental rights which the State must respect, just as they themselves must respect their obligations to the State. In our system, students may not be regarded as closed-circuit recipients of only that which the State chooses

to communicate. They may not be confined to the expression of those sentiments that are officially approved. In the absence of a specific showing of constitutionally valid reasons to regulate their speech, students are entitled to freedom of expression of their views. As Judge Gewin, speaking for the Fifth Circuit, said, school officials cannot suppress "expressions of feelings with which they do not wish to contend." *Burnside v. Byars*, supra, at 749. [footnotes omitted]

New York Times v. United States, 403 U.S. 713 (1971)

The *New York Times* obtained excerpts from classified documents dealing with U.S. foreign policy in Vietnam. The Justice Department claimed the documents, popularly known as the Pentagon Papers, were classified as a matter of national security and sought to prevent further publication of the documents. Critics argued that the government relied on excessive classification of documents to mask the fact that it had not consulted Congress on a number of major political decisions. A divided Supreme Court ruled in favor of the newspaper's right to publish the material. Justice Hugo L. Black wrote:

> In the First Amendment the Founding Fathers gave the free press the protection it must have to fulfill its essential role in our democracy. The press was to serve the governed, not the governors. The Government's power to censor the press was abolished so that the press would remain forever free to censure the Government. The press was protected so that it could bare the secrets of government and inform the people. Only a free and unrestrained press can effectively expose deception in government. And paramount among the responsibilities of a free press is the duty to prevent any part of the government from deceiving the people and sending them off to distant lands to die of foreign fevers and foreign shot and shell. In my view, far from deserving condemnation for their courageous reporting, the *New York Times,* the *Washington Post,* and other newspapers should be commended for serving the purpose that the Founding Fathers saw so clearly. In revealing the workings of

government that led to the Vietnam war, the newspapers nobly did precisely that which the Founders hoped and trusted they would do.

Miller v. California, 413 U.S. 15 (1973)

A man who mailed unsolicited obscene materials was convicted of violating obscenity laws, and though he protested the judgment that the materials he mailed were obscene, they were found to be obscene under the "community standards" test. The Court affirmed the decision, ruling that obscene materials were not protected by the First Amendment. The Court also defined obscenity as that which is "patently offensive . . . and taken as a whole, does not have serious literary, artistic, political, or scientific value." Chief Justice Warren C. Burger explained:

> This case involves the application of a State's criminal obscenity statute to a situation in which sexually explicit materials have been thrust by aggressive sales action upon unwilling recipients who had in no way indicated any desire to receive such materials. This Court has recognized that the States have a legitimate interest in prohibiting dissemination or exhibition of obscene material when the mode of dissemination carries with it a significant danger of offending the sensibilities of unwilling recipients or of exposure to juveniles. . . . It is in this context that we are called on to define the standards which must be used to identify obscene material that a State may regulate without infringing on the First Amendment as applicable to the States through the Fourteenth Amendment. . . .
>
> Under a National Constitution, fundamental First Amendment limitations on the powers of the States do not vary from community to community, but this does not mean that there are, or should or can be, fixed, uniform national standards of precisely what appeals to the "prurient interest" or is "patently offensive." These are essentially questions of fact, and our Nation is simply too big and too diverse for this Court to reasonably expect that such standards could be articulated for all 50 States in a single formulation, even assuming the prerequisite consensus exists. When triers of fact are asked to decide whether "the

average person, applying contemporary community standards" would consider certain materials "prurient," it would be unrealistic to require that the answer be based on some abstract formulation. The adversary system, with lay jurors as the usual ultimate factfinders in criminal prosecutions, has historically permitted triers of fact to draw on the standards of their community, guided always by limiting instructions on the law. To require a State to structure obscenity proceedings around evidence of a national "community standard" would be an exercise in futility. . . .

Sex and nudity may not be exploited without limit by films or pictures exhibited or sold in places of public accommodation any more than live sex and nudity can be exhibited or sold without limit in such public places. At a minimum, prurient, patently offensive depiction or description of sexual conduct must have serious literary, artistic, political, or scientific value to merit First Amendment protection. For example, medical books for the education of physicians and related personnel necessarily use graphic illustrations and descriptions of human anatomy. In resolving the inevitably sensitive questions of fact and law, we must continue to rely on the jury system, accompanied by the safeguards that judges, rules of evidence, presumption of innocence, and other protective features provide, as we do with rape, murder, and a host of other offenses against society and its individual members.

One can concede that the "sexual revolution" of recent years may have had useful byproducts in striking layers of prudery from a subject long irrationally kept from needed ventilation. But it does not follow that no regulation of patently offensive "hard core" materials is needed or permissible; civilized people do not allow unregulated access to heroin because it is a derivative of medicinal morphine. [footnotes omitted]

FCC v. Pacifica Foundation, 438 U.S. 726 (1978)

Comedian George Carlin delivered a monologue called "Filthy Words" before a live audience, and the recording of this monologue was later broadcast by a New York radio station. The Federal Communication Commission (FCC) ruled that this broadcast was indecent and illegal, under statutes forbidding obscene, indecent, and profane language from radio broadcasts. The radio station charged that the FCC was exercising censorship. The Supreme Court, deciding that sexual and excretory functions and words were indecent, especially at hours when children might be listening, ruled that the FCC had not violated the First Amendment in its decision. Justice John P. Stevens delivered the opinion of the court:

> The question in this case is whether a broadcast of patently offensive words dealing with sex and excretion may be regulated because of its content. Obscene materials have been denied the protection of the First Amendment because their content is so offensive to contemporary moral standards. *Roth v. United States,* 354 U.S. 476. But the fact that society may find speech offensive is not a sufficient reason for suppressing it. Indeed, if it is the speaker's opinion that gives offense, that consequence is a reason for according it constitutional protection. For it is a central tenet of the First Amendment that the government must remain neutral in the marketplace of [438 U.S. 726, 746] ideas. If there were any reason to believe that the Commission's characterization of the Carlin monologue as offensive could be traced to its political content—or even to the fact that it satirized contemporary attitudes about four-letter words—First Amendment protection might be required. But that is simply not this case. These words offend for the same reasons that obscenity offends. Their place in the hierarchy of First Amendment values was aptly sketched by Mr. Justice Murphy when he said: "[S]uch utterances are no essential part of any exposition of ideas, and are of such slight social value as a step to truth that any benefit that may be derived from them is clearly outweighed by the social interest in order and morality." *Chaplinsky v. New Hampshire,* 315 U.S., at 572.
>
> Although these words ordinarily lack literary, political, or scientific value, they are not entirely outside the protection of the First Amendment. Some uses of even the most offensive words are unquestionably

protected. See, e.g., *Hess v. Indiana*, 414 U.S. 105. Indeed, we may assume, arguendo, that this monologue would be protected in other contexts. Nonetheless, [438 U.S. 726, 747] the constitutional protection accorded to a communication containing such patently offensive sexual and excretory language need not be the same in every context. It is a characteristic of speech such as this that both its capacity to offend and its "social value," to use Mr. Justice Murphy's term, vary with the circumstances. Words that are commonplace in one setting are shocking in another. To paraphrase Mr. Justice Harlan, one occasion's lyric is another's vulgarity. Cf. *Cohen v. California*, 403 U.S. 15, 25. [footnotes omitted]

Smith v. Collin, 439 U.S. 916 (1978)

The National Socialist Party of America, a Nazi organization, planned to assemble and demonstrate in front of Skokie Village Hall in Skokie, Illinois, a predominantly Jewish suburb of Chicago where many Holocaust survivors lived. The town of Skokie attempted to block the Nazis from demonstrating in their community and denied them a permit for a parade and public assembly. The case made its way to the Supreme Court, which ruled in favor of the Nazis and their right, under the First Amendment, to assembly. One justice, however, Harry A. Blackmun, offered a dissenting opinion:

> On the one hand, we have precious First Amendment rights vigorously asserted and an obvious concern that if those asserted rights are not recognized, the precedent of a "hard" case might offer a justification for repression in the future. On the other hand, we are presented with evidence of a potentially explosive and dangerous situation, enflamed by unforgettable recollections of traumatic experiences in the second world conflict. Finally, Judge Sprecher of the Seventh Circuit observed that "each court dealing with these precise problems (the Illinois Supreme Court, the District Court and this Court) feels the need to apologize for its result." 578 F.2d at 1211. [439 U.S. 916, 919] Furthermore, in *Beauharnais v. Illinois*, 343 U.S. 250 (1952), this Court faced up to an Illinois statute that made it a

crime to exhibit in any public place a publication that portrayed "depravity, criminality, unchastity, or lack of virtue of a class of citizens, of any race, color, creed or religion," thereby exposing such citizens "to contempt, derision, or obloquy." The Court, by a divided vote, held that, as construed and applied, the statute did not violate the liberty of speech guaranteed as against the States by the Due Process Clause of the Fourteenth Amendment.

I stated in dissent when the application for stay in the present litigation was denied, 436 U.S., at 953, that I feel the Seventh Circuit's decision is in some tension with Beauharnais. That case has not been overruled or formally limited in any way.

I therefore would grant certiorari in order to resolve any possible conflict that may exist between the ruling of the Seventh Circuit here and Beauharnais. I also feel that the present case affords the Court an opportunity to consider whether, in the context of the facts that this record appears to present, there is no limit whatsoever to the exercise of free speech. There indeed may be no such limit, but when citizens assert, not casually but with deep conviction, that the proposed demonstration is scheduled at a place and in a manner that is taunting and overwhelmingly offensive to the citizens of that place, that assertion, uncomfortable though it may be for judges, deserves to be examined. It just might fall into the same category as one's "right" to cry "fire" in a crowded theater, for "the character of every act depends upon the circumstances in which it is done." *Schenck v. United States*, 249 U.S. 47, 52 (1919). [footnotes omitted]

Board of Education v. Pico, 457 U.S. 853 (1982)

A New York state board of education, overruling the wishes of a parents' committee and the school staff that it had appointed, removed books they alleged were antireligious and obscene from junior high and high school libraries. Students claimed the board's removal of the books violated their First Amendment rights. The Supreme Court ruled in favor of the students, writing that the authority of school boards was limited by the First

Amendment and that the school board could not remove books because of partisan or political beliefs or for the purpose of restricting access to certain ideas or points of view. Justice William J. Brennan Jr. wrote:

> The First Amendment imposes limitations upon a local school board's exercise of its discretion to remove books from high school and junior high school libraries. Local school boards have broad discretion in the management of school affairs, but such discretion must be exercised in a manner that comports with the transcendent imperatives of the First Amendment. Students do not "shed their constitutional rights to freedom of speech or expression at the schoolhouse gate" [*Tinker v. Des Moines School Dist.*, 393 U.S. 503, 506], and such rights may be directly and sharply implicated by the removal of books from the shelves of a school library. While students' First Amendment rights must be construed "in light of the special characteristics of the school environment," ibid., the special characteristics of the school library make that environment especially appropriate for the recognition of such rights.
>
> While petitioners might rightfully claim absolute discretion in matters of curriculum by reliance upon their duty to inculcate community values in schools, petitioners' reliance upon that duty is misplaced [457 U.S. 853, 854] where they attempt to extend their claim of absolute discretion beyond the compulsory environment of the classroom into the school library and the regime of voluntary inquiry that there holds sway.
>
> Petitioners possess significant discretion to determine the content of their school libraries, but that discretion may not be exercised in a narrowly partisan or political manner. Whether petitioners' removal of books from the libraries denied respondents their First Amendment rights depends upon the motivation behind petitioners' actions.
>
> Local school boards may not remove books from school libraries simply because they dislike the ideas contained in those books and seek by their removal to "prescribe what shall be orthodox in politics, nationalism, religion, or other matters of opinion." *West Vir-*

ginia Board of Education v. Barnette, 319 U.S. 624, 642. If such an intention was the decisive factor in petitioners' decision, then petitioners have exercised their discretion in violation of the Constitution. [footnotes omitted]

New York v. Ferber, 458 U.S. 747 (1982)

A New York bookstore owner who sold films that showed young boys masturbating was convicted under a state law that prohibited the distribution of material depicting children under the age of 16 engaged in sexual conduct. The New York Court of Appeals reversed his conviction on the grounds that the state law was unconstitutional, but the Supreme Court upheld the conviction, arguing that the states were allowed to regulate pornography and that the statute was neither overly broad nor underinclusive. With this ruling, the Court sent a message that child pornography laws would be upheld. Justice Byron R. White delivered the opinion of the court:

> We consider this the paradigmatic case of a state statute whose legitimate reach dwarfs its arguably impermissible applications. New York, as we have held, may constitutionally prohibit dissemination of material specified in 263.15. While the reach of the statute is directed at the hard core of child pornography, the Court of Appeals was understandably concerned that some protected expression, ranging from medical textbooks to pictorials in the *National Geographic* would fall prey to the statute. How often, if ever, it may be necessary to employ children to engage in conduct clearly within the reach of 263.15 in order to produce educational, medical, or artistic works cannot be known with certainty. Yet we seriously doubt, and it has not been suggested, that these arguably impermissible applications of the statute amount to more than a tiny fraction of the materials within the statute's reach. Nor will we assume that the New York courts will widen the possibly invalid reach of the statute by giving an expansive construction to the proscription on "lewd exhibition[s] of the genitals." Under these circumstances, 263.15 is "not substantially overbroad and . . . whatever overbreadth may

exist [458 U.S. 747, 774] should be cured through case-by-case analysis of the fact situations to which its sanctions, assertedly, may not be applied." *Broadrick v. Oklahoma*, 413 U.S., at 615–616. [footnotes omitted]

Wallace v. Jaffree, 466 U.S. 924 (1984)

An Alabama practice of holding a moment of silence in public schools each morning, during which students and teachers could pray if they so chose, was ruled unconstitutional by the Supreme Court because of the First Amendment's insistence that there be no laws "respecting an establishment of religion." Justice John P. Stevens wrote:

> The addition of "or voluntary prayer" indicates that the State intended to characterize prayer as a favored practice. Such an endorsement is not consistent with the established principle that the government must pursue a course of complete neutrality toward religion.
>
> The importance of that principle does not permit us to treat this as an inconsequential case involving nothing more than a few words of symbolic speech on behalf of the political majority. For whenever the State itself speaks on a religious [472 U.S. 38, 61] subject, one of the questions that we must ask is "whether the government intends to convey a message of endorsement or disapproval of religion." The well-supported concurrent findings of the District Court and the Court of Appeals—that 16-1-20.1 was intended to convey a message of state approval of prayer activities in the public schools—make it unnecessary, and indeed inappropriate, to evaluate the practical significance of the addition of the words "or voluntary prayer" to the statute. Keeping in mind, as we must, "both the fundamental place held by the Establishment Clause in our constitutional scheme and the myriad, subtle ways in which Establishment Clause values can be eroded," we conclude that 16–1–20.1 violates the First Amendment. [footnotes omitted]

Hazelwood School District v. Kuhlmeier, 484 U.S. 260 (1988)

High school students writing for the school's newspaper had their writing censored by school officials because some of their articles dealt with controversial topics such as teen pregnancy and the impact of divorce on children. The students filed suit, alleging that their First Amendment rights had been violated. The Supreme Court, however, ruled in favor of the school officials, arguing that the school environment was different than the outside environment and that schools did not have to accept student speech that was incompatible with the goals or mission of the school. Justice Byron R. White delivered the opinion of the Court:

> Students in the public schools do not "shed their constitutional rights to freedom of speech or expression at the schoolhouse gate." *Tinker,* supra, at 506. They cannot be punished merely for expressing their personal views on the school premises—whether "in the cafeteria, or on the playing field, or on the campus during the authorized hours," 393 U.S., at 512–513—unless school authorities have reason to believe that such expression will "substantially interfere with the work of the school or impinge upon the rights of other students." Id., at 509.
>
> We have nonetheless recognized that the First Amendment rights of students in the public schools "are not automatically coextensive with the rights of adults in other settings," *Bethel School District No. 403 v. Fraser,* 478 U.S. 675, 682 (1986), and must be "applied in light of the special characteristics of the school environment." *Tinker,* supra, at 506; cf. *New Jersey v. T. L. O.,* 469 U.S. 325, 341–343 (1985). A school need not tolerate student speech that is inconsistent with its "basic educational mission," *Fraser,* supra, at 685, even though the government could not censor similar speech outside the school. Accordingly, we held in *Fraser* that a student could be disciplined for having delivered a speech that was "sexually explicit" but not legally obscene at an official school assembly, because the school was entitled to "disassociate itself" from the speech in a manner [484 U.S. 260, 267] that would demonstrate to others that such vulgarity is "wholly

inconsistent with the 'fundamental values' of public school education." 478 U.S., at 685–686. We thus recognized that "[t]he determination of what manner of speech in the classroom or in school assembly is inappropriate properly rests with the school board," id., at 683, rather than with the federal courts. [footnotes omitted]

United States v. Eichman, et al., *496 U.S. 310 (1990)*

Congress passed the Flag Protection Act in 1989, criminalizing the mutilation or burning of the U.S. flag except in cases of disposal. Several demonstrators, including those who burned a flag on the steps of the U.S. capitol to protest U.S. foreign policy, were convicted under this act and sought to dismiss the charges on the grounds that the act violated their First Amendment rights. The Supreme Court ruled in favor of the demonstrators, finding the act to be an unconstitutional violation of free expression. Justice William J. Brennan Jr. wrote:

> Although the Flag Protection Act contains no explicit content-based limitation on the scope of prohibited conduct, it is nevertheless clear that the Government's asserted interest is "related 'to the suppression of free expression,'" 491 U.S., at 410, and concerned with the content of such expression. The Government's interest in protecting the "physical integrity" [496 U.S. 310, 316] of a privately owned flag rests upon a perceived need to preserve the flag's status as a symbol of our Nation and certain national ideals. But the mere destruction or disfigurement of a particular physical manifestation of the symbol, without more, does not diminish or otherwise affect the symbol itself in any way. For example, the secret destruction of a flag in one's own basement would not threaten the flag's recognized meaning. Rather, the Government's desire to preserve the flag as a symbol for certain national ideals is implicated "only when a person's treatment of the flag communicates [a] message" to others that is inconsistent with those ideals. Ibid. [496 U.S. 310, 317] . . .
> We are aware that desecration of the flag is deeply

offensive to many. But the same might be said, for example, of virulent ethnic and religious epithets, see *Terminiello v. Chicago*, 337 U.S. 1 (1949); vulgar repudiations of the draft, see [496 U.S. 310, 319] *Cohen v. California*, 403 U.S. 15 (1971); and scurrilous caricatures, see *Hustler Magazine, Inc. v. Falwell*, 485 U.S. 46 (1988). "If there is a bedrock principle underlying the First Amendment, it is that the Government may not prohibit the expression of an idea simply because society finds the idea itself offensive or disagreeable." *Johnson*, supra, at 414. Punishing desecration of the flag dilutes the very freedom that makes this emblem so revered, and worth revering. [footnotes omitted]

Wisconsin v. Mitchell, 508 U.S. 476 (1993)

A man convicted of battery had his sentence enhanced under a Wisconsin hate crime statute because he had specifically selected his victim because of the victim's race. The man challenged the hate crime statute, arguing that it interfered with his right to think freely. The Court rejected this argument, deciding that the statute did not violate the First Amendment because it only punished racists acts, not racist thoughts. Chief Justice William Rehnquist delivered the opinion of a unanimous Court:

> The sort of chill envisioned here is far more attenuated and unlikely than that contemplated in traditional "overbreadth" cases. We must conjure up a vision of a Wisconsin citizen suppressing his unpopular bigoted opinions for fear that, if he later commits an offense covered by the statute [508 U.S. 476, 489], these opinions will be offered at trial to establish that he selected his victim on account of the victim's protected status, thus qualifying him for penalty-enhancement. To stay within the realm of rationality, we must surely put to one side minor misdemeanor offenses covered by the statute, such as negligent operation of a motor vehicle (Wis.Stat. 941.01 (1989–1990), for it is difficult, if not impossible, to conceive of a situation where such offenses would be racially motivated. We are left, then, with the prospect of a citizen suppressing his bigoted beliefs for fear that evidence of such beliefs will be introduced against him at

trial if he commits a more serious offense against person or property. This is simply too speculative a hypothesis to support Mitchell's overbreadth claim.

The First Amendment, moreover, does not prohibit the evidentiary use of speech to establish the elements of a crime or to prove motive or intent. Evidence of a defendant's previous declarations or statements is commonly admitted in criminal trials subject to evidentiary rules dealing with relevancy, reliability, and the like. Nearly half a century ago, in *Haupt v. United States,* 330 U.S. 631 (1947), we rejected a contention similar to that advanced by Mitchell here. Haupt was tried for the offense of treason, which, as defined by the Constitution (Art. III, 3), may depend very much on proof of motive. To prove that the acts in question were committed out of "adherence to the enemy" rather than "parental solicitude," id. At 641, the Government introduced evidence of conversations that had taken place long prior to the indictment, some of which consisted of statements showing Haupt's sympathy with Germany and Hitler and hostility towards the United States. We rejected Haupt's argument that this evidence was improperly admitted. While "[s]uch testimony is to be scrutinized with care to be certain the statements are not expressions of mere lawful and permissible difference of opinion with our own government or quite proper appreciation of the land of birth," we held that "these statements . . . [508 U.S. 476, 490] clearly were admissible on the question of intent and adherence to the enemy." Id. at 642. See also *Price Waterhouse v. Hopkins,* 490 U.S. 228, 251–252 (1989) (plurality opinion) (allowing evidentiary use of defendant's speech in evaluating Title VII discrimination claim); *Street v. New York,* 394 U.S. 576, 594 (1969).

For the foregoing reasons, we hold that Mitchell's First Amendment rights were not violated by the application of the Wisconsin penalty-enhancement provision in sentencing him. The judgment of the Supreme Court of Wisconsin is therefore reversed, and the case is remanded for further proceedings not inconsistent with this opinion. [footnotes omitted]

Reno, Attorney General of the United States, et al., v. American Civil Liberties Union, et al.; appeal from the U.S. District Court for the eastern district of Pennsylvania; No. 96-511; decided June 26, 1997

In *Reno v. ACLU*, cyber-liberties groups argued that two provisions of the Communications Decency Act of 1996 (CDA) were unconstitutional. These CDA provisions were designed to protect minors from harmful material on the Internet, and in the language of the CDA this material was broadly defined as that which was found to be "indecent" or "patently offensive." However, the Supreme Court ruled that these provisions violated the guarantee of free speech provided by the First Amendment and declared the CDA unconstitutional. The overturning of the CDA set a clear precedent for the safeguarding of constitutional liberties in cyberspace. Justice John P. Stevens delivered the opinion of the Court:

> Regardless of whether the CDA is so vague that it violates the Fifth Amendment, the many ambiguities concerning the scope of its coverage render it problematic for purposes of the First Amendment. For instance, each of the two parts of the CDA uses a different linguistic form. The first uses the word "indecent," 47 U.S.C.A. §223(a) (Supp. 1997), while the second speaks of material that "in context, depicts or describes, in terms patently offensive as measured by contemporary community standards, sexual or excretory activities or organs," §223(d). Given the absence of a definition of either term, this difference in language will provoke uncertainty among speakers about how the two standards relate to each other and just what they mean. Could a speaker confidently assume that a serious discussion about birth control practices, homosexuality, the First Amendment issues raised by the Appendix to our *Pacifica* opinion, or the consequences of prison rape would not violate the CDA? This uncertainty undermines the likelihood that the CDA has been carefully tailored to the congressional goal of protecting minors from potentially harmful materials.
>
> The vagueness of the CDA is a matter of special concern for two reasons. First, the CDA is a content

based regulation of speech. The vagueness of such a regulation raises special First Amendment concerns because of its obvious chilling effect on free speech. See, e.g., *Gentile v. State Bar of Nev.*, 501 U.S. 1030, 1048–1051 (1991). Second, the CDA is a criminal statute. In addition to the opprobrium and stigma of a criminal conviction, the CDA threatens violators with penalties including up to two years in prison for each act of violation. The severity of criminal sanctions may well cause speakers to remain silent rather than communicate even arguably unlawful words, ideas, and images. See, e.g., *Dombrowski v. Pfister*, 380 U.S. 479, 494 (1965). As a practical matter, this increased deterrent effect, coupled with the "risk of discriminatory enforcement" of vague regulations, poses greater First Amendment concerns than those implicated by the civil regulation reviewed in *Denver Area Ed. Telecommunications Consortium, Inc. v. FCC*, 518 U.S. ___ (1996). . . .

We are persuaded that the CDA lacks the precision that the First Amendment requires when a statute regulates the content of speech. In order to deny minors access to potentially harmful speech, the CDA effectively suppresses a large amount of speech that adults have a constitutional right to receive and to address to one another. That burden on adult speech is unacceptable if less restrictive alternatives would be at least as effective in achieving the legitimate purpose that the statute was enacted to serve. . . .

The record demonstrates that the growth of the Internet has been and continues to be phenomenal. As a matter of constitutional tradition, in the absence of evidence to the contrary, we presume that governmental regulation of the content of speech is more likely to interfere with the free exchange of ideas than to encourage it. The interest in encouraging freedom of expression in a democratic society outweighs any theoretical but unproven benefit of censorship. [footnotes omitted]

Graphs and Tables

The Office for Intellectual Freedom (OIF) at the American Library Association maintains a database of statistics that reflects the number of challenges to books, textbooks, film, and other materials that are reported each year. Though these challenges represent objections to specific materials, not all of them resulted in the censoring of the material. The OIF maintains that for each challenge that is reported, four or five may go unreported, so the statistics need to be interpreted in light of this discrepancy between recorded and unrecorded events.

Figures 4.1 through 4.4 are reprinted by permission of the American Library Association. Figure 4.1 shows how annual challenges stack up over the course of the 1990s, with challenges peaking in 1995 and dropping off thereafter. Figure 4.2 graphs challenges to books and other materials in the 1990s based on the *objection of the person* who made the challenge. The primary objections to materials in the 1990s were that they were sexually explicit, that they used offensive language, and that they were inappropriate for the age group exposed to them. Figure 4.3 depicts the *initiators* of challenges in the 1990s and shows that among initiators, parents are the overwhelmingly majority, with library patrons a distant second. Figure 4.4 graphs challenges to materials in the 1990s *by venue* and shows that school libraries, schools, and public libraries are the top three institutions where books and other educational materials are challenged.

People for the American Way, a nonprofit organization devoted to the advancement of democratic values, publishes an annual report, *Attacks on the Freedom to Learn*, which also chronicles challenges and attempts to censor books and other materials in the nation's public schools. The most current version of this report is available on the PAW web site, http://www.pfaw.org. Figure 4.5, from *Attacks on the Freedom to Learn, 1996,* ranks the ten states where the highest number of challenges to books and other materials took place from 1982 to 1996.

Figure 4.6, "Internet Use Policies in Public Library Outlets," shows the percentage of public libraries that use filters in order to screen Internet content from minors. The data are derived from "The 1998 National Survey of U.S. Public Library Outlet Internet Connectivity: Summary Results," published by the ALA Office for Information Technology Policy.

Table 4.1, "Public Libraries that Have an Acceptable Use Policy for their Public Internet Stations," illustrates the number of public libraries that have adopted some kind of acceptable use policy in order to regulate public access to the Internet.

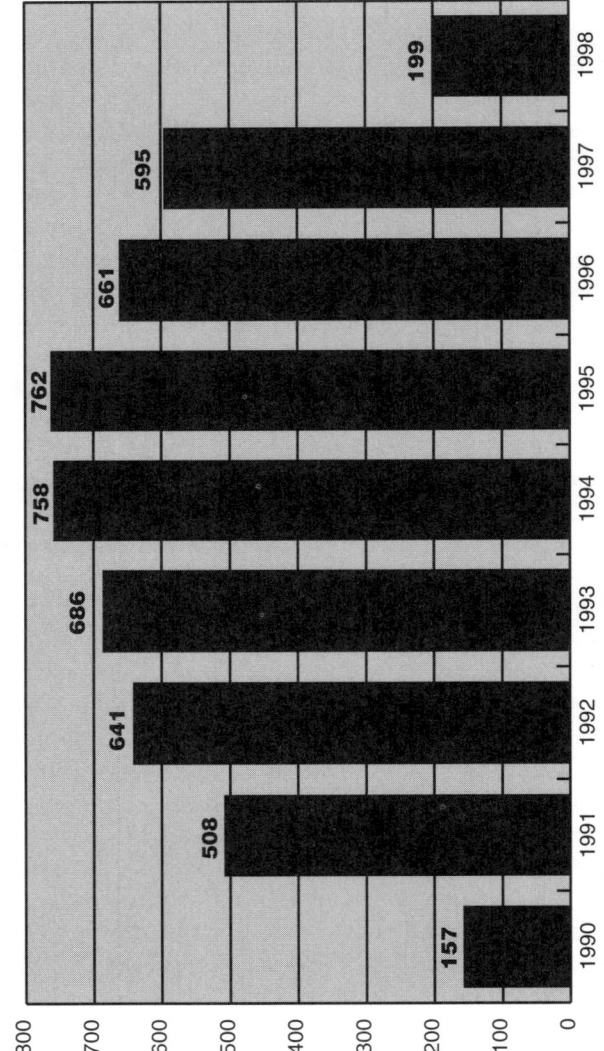

Figure 4.1 OIF Censorship Database-Challenges by Year

As of October 9, 1998, as compiled by the Office for Intellectual Freedom, American Library Association. The Office for Intellectual Freedom does not claim comprehensiveness in recording challenges. Research suggests that for each challenge reported there are as many as four or five which go unreported. Reprinted by permission of the American Library Association.

Figure 4.2 OIF Censorship Database 1990-Present Challenges by Type

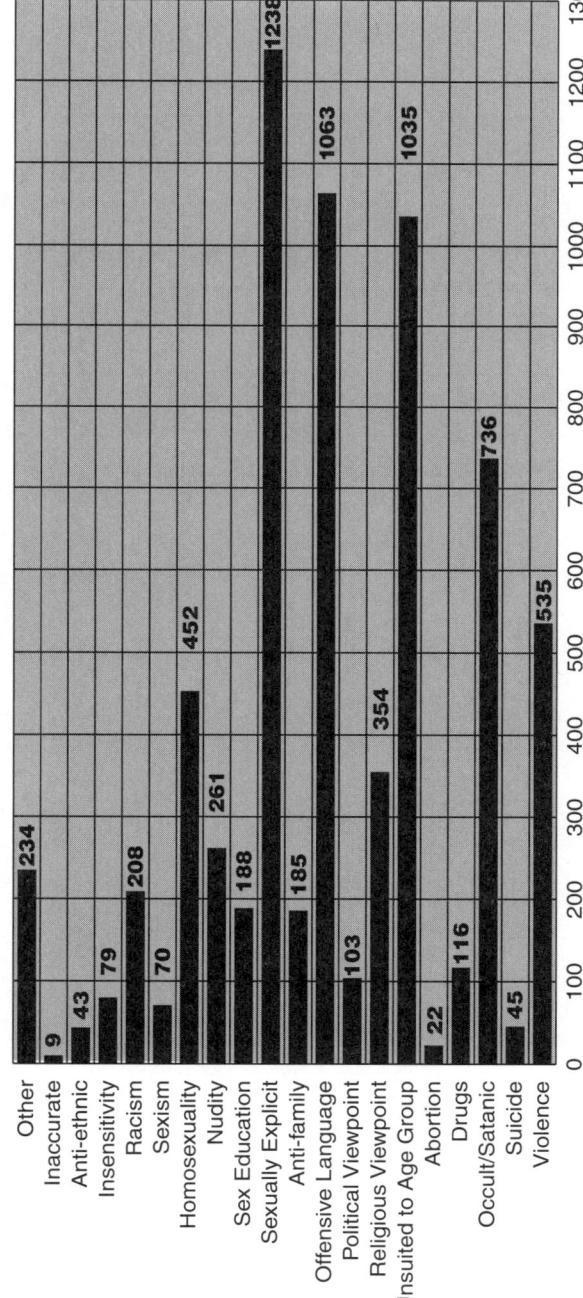

As of October 9, 1998, as compiled by the Office for Intellectual Freedom, American Library Association. The Office for Intellectual Freedom does not claim comprehensiveness in recording challenges. Research suggests that for each challenge reported there are as many as four or five which go unreported. Reprinted by permission of the American Library Association.

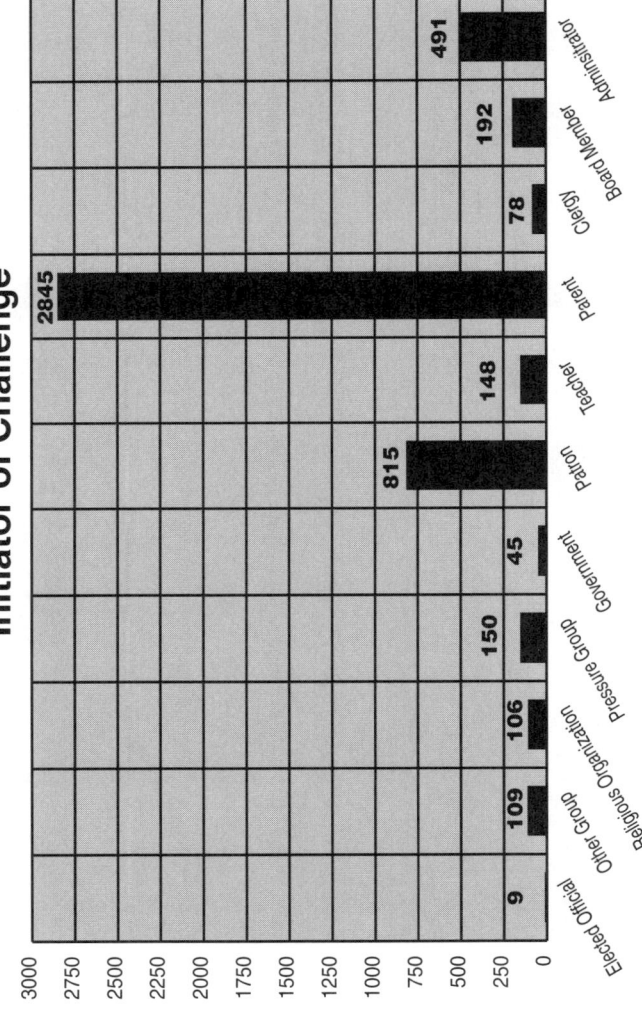

Figure 4.3 OIF Censorship Database 1990-Present Initiator of Challenge

As of October 9, 1998, as compiled by the Office for Intellectual Freedom, American Library Association. The Office for Intellectual Freedom does not claim comprehensiveness in recording challenges. Research suggests that for each challenge reported there are as many as four or five which go unreported. Reprinted by permission of the American Library Association.

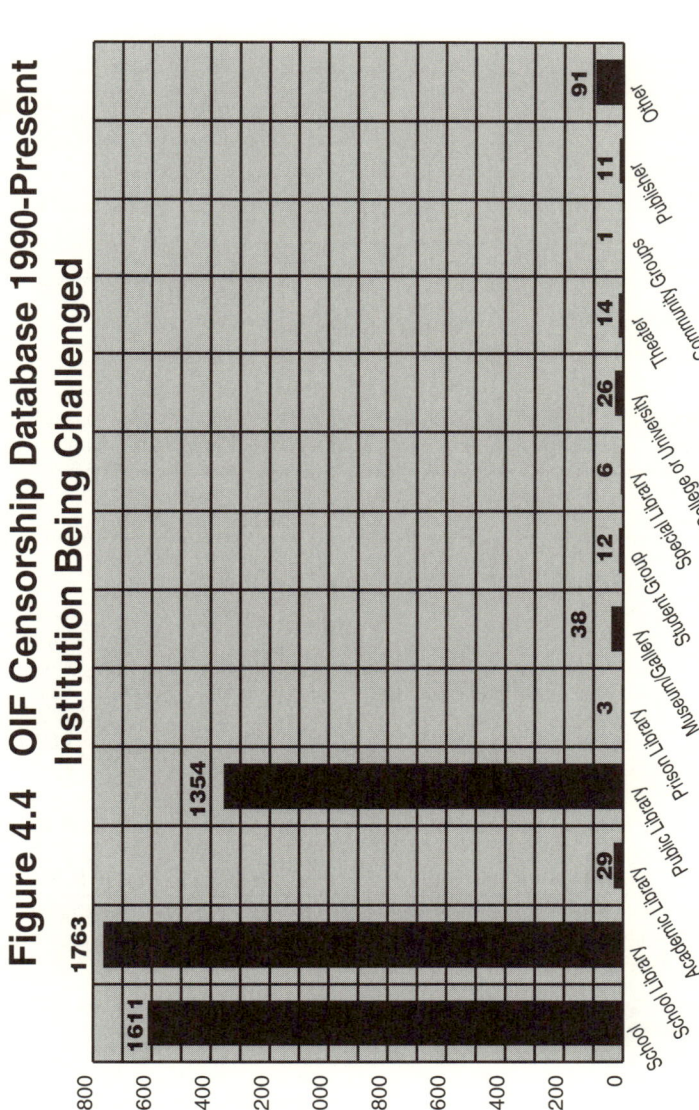

Figure 4.4 OIF Censorship Database 1990-Present Institution Being Challenged

As of October 9, 1998, as compiled by the Office for Intellectual Freedom, American Library Association. The Office for Intellectual Freedom does not claim comprehensiveness in recording challenges. Research suggests that for each challenge reported there are as many as four or five which go unreported. Reprinted by permission of the American Library Association.

Figure 4.5 States with the Highest Number of Challenges, 1982–1996

1. California
2. Texas
3. Oregon
4. Florida
5. Pennsylvania
6. Washington
7. New York
8. Ohio
9. MIchigan
10. Colorado

Attacks on the Freedom to Learn, 1996, People For the American Way. Reprinted with permission.

Table 4.1
Public Library Outlets that Have an Acceptable Use Policy for their Public Access Internet Workstations by Metropolitan Status and Poverty (As a Percentage of Library Outlets Offering Public Internet Access)

Base=11,519	Less than 20%	Poverty 20%–40%	More than 40%	Overall
Metropolitan Status				
Urban	85.8%	89.9%	88.5%	87.3%
	(n=1,162)	(n=641)	(n=162)	(±3.3%)
				(n=1,965)
Suburban	86.0%	85.5%	64.3%	85.9%
	(n=3,064)	(n=178)	(n=9)	±3.5%
				(n=3,250)
Rural	82.8%	84.5%	85.5%	83.1%
	(n=3,665)	(n=841)	(n=47)	±3.7%
				(n=4,553)
Overall	84.5%	86.6%	86.3%	**84.8%**
	±3.6%	±3.4%	±3.4%	±3.6%
	(n=7,891)	(n=1,660)	(n=214)	(n=9,769)

Note 1: The cell n's represent weighted estimates of connected public library outlets that have an acceptable use policy in place for their public access Internet services.
Note 2: Readers should refer to Figure 6 for the total number of connected public library outlets that provide public access to the Internet.
Note 3: Due to the weighted statistical analysis technique used to analyze the data and rounding, not all cell n's will sum or cell percentages will total to 100.0%.

Bertot, John Carlo, and McClure, Charles R. (1998). *The 1998 National Survey of U.S. Public Library Outlet Internet Connectivity: Final Report.* Washington, D.C.: U.S. National Commission on Libraries and Information Science. Reprinted with permission.

Figure 4.6 Internet Use Policies in Public Library Outlets (n=11,519)

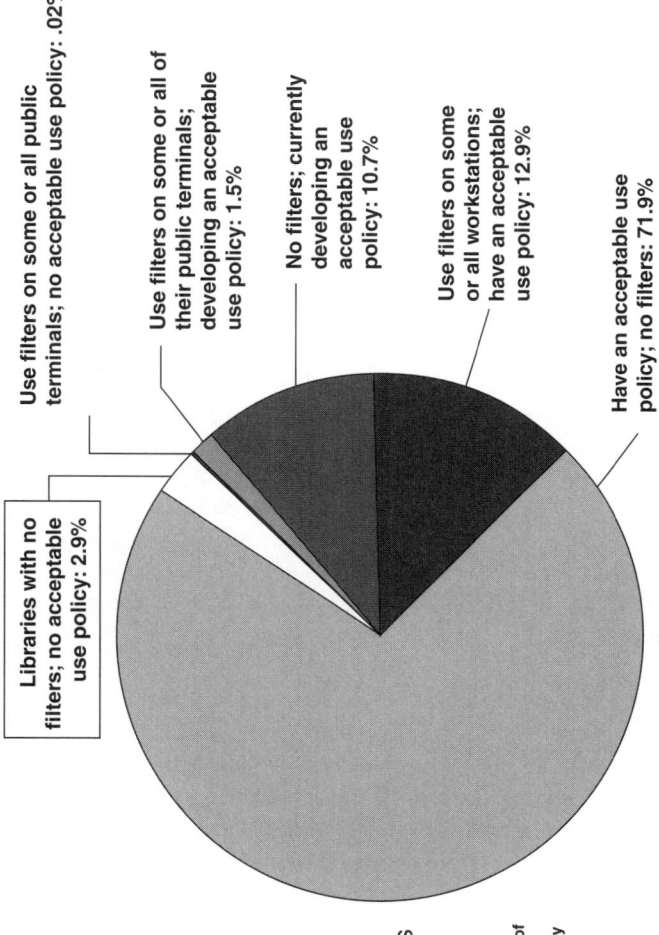

Use filters on some or all public terminals; no acceptable use policy: .02%

Use filters on some or all of their public terminals; developing an acceptable use policy: 1.5%

No filters; currently developing an acceptable use policy: 10.7%

Use filters on some or all workstations; have an acceptable use policy: 12.9%

Have an acceptable use policy; no filters: 71.9%

Libraries with no filters; no acceptable use policy: 2.9%

Nearly every public library outlet has or is developing an Internet acceptable use policy for patrons using their facilities. More than 8 in 10 public library outlets have an acceptable use policy and another 1 in 10 are developing such policies. About 1 in 7 public library outlets use filters on some or all of their public workstations

Copyright © 1998 by the American Library Association. Bertot, John Carlo, and McClure, Charles R. (1998). "The 1998 National Survey of U.S. Public Library Outlet Internet Connectivity: Summary Results." Published by the ALA Office for Information Technology Policy. Reprinted with permission

Documents

American Library Association's Library Bill of Rights

The American Library Association is a private, not-for-profit organization dedicated to promoting responsible library stewardship in the United States. In response to attacks on intellectual freedom encountered by member librarians, the ALA created the Office of Intellectual Freedom and the Freedom to Read Foundation, which support the right of libraries to include all kinds of works in their collections and the right of patrons to read any work that a library might legally acquire. The following document is the ALA's Library Bill of Rights, *adopted by the American Library Association Council on June 18, 1948, Amended February 2, 1961, and January 23, 1980, reaffirmed January 23, 1996, by the ALA Council. The principles outlined in the* Library Bill of Rights *form the primary model that most American libraries follow. The* Library Bill of Rights *is reprinted here with permission from the American Library Association. For more information on the ALA, contact their web site at http//:www.ala.org.*

The American Library Association affirms that all libraries are forums for information and ideas, and that the following basic policies should guide their services.

I. Books and other library resources should be provided for the interest, information, and enlightenment of all people of the community the library serves. Materials should not be excluded because of the origin, background, or views of those contributing to their creation.

II. Libraries should provide materials and information presenting all points of view on current and historical issues. Materials should not be proscribed or removed because of partisan or doctrinal disapproval.

III. Libraries should challenge censorship in the fulfillment of their responsibility to provide information and enlightenment.

IV. Libraries should cooperate with all persons and groups concerned with resisting abridgment of free expression and free access to ideas.

V. A person's right to use a library should not be denied or abridged because of origin, age, background, or views.

VI. Libraries which make exhibit spaces and meeting rooms

available to the public they serve should make such facilities available on an equitable basis, regardless of the beliefs or affiliations of individuals or groups requesting their use.
Adopted June 18, 1948
Amended February 2, 1961, and January 23, 1980; reaffirmed January 23, 1996, by the ALA Council

American Library Association's *Diversity in Collection Development*

The American Library Association has also issued Diversity in Collection Development, *a statement on the need for diversity in the building of library collections, which is an interpretation of the* Library Bill of Rights. *This statement, which justifies building a diverse collection of books on all—even controversial—topics, was adopted July 14, 1982, by the ALA Council and amended January 10, 1990, by the ALA Council. It is reprinted here by permission of the American Library Association.*

Throughout history, the focus of censorship has fluctuated from generation to generation. Books and other materials have not been selected or have been removed from library collections for many reasons, among which are prejudicial language and ideas, political content, economic theory, social philosophies, religious beliefs, sexual forms of expression, and other topics of a potentially controversial nature.

Some examples of censorship may include removing or not selecting materials because they are considered by some as racist or sexist; not purchasing conservative religious materials; not selecting materials about or by minorities because it is thought these groups or interests are not represented in a community; or not providing information on or materials from non-mainstream political entities.

Librarians may seek to increase user awareness of materials on various social concerns by many means, including, but not limited to, issuing bibliographies and presenting exhibits and programs.

Librarians have a professional responsibility to be inclusive, not exclusive, in collection development and in the provision of interlibrary loan. Access to all materials legally obtainable should be assured to the user, and policies should not unjustly exclude materials even if they are offensive to the librarian or the user. Collection development should reflect the philosophy inherent in Article II of the *Library Bill of Rights:* "Libraries should provide materials and information presenting all points of view on current and historical issues. Materials should not be proscribed or removed because of partisan or doctrinal disapproval." A balanced collection reflects a diversity of materials, not an equality of numbers. Collection development responsibilities include selecting materials in the languages in common use in the community which the library serves. Collection development and the selection of materials should be done according to professional standards and established selection and review procedures.

There are many complex facets to any issue, and variations of context in which issues may be expressed, discussed, or interpreted. Librarians have a professional responsibility to be fair, just, and equitable and to give all library users equal protection in guarding against violation of the library patron's right to read, view, or listen to materials and resources protected by the First Amendment, no matter what the viewpoint of the author, creator, or selector. Librarians have an obligation to protect library collections from removal of materials based on personal bias or prejudice, and to select and support the access to materials on all subjects that meet, as closely as possible, the needs and interests of all persons in the community which the library serves. This includes materials that reflect political, economic, religious, social, minority, and sexual issues.

Intellectual freedom, the essence of equitable library services, provides for free access to all expressions of ideas through which any and all sides of a question, cause, or movement may be explored. Toleration is meaningless without tolerance for what some may consider detestable. Librarians cannot justly permit their own preferences to limit their degree of tolerance in collection development, because freedom is indivisible.

Adopted July 14, 1982; amended January 10, 1990, by the ALA Council. [ISBN 838965520]

Family Friendly Library's *Charter for a Family Friendly Library System*

Family Friendly Libraries is a not-for-profit organization that encourages libraries to uphold traditional family values in the selection and sponsorship of books. The following document is the group's Charter for a Family Friendly Library System. *The charter was proposed as an alternative to the vision set forth in the American Library Association's* Library Bill of Rights, *which Family Friendly Libraries perceives as hostile to traditional family values and to parental and civic participation in the library system. The* Charter for a Family Friendly Library System, *drafted in 1995, promotes parental rights and involvement in library policy. It is reprinted here with permission from Family Friendly Libraries. For more information on Family Friendly Libraries, contact their web site at http://fflibraries.org.*

Article One: Traditional Family Emphasis

The library system clearly acknowledges the importance and superiority of the traditional family—mother and father married to each other, committed to a lifetime, monogamous relationship and to caring responsibly together for their children.

Policy translation: As a branch of the government charged with protecting and preserving our society, the policies of the library system will not be neutral on the subject of traditional family and family values. They will be supportive.

a. The libraries will actively seek out books and other relevant materials that help our citizens understand the importance of traditional family and aid in its preservation.

b. The libraries will actively seek out books and other relevant materials that help our citizens understand the importance of traditional family values (lawful and moral behavior helpful to preserving the traditional family) and aid in its preservation.

c. While providing helpful resources to non-traditional families (such as single parent households, families "blended" after divorce or death, etc.) the standard of emphasizing traditional family and relevant values will not be forgotten in what is purchased, displayed, and celebrated.

d. Where American Library Association standards fail to uphold the traditional family and relevant supportive values, those standards will be discarded and standards upholding traditional family values will take precedence.

e. While works discrediting and devaluing traditional family and traditional family values will not be automatically excluded from the collection of a "Family-Friendly Libraries" library, there will be no mandate to give this proven destructive point of view "equal time," space, and emphasis for the sake of "intellectual freedom" or perceived "political correctness." The point will be not to disallow opposing points of view from the public library system but to give more emphasis, time, space, and tax-money toward sponsorship of those materials which contribute toward the building rather than the destruction of society. Books which are not bought with tax money for free borrowing are still freely published and available for purchase by any citizen from book retail dealers. This is not a call for censorship, but for responsible sponsorship.

Article Two: Parental Library Rights

The library system clearly acknowledges parents as having primary authority over the lives and activities, including reading activities, of their minor children.

Policy translation:

a. Minor children must have the signed permission of a parent or legal guardian in order to obtain a card for library borrowing privileges.

b. Parents, with proper identification that they are the parents, will have full access to their minor children's reading records, such as the list of items checked out on their cards, past (if such records exist) and present.

c. Minors will not have access to explicitly adult materials without a parent's or guardian's permission.

d. Libraries will also offer parents other options for limiting what their minor children check out when parents or guardians are not present.

e. Library administrators will actively seek out parental opinion for guidelines in handling other materials that may need to be in a general "parental guidance only" category. These other topics may vary from community to community, but they will all have one thing in common: parents in the community have input into the ideas for these guidelines, and their input is given fair and respectful consideration by the library governing body.

Article Three: Respect for Standards and Laws

The library system clearly acknowledges "Community Standards" and statutory law, both local and state, as being relevant to the selection, display, and access policies concerning materials for the public library system.

Policy translation:

a. American Library Association guidelines may be adopted but are not required.

b. Where American Library Association guidelines and local "community standards" are in opposition, community standards will take precedence.

c. The governing body of the library system will consider the law-abiding taxpayers of the community the ultimate source of their authority, not the ALA.

d. Library administrators should periodically provide feedback and encouragement to the ALA on helpful changes the ALA needs to make in their policies in order to become more "Family-Friendly" as they once were earlier in their history.

Article Four: Respect for Minors

The library system clearly acknowledges that minor patrons have sensibilities and vulnerabilities different from that of adults and deserving of protection.

Policy translation:

a. Displays

1. Policies affecting open displays of new books, seasonal celebrations, special reading themes, and other library materials will consider the sensibilities of the libraries' youngest patrons.

2. No open displays will include material of an adult sexual nature.

3. No open displays will include any other material which community standards would consider inappropriate or potentially harmful to minors.

b. Shelving

1. Books and materials which community standards would consider potentially harmful to minors will be considered for a "parental guidance" section accessible only to adults and minors accompanied by adults, preferably parents or guardians.

2. All other regular library materials will be separated into age-appropriate sections.

3. Free handouts of an adult sexual nature or with advertisements for adult sexual partners or activities will be made inaccessible to unaccompanied minors.

Article Five: Parent and Citizen Participation

The library system clearly acknowledges that regular communication with parents and other concerned citizens is a necessary and important part of maintaining a library that successfully serves the needs of families, and does not undermine their strength.

Policy translation:

a. The library administration and other personnel will treat citizen/parental input with respect and appreciation both in public and behind the scenes when conducting library business.

b. The library administration and personnel will provide regular encouragement and opportunity for citizen/parental input for suggestions, criticisms, and comments both positive and negative, regarding library purchases, policies, people, and programs.

American Library Association's Freedom to Read

The Freedom to Read Foundation was established in 1969 by the American Library Association as an independent organization devoted to the legal and financial defense of intellectual freedom in libraries. The Freedom to Read *statement is a joint statement by the American Library Association and the Association of American Publishers, subsequently endorsed by the Freedom to Read Foundation. The* Freedom to Read *statement, which was adopted in 1953 and last revised in 1991, outlines the reasons why intellectual freedom is essential to a democracy. It is reprinted here by permission of the American Library Association.*

The freedom to read is essential to our democracy. It is continuously under attack. Private groups and public authorities in various parts of the country are working to remove books from sale, to censor textbooks, to label "controversial" books, to distribute lists of "objectionable" books or authors, and to purge libraries. These actions apparently rise from a view that our national tradition of free expression is no longer valid; that censorship and suppression are needed to avoid the subversion of politics and the corruption of morals. We, as citizens devoted to the use of books and as librarians and publishers responsible for disseminating them, wish to assert the public interest in the preservation of the freedom to read.

We are deeply concerned about these attempts at suppression. Most such attempts rest on a denial of the fundamental premise of democracy: that the ordinary citizen, by exercising critical judgment, will accept the good and reject the bad. The censors, public and private, assume that they should determine what is good and what is bad for their fellow-citizens.

We trust Americans to recognize propaganda, and to reject it. We so not believe they need the help of censors to assist them in this task. We do not believe that they are prepared to sacrifice their heritage of a free press in order to be "protected" against what others think may be bad for them. We believe they still favor free enterprise in ideas and expression.

We are aware, of course, that books are not alone in being subjected to efforts at suppression. We are aware that these efforts are related to a larger pattern of pressures being brought against education, the press, films, radio, and television. The problem is not only one of actual censorship. The shadow of fear cast by these pressures leads, we suspect, to an even larger voluntary curtailment of expression by those who seek to avoid controversy.

Such pressure toward conformity is perhaps natural to a time of uneasy change and pervading fear. Especially when so many of our apprehensions are directed against an ideology, the expression of a dissident idea becomes a thing feared in itself, and we tend to move against it as against a hostile deed, with suppression.

And yet suppression is never more dangerous than in such a time of social tension. Freedom has given the United States the elasticity to endure strain. Freedom keeps open the path of novel and creative solutions, and enables change to come by choice. Every silencing of a heresy, every enforcement of an orthodoxy, diminishes the toughness and resilience of our society and leaves it the less able to deal with stress.

Now as always in our history, books are among our greatest instruments of freedom. They are almost the only means for making generally available ideas or manners of expression that can initially command only a small audience. They are the natural medium for the new idea and the untried voice from which come the original contributions to social growth. They are essential to the extended discussion which serious thought requires, and to the accumulation of knowledge and ideas into organized collections.

We believe that free communication is essential to the preservation of a free society and a creative culture. We believe that these pressures towards conformity present the danger of limiting the range and variety of inquiry and expression on which our democracy and our culture depend. We believe that every American community must jealously guard the freedom to publish and to circulate, in order to preserve its own freedom to read. We believe that publishers and librarians have a profound responsibility to give validity to that freedom to read by making it possible for the readers to choose freely from a variety of offerings.

The freedom to read is guaranteed by the Constitution. Those with faith in free people will stand firm on these constitutional guarantees of essential rights and will exercise the responsibilities that accompany these rights.

We therefore affirm these propositions:

1. It is in the public interest for publishers and librarians to make available the widest diversity of views and expressions, including those which are unorthodox or unpopular with the majority.

Creative thought is by definition new, and what is new is different. The bearer of every new thought is a rebel until that idea is refined and tested. Totalitarian systems attempt to maintain themselves in power by the ruthless suppression of any concept which challenges the established orthodoxy. The power of a democratic system to adapt to change is vastly strengthened by the freedom of its citizens to choose widely from among conflicting opinions offered freely to them. To stifle every nonconformist idea at birth would mark the end of the democratic process. Furthermore, only through the constant activity of weighing and selecting can the democratic mind attain the strength demanded by times like these. We need to know not only what we believe but why we believe it.

2. Publishers, librarians and booksellers do not need to endorse every idea or presentation contained in the books they make available. It would conflict with the public interest for them to establish their own political, moral or aesthetic views as a standard for determining what books should be published or circulated.

Publishers and librarians serve the educational process by helping to make available knowledge and ideas required for the growth of the mind and the increase of learning. They do not foster education by imposing as mentors the patterns of their own thought. The people should have the freedom to read and consider a broader range of ideas than those that may be held by any single librarian or publisher or government or church. It is wrong that what one can read should be confined to what another thinks proper.

3. It is contrary to the public interest for publishers or librarians to determine the acceptability of a book on the basis of the personal history or political affiliations of the author.

A book should be judged as a book. No art or literature can flourish if it is to be measured by the political views or private lives of its creators. No society of free people can flourish which draws up lists of writers to whom it will not listen, whatever they may have to say.

4. There is no place in our society for efforts to coerce the taste of others, to confine adults to the reading matter deemed suitable for adolescents, or to inhibit the efforts of writers to achieve artistic expression.

To some, much of modern literature is shocking. But is not much of life itself shocking? We cut off literature at the source if we prevent writers from dealing with the stuff of life. Parents and teachers have a responsibility to prepare the young to meet the diversity of experiences in life to which they will be exposed, as they have a responsibility to help them learn to think critically for themselves. These are affirmative responsibilities, not to be discharged simply by preventing them from reading works for which they are not yet prepared. In these matters taste differs, and taste cannot be legislated; nor can machinery be devised which will suit the demands of one group without limiting the freedom of others.

5. It is not in the public interest to force a reader to accept with any book the prejudgment of a label characterizing the book or author as subversive or dangerous.

The ideal of labeling presupposes the existence of individuals or groups with wisdom to determine by authority what is good or bad for the citizen. It presupposes that individuals must be directed in making up their minds about the ideas they examine. But Americans do not need others to do their thinking for them.

6. It is the responsibility of publishers and librarians, as guardians of the people's freedom to read, to contest encroachments upon that freedom by individuals or groups seeking to impose their own standards or tastes upon the community at large.

It is inevitable in the give and take of the democratic process that the political, the moral, or the aesthetic concepts of an individual or group will occasionally collide with those of another individual or group. In a free society individuals are free to determine for themselves what they wish to read, and each group is free to determine what it will recommend to its freely associated members. But no group has the right to take the law into its own hands, and to impose its own concept of politics or morality upon other members of a democratic society. Freedom is no freedom if it is accorded only to the accepted and the inoffensive.

7. It is the responsibility of publishers and librarians to give full meaning to the freedom to read by providing books that

enrich the quality and diversity of thought and expression. By the exercise of this affirmative responsibility, they can demonstrate that the answer to a bad book is a good one, the answer to a bad idea is a good one.

The freedom to read is of little consequence when expended on the trivial; it is frustrated when the reader cannot obtain matter fit for that reader's purpose. What is needed is not only the absence of restraint, but the positive provision of opportunity for the people to read the best that has been thought and said. Books are the major channel by which the intellectual inheritance is handed down, and the principal means of its testing and growth. The defense of their freedom and integrity, and the enlargement of their service to society, requires of all publishers and librarians the utmost of their faculties, and deserves of all citizens the fullest of their support.

We state these propositions neither lightly nor as easy generalizations. We here stake out a lofty claim for the value of books. We do so because we believe that they are good, possessed of enormous variety and usefulness, worthy of cherishing and keeping free. We realize that the application of these propositions may mean the dissemination of ideas and manners of expression that are repugnant to many persons. We do not state these propositions in the comfortable belief that what people read is unimportant. We believe rather that what people read is deeply important; that ideas can be dangerous; but that the suppression of ideas is fatal to a democratic society. Freedom itself is a dangerous way of life, but it is ours.

This statement was originally issued in May of 1953 by the Westchester Conference of the American Library Association and the American Book Publishers Council, which in 1970 consolidated with the American Educational Publishers Institute to become the Association of American Publishers.

Adopted June 25, 1953; revised January 28, 1972, January 16, 1991, by the ALA Council and the AAP Freedom to Read Committee.

A Joint Statement by: American Library Association & Association of American Publishers
    Subsequently Endorsed by:
    American Booksellers Association
    American Booksellers Foundation for Free Expression
    American Civil Liberties Union
    American Federation of Teachers AFL-CIO
    Anti-Defamation League of B'nai B'rith

Association of American University Presses
Children's Book Council
Freedom to Read Foundation
International Reading Association
Thomas Jefferson Center for the Protection of Free Expression
National Association of College Stores
National Council of Teachers of English
PEN American Center
People for the American Way
Periodical and Book Association of America
Sexuality Information and Education Council of the United States
Society of Professional Journalists
Women's National Book Association
The YWCA of the USA

American Civil Liberties Union's Briefing Paper Number 14

The ACLU publishes a number of briefing papers that reflect its position on various freedoms. The ACLU's Briefing Paper Number 14, written in 1997, defends the freedom of artistic expression as guaranteed by the First and Fourteenth Amendments of the U.S. Constitution and outlines some important Supreme Court rulings on censorship issues. It is reprinted here, courtesy of the American Civil Liberties Union, 1998.

Freedom of Expression in the Arts and Entertainment

In the late 1980s, state prosecutors brought a criminal obscenity charge against the owner of a record store for selling an album by the rap group *2 Live Crew*. Although this was the first time that obscenity charges had ever been brought against song lyrics, the *2 Live Crew* case focused the nation's attention on an old question: should the government ever have the authority to dictate to its citizens what they may or may not listen to, read, or watch?

American society has always been deeply ambivalent about this question. On the one hand, our history is filled with examples of overt government censorship, from the 1873 Comstock Law to the 1996 Communications Decency Act. Anthony Comstock, head of the Society for the Suppression of Vice, boasted 194,000 "questionable pictures" and 134,000 pounds of books of "improper character" were destroyed under the Comstock Law—in the first year alone. The Communications Decency Act imposed an unconstitutional censorship scheme on the Internet, accurately described by a federal judge as "the most participatory form of mass speech yet developed."

On the other hand, the commitment to freedom of imagination and expression is deeply embedded in our national psyche, buttressed by the First Amendment, and supported by a long line of Supreme Court decisions.

Provocative and controversial art and in-your-face entertainment put our commitment to free speech to the test. Why should we oppose censorship when scenes of murder and mayhem dominate the TV screen, when works of art can be seen as a direct insult to people's religious beliefs, and when much sexually explicit material can be seen as degrading to women? Why not let the majority's morality and taste dictate what others can look at or listen to?

The answer is simple, and timeless: a free society is based on the principle that each and every individual has the right to decide what art or entertainment he or she wants—or does not want—to receive or create. Once you allow the government to censor someone else, you cede to it the power to censor you, or something you like. Censorship is like poison gas: a powerful weapon that can harm you when the wind shifts.

Freedom of expression for ourselves requires freedom of expression for others. It is at the very heart of our democracy.

Sexual Speech

Sex in art and entertainment is the most frequent target of censorship crusades. Many examples come to mind. A painting of the classical statue of Venus de Milo was removed from a store because the managers of the shopping mall found its seminudity "too shocking." Hundreds of works of literature, from Maya Angelou's *I Know Why the Caged Bird Sings* to John Steinbeck's *Grapes of Wrath*, have been banned from public schools based on their sexual content.

A museum director was charged with a crime for including sexually explicit photographs by Robert Mapplethorpe in an art exhibit.

American law is, on the whole, the most speech-protective in the world—but sexual expression is treated as a second-class citizen. No causal link between exposure to sexually explicit materials and anti-social or violent behavior has ever been scientifically established, in spite of many efforts to do so. Rather, the Supreme Court has allowed censorship of sexual speech on moral grounds—a remnant of our nation's Puritan heritage.

This does not mean that all sexual expression can be censored, however. Only a narrow range of "obscene" material can be suppressed; a term like "pornography" has no legal meaning. Nevertheless, even the relatively narrow obscenity exception serves as a vehicle for abuse by government authorities as well as pressure groups who want to impose their personal views on other people.

Is Media Violence a Threat to Society?

Today's calls for censorship are not motivated solely by morality and taste, but also by the widespread belief that exposure to images of violence causes people to act in destructive ways. Pro-censorship forces, including many politicians, often cite a multitude of "scientific studies" that allegedly prove fictional violence leads to real-life violence.

There is, in fact, virtually no evidence that fictional violence causes otherwise stable people to become violent. And if we suppressed material based on the actions of unstable people, no work of fiction or art would be safe from censorship. Serial killer Ted Bundy collected cheerleading magazines. And the work most often cited by psychopaths as justification for their acts of violence is the Bible.

But what about the rest of us? Does exposure to media violence actually lead to criminal or anti-social conduct by otherwise stable people, including children, who spend an average of 28 hours watching television each week? These are important questions. If there really were a clear cause-and-effect relationship between what normal children see on TV and harmful actions, then limits on such expression might arguably be warranted.

What the Studies Show

Studies on the relationship between media violence and real violence are the subject of considerable debate. Children have been shown TV programs with violent episodes in a laboratory setting and then tested for "aggressive" behavior. Some of these studies suggest that watching TV violence may temporarily induce "object aggression" in some children (such as popping balloons or hitting dolls or playing sports more aggressively) but not actual criminal violence against another person.

Correlational studies that seek to explain why some aggressive people have a history of watching a lot of violent TV suffer from the chicken-and-egg dilemma: does violent TV cause such people to behave aggressively, or do aggressive people simply prefer more violent entertainment? There is no definitive answer. But all scientists agree that statistical correlations between two phenomena do not mean that one causes the other.

International comparisons are no more helpful. Japanese TV and movies are famous for their extreme, graphic violence, but Japan has a very low crime rate—much lower than many other societies in which television watching is relatively rare. What the studies reveal on the issue of fictional violence and real world aggression is—not much.

The only clear assertion that can be made is that the relationship between art and human behavior is a very complex one. Violent and sexually explicit art and entertainment have been a staple of human cultures from time immemorial. Many human behavioralists believe that these themes have a useful and constructive societal role, serving as a vicarious outlet for individual aggression.

Where Do the Experts Agree?

Whatever influence fictional violence has on behavior, most experts believe its effects are marginal compared to other factors. Even small children know the difference between fiction and reality, and their attitudes and behavior are shaped more by their life circumstances than by the books they read or the TV they watch. In 1972, the U.S. Surgeon General's Advisory Committee on Television and Social Behavior released a 200-page report, "Television and Growing Up: The Impact of Televised Violence," which concluded, "The Effect [of television] is small compared with many other possible causes, such as parental attitudes or knowledge of and experience with the real violence of our society." Twenty-one years later, the American Psychological Association published its 1993 report, "Violence and Youth," and concluded, "The greatest predictor of future violent behavior is a previous history of violence." In 1995, the Center for Communication Policy at UCLA, which monitors TV violence, came to a similar conclusion in its yearly report: "It is known that television does not have a simple, direct stimulus-response effect on its audiences."

Blaming the media does not get us very far, and, to the extent that it diverts the public's attention from the real causes of violence in society, it may do more harm than good.

Which Media Violence Would You Ban?

A pro-censorship member of Congress once attacked the following shows for being too violent: *The Miracle Worker, Civil War Journal, Star Trek 9, The Untouchables,* and *Teenage Mutant Ninja Turtles*. What would be left if all these kinds of programs were purged from the airwaves? Is there good violence and bad violence? If so, who decides? Sports and news are at least as violent as fiction, from the fights that erupt during every televised hockey game, to the videotaped beating of Rodney King by the L.A. Police Department, shown over and over again on prime time TV. If we accept censorship of violence in the media, we will have to censor sports and news programs.

Individual Rights, Individual Decisions

The First Amendment is based upon the belief that in a free and democratic society, individual adults must be free to decide for themselves what to read, write, paint, draw, see and hear. If we are disturbed by images of violence or sex, we can change the channel, turn off the TV, and decline to go to certain movies or museum exhibits.

We can also exercise our freedom of speech rights by voicing our objections to forms of expression that we don't like. Justice Louis Brandeis' advice that the remedy for messages we disagree with or dislike in art, entertainment, or politics is "more speech, not enforced silence," is as true today as it was when given in 1927.

Further, we can exercise our prerogative as parents without resorting to censorship. Devices now exist that make it possible to block access to specific TV programs and Internet sites. Periodicals that review books, recordings, and films can help parents determine what they feel is appropriate for their youngsters. Viewing decisions can, and should, be made at home, without government interference.

Pornographic! Indecent! Obscene!

Justice John Marshall Harlan's line "one man's vulgarity is another's lyric," sums up the impossibility of developing a definition of obscenity that isn't hopelessly vague and subjective. And Justice Potter Stewart's famous assurance, "I know it when I see it," is of small comfort to artists, writers, movie directors, and lyricists who must navigate the murky waters of obscenity law trying to figure out what police, prosecutors, and judges and juries think.

The Supreme Court's current definition of constitutionally unprotected obscenity, first announced in a 1973 case called *Miller v. California*, has three requirements. The work must: 1. Appeal to the average person's prurient (shameful, morbid) interest in sex; 2. Depict sexual conduct in a "patently offensive way" as defined by community standards; and 3. Taken as a whole, lack serious literary, artistic, political, or scientific value.

The Supreme Court has held that indecent expression—in contrast with "obscenity"—is entitled to some constitutional protection, but that indecency in some media (broadcasting, cable, and telephone) may be regulated. In its 1978 decision in *Federal Communications Commission v. Pacifica*, the Court ruled that the government could require radio and television stations to air "indecent" material only during those hours when children would be unlikely listeners or viewers. Broadcast indecency was defined as "language that describes, in terms patently offensive as measured by contemporary community standards for the broadcast medium, sexual or excretory activities or organs." This vague concept continues to baffle both the public and the courts.

Pornography is not a legal term at all. Its dictionary definition is "writing or pictures intended to arouse sexual desire." Pornography comes in as many varieties as the human sexual impulse and is protected by the First Amendment unless it meets the definition for illegal obscenity.

What Is Censorship?

Censorship, the suppression of words, images, or ideas that are "offensive," happens whenever some people succeed in imposing their personal political or moral values on others. Censorship can be carried out by the government as well as private pressure groups. Censorship by the government is unconstitutional.

In contrast, when private individuals or groups organize boycotts against stores that sell magazines of which they disapprove, their actions are protected by the First Amendment, although they can become dangerous in the extreme. Private pressure groups, not the government, promulgated and enforced the infamous Hollywood blacklists during the McCarthy period. But these private censorship campaigns are best countered by groups and individuals speaking out and organizing in defense of the threatened expression.

What Does Artistic Freedom Include?

The Supreme Court has interpreted the First Amendment's protection of artistic expression very broadly. It extends not only to books, theatrical works, and paintings, but also to posters, television, music videos, and comic books—whatever the human creative impulse produces.

Two fundamental principles come into play whenever a court must decide a case involving freedom of expression. The first is "content neutrality"—the government cannot limit expression just because any listener, or even the majority of a community, is offended by its content. In the context of art and entertainment, this means tolerating some works that we might find offensive, insulting, outrageous—or just plain bad.

The second principle is that expression may be restricted only if it will clearly cause direct and imminent harm to an important societal interest. The classic example is falsely shouting fire in a crowded theater and causing a stampede. Even then, the speech may be silenced or punished only if there is no other way to avert the harm.

The Motion Picture Production Code of 1930

The next document, the Motion Picture Production Code of 1930, was designed to regulate the powerful new medium of film and ensure that "taboo" subjects such as sex, nudity, childbirth, adultery, and homosexuality were not shown to audiences. The production code highlights the moral concerns of the time and also alludes to the power and possibility inherent in film. This production code was voluntarily adopted by the Motion Picture Producers and Distributors of America (MPPDA) as an alternative to government regulation of their industry. It is also known as the Hays Code, after the first director of the MPPDA, Will Hays. Among the movies subject to censure under this code were the screen adaptations of the novels Anna Karenina, The Grapes of Wrath, A Farewell to Arms, *and* Of Human Bondage. *The 1930 code remained intact and was not changed until 1966 when the Motion Picture Association of America updated it in order to suit new tastes and new film audiences.*

Motion picture producers recognize the high trust and confidence which have been placed in them by the people of the world and which have made motion pictures a universal form of entertainment.

They recognize their responsibility to the public because of this trust and because entertainment and art are important influences in the life of a nation.

Hence, though regarding motion pictures primarily as entertainment without any explicit purpose of teaching or propaganda, they know that the motion picture within its own field of entertainment may be directly responsible for spiritual or moral progress, for higher types of social life, and for much correct thinking.

During the rapid transition from silent to talking pictures they have realized the necessity and the opportunity of subscribing to a Code to govern the production of talking pictures and of re-acknowledging this responsibility.

On their part, they ask from the public and from public leaders a sympathetic understanding of their purposes and problems and a spirit of cooperation that will allow them the freedom and opportunity necessary to bring the motion picture to a still higher level of wholesome entertainment for all the people.

General Principles

1. No picture shall be produced that will lower the moral standards of those who see it. Hence the sympathy of the audience should never be thrown to the side of crime, wrongdoing, evil or sin.

2. Correct standards of life, subject only to the requirements of drama and entertainment, shall be presented.

3. Law, natural or human, shall not be ridiculed, nor shall sympathy be created for its violation.

Particular Applications

I. Crimes Against the Law

These shall never be presented in such a way as to throw sympathy with the crime as against law and justice or to inspire others with a desire for imitation.

 1. Murder

  a. The technique of murder must be presented in a way that will not inspire imitation.

  b. Brutal killings are not to be presented in detail.

  c. Revenge in modern times shall not be justified.

 2. Methods of crime should not be explicitly presented.

a. Theft, robbery, safe-cracking, and dynamiting of trains, mines, buildings, etc., should not be detailed in method.

b. Arson must be subject to the same safeguards.

c. The use of firearms should be restricted to the essentials.

d. Methods of smuggling should not be presented.

3. Illegal drug traffic must never be presented.

4. The use of liquor in American life, when not required by the plot or for proper characterization, will not be shown.

II. Sex

The sanctity of the institution of marriage and the home shall be upheld.

Pictures shall not infer that low forms of sex relationship are the accepted or common thing.

1. Adultery, sometimes necessary plot material, must not be explicitly treated, or justified, or presented attractively.

2. Scenes of Passion

a. They should not be introduced when not essential to the plot.

b. Excessive and lustful kissing, lustful embraces, suggestive postures and gestures, are not to be shown.

c. In general passion should so be treated that these scenes do not stimulate the lower and baser element.

3. Seduction or Rape

a. They should never be more than suggested, and only when essential for the plot, and even then never shown by explicit method.

b. They are never the proper subject for comedy.

4. Sex perversion or any inference to it is forbidden.

5. White slavery shall not be treated.

6. Miscegenation (sex relationships between the white and black races) is forbidden.

7. Sex hygiene and venereal diseases are not subjects for motion pictures.

8. Scenes of actual child birth, in fact or in silhouette, are never to be presented.

9. Children's sex organs are never to be exposed.

III. Vulgarity

The treatment of low, disgusting, unpleasant, though not necessarily evil, subjects should always be subject to the dictates of good taste and a regard for the sensibilities of the audience.

IV. Obscenity

Obscenity in word, gesture, reference, song, joke, or by

suggestion (even when likely to be understood only by part of the audience) is forbidden.

V. Profanity

Pointed profanity (this includes the words God, Lord, Jesus, Christ—unless used reverently—Hell, S.O.B., damn, Gawd), or every other profane or vulgar expression however used, is forbidden.

VI. Costume

1. Complete nudity is never permitted. This includes nudity in fact or in silhouette, or any lecherous or licentious notice thereof by other characters in the picture.

2. Undressing scenes should be avoided, and never used save where essential to the plot.

3. Indecent or undue exposure is forbidden.

4. Dancing or costumes intended to permit undue exposure or indecent movements in the dance are forbidden.

VII. Dances

1. Dances suggesting or representing sexual actions or indecent passions are forbidden.

2. Dances which emphasize indecent movements are to be regarded as obscene.

VIII. Religion

1. No film or episode may throw ridicule on any religious faith.

2. Ministers of religion in their character as ministers of religion should not be used as comic characters or as villains.

3. Ceremonies of any definite religion should be carefully and respectfully handled.

IX. Locations

The treatment of bedrooms must be governed by good taste and delicacy.

X. National Feelings

1. The use of the Flag shall be consistently respectful.

2. The history, institutions, prominent people and citizenry of other nations shall be represented fairly.

XI. Titles

Salacious, indecent, or obscene titles shall not be used.

XII. Repellent Subjects

The following subjects must be treated within the careful limits of good taste:

1. Actual hangings or electrocutions as legal punishments for crime.

2. Third degree methods.

3. Brutality and possible gruesomeness.
4. Branding of people or animals.
5. Apparent cruelty to children or animals.
6. The sale of women, or a woman selling her virtue.
7. Surgical operations.

Reasons Supporting the Preamble of the Code

I. Theatrical motion pictures, that is, pictures intended for the theatre as distinct from pictures intended for churches, schools, lecture halls, educational movements, social reform movements, etc., are primarily to be regarded as *entertainment*.

Mankind has always recognized the importance of entertainment and its value in rebuilding the bodies and souls of human beings.

But it has always recognized that entertainment can be a character either *helpful* or *harmful* to the human race, and in consequence has clearly distinguished between:

a. Entertainment which tends to improve the race, or at least to re-create and rebuild human beings exhausted with the realities of life; and

b. Entertainment which tends to degrade human beings, or to lower their standards of life and living.

Hence the *moral importance* of entertainment is something which has been universally recognized. It enters intimately into the lives of men and women and affects them closely; it occupies their minds and affections during leisure hours; and ultimately touches the whole of their lives. A man may be judged by his standard of entertainment as easily as by the standard of his work.

So correct entertainment raises the whole standard of a nation.

Wrong entertainment lowers the whole living conditions and moral ideals of a race.

Note, for example, the healthy reactions to healthful sports, like baseball, golf; the unhealthy reactions to sports like cockfighting, bullfighting, bear baiting, etc.

Note, too, the effect on ancient nations of gladiatorial combats, the obscene plays of Roman times, etc.

II. Motion pictures are very important as *art*.

Though a new art, possibly a combination art, it has the same object as the other arts, the presentation of human thought, emotion, and experience, in terms of an appeal to the soul through the senses.

Here, as in entertainment,
Art enters intimately into the lives of human beings.

Art can be morally good, lifting men to higher levels. This has been done through good music, great painting, authentic fiction, poetry, drama.

Art can be morally evil in its effects. This is the case clearly enough with unclean art, indecent books, suggestive drama. The effect on the lives of men and women are obvious.

Note: It has often been argued that art itself is unmoral, neither good nor bad. This is true of the *thing* which is music, painting, poetry, etc. But the *thing* is the *product* of some person's mind, and the intention of that mind was either good or bad morally when it produced the thing.

Besides, the thing has its *effect* upon those who come into contact with it. In both these ways, that is, as a product of a mind and as the cause of definite effects, it has a deep moral significance and unmistakable moral quality.

Hence: The motion pictures, which are the most popular of modern arts for the masses, have their moral quality from the intention of the minds which produce them and from their effects on the moral lives and reactions of their audiences. This gives them a most important morality.

1. They reproduce the morality of the men who use the pictures as a medium for the expression of their ideas and ideals.

2. They affect the moral standards of those who, through the screen, take in these ideas and ideals.

In the case of motion pictures, the effect may be particularly emphasized because no art has so quick and so widespread an appeal to the masses. It has become in an incredibly short period the art of the multitudes.

III. The motion picture, because of its importance as entertainment and because of the trust placed in it by the peoples of the world, has special *moral obligations:*

A. Most arts appeal to the mature. This art appeals at once to every class, mature, immature, developed, undeveloped, law abiding, criminal. Music has its grades for different classes; so has literature and drama. This art of the motion picture, combining as it does the two fundamental appeals of looking at a picture and listening to a story, at once reaches every class of society.

B. By reason of the mobility of film and the ease of picture distribution, and because the possibility of duplicating positives in large quantities, this art reaches places unpenetrated by other forms of art.

C. Because of these two facts, it is difficult to produce films intended for only certain classes of people. The exhibitors' theatres are built for the masses, for the cultivated and the rude, the mature and the immature, the self-respecting and the criminal. Films, unlike books and music, can with difficulty be confined to certain selected groups.

D. The latitude given to film material cannot, in consequence, be as wide as the latitude given to book material. In addition:

a. A book describes; a film vividly presents. One presents on a cold page; the other by apparently living people.

b. A book reaches the mind through words merely; a film reaches the eyes and ears through the reproduction of actual events.

c. The reaction of a reader to a book depends largely on the keenness of the reader's imagination; the reaction to a film depends on the vividness of presentation.

Hence many things which might be described or suggested in a book could not possibly be presented in a film.

E. This is also true when comparing the film with the newspaper.

a. Newspapers present by description, films by actual presentation.

b. Newspapers are after the fact and present things as having taken place; the film gives the events in the process of enactment and with apparent reality of life.

F. Everything possible in a play is not possible in a film:

a. Because of the larger audience of the film, and its consequential mixed character. Psychologically, the larger the audience, the lower the moral mass resistance to suggestion.

b. Because through light, enlargement of character, presentation, scenic emphasis, etc., the screen story is brought closer to the audience than the play.

c. The enthusiasm for and interest in the film actors and actresses, developed beyond anything of the sort in history, makes the audience largely sympathetic toward the characters they portray and the stories in which they figure. Hence the audience is more ready to confuse actor and actress and the characters they portray, and it is most receptive of the emotions and ideals presented by the favorite stars.

G. Small communities, remote from sophistication and from the hardening process which often takes place in the ethical and moral standards of larger cities, are easily and readily reached by any sort of film.

H. The grandeur of mass settings, large action, spectacular features, etc., affects and arouses more intensely the emotional side of the audience.

In general, the mobility, popularity, accessibility, emotional appeal, vividness, straightforward presentation of fact in the film make for more intimate contact with a larger audience and for greater emotional appeal.

Hence the larger moral responsibilities of the motion pictures.

Reasons Underlying the General Principles

I. No picture shall be produced which will lower the moral standards of those who see it. Hence the sympathy of the audience should never be thrown to the side of crime, wrong-doing, evil or sin.

This is done:

1. When evil is made to appear attractive and alluring, and good is made to appear unattractive.

2. When the sympathy of the audience is thrown on the side of crime, wrong-doing, evil, sin. The same is true of a film that would throw sympathy against goodness, honor, innocence, purity or honesty.

Note: Sympathy with a person who sins is not the same as sympathy with the sin or crime of which he is guilty. We may feel sorry for the plight of the murderer or even understand the circumstances which led him to his crime: we may not feel sympathy with the wrong which he has done. The presentation of evil is often essential for art or fiction or drama. This in itself is not wrong provided:

a. That evil is not presented alluringly. Even if later in the film the evil is condemned or punished, it must not be allowed to appear so attractive that the audience's emotions are drawn to desire or approve so strongly that later the condemnation is forgotten and only the apparent joy of sin is remembered.

b. That throughout, the audience feels sure that evil is wrong and good is right.

II. Correct standards of life shall, as far as possible, be presented.

A wide knowledge of life and of living is made possible through the film.

When right standards are consistently presented, the motion picture exercises the most powerful influences. It builds character, develops right ideals, inculcates correct principles, and all this in attractive story form.

If motion pictures consistently hold up for admiration high types of characters and present stories that will affect lives for the better, they can become the most powerful force for the improvement of mankind.

III. Law, natural or human, shall not be ridiculed, nor shall sympathy be created for its violation.

By natural law is understood the law which is written in the hearts of all mankind, the greater underlying principles of right and justice dictated by conscience.

By human law is understood the law written by civilized nations.

1. The presentation of crimes against the law is often necessary for the carrying out of the plot. But the presentation must not throw sympathy with the crime as against the law nor with the criminal as against those who punish him.

2. The courts of the land should not be presented as unjust. This does not mean that a single court may not be presented as unjust, much less that a single court official must not be presented this way. But the court system of the country must not suffer as a result of this presentation.

Reasons Underlying the Particular Applications

I. Sin and evil enter into the story of human beings and hence in themselves are valid dramatic material.

II. In the use of this material, it must be distinguished between sin which repels by its very nature, and sins which often attract.

a. In the first class come murder, most theft, many legal crimes, lying, hypocrisy, cruelty, etc.

b. In the second class come sex sins, sins and crimes of apparent heroism, such as banditry, daring thefts, leadership in evil, organized crime, revenge, etc.

The first class needs less care in treatment, as sins and crimes of this class are naturally unattractive. The audience instinctively condemns all such and is repelled.

Hence the important objective must be to avoid the hardening of the audience, especially of those who are young and impressionable, to the thought and fact of crime. People can become accustomed even to murder, cruelty, brutality, and repellent crimes, if these are too frequently repeated.

The second class needs great care in handling, as the response of human nature to their appeal is obvious. This is treated more fully below.

III. A careful distinction can be made between films intended for general distribution, and films intended for use in theatres restricted to a limited audience. Themes and plots quite appropriate for the latter would be altogether out of place and dangerous in the former.

Note: The practice of using a general theatre and limiting its patronage to "Adults Only" is not completely satisfactory and is only partially effective.

However, maturer minds may easily understand and accept without harm subject matter in plots which do younger people positive harm.

Hence: If there should be created a special type of theatre, catering exclusively to an adult audience, for plays of this character (plays with problem themes, difficult discussions and maturer treatment) it would seem to afford an outlet, which does not now exist, for pictures unsuitable for general distribution but permissible for exhibitions to a restricted audience.

I. Crimes Against the Law

The treatment of crimes against the law must not:

1. Teach methods of crime.
2. Inspire potential criminals with a desire for imitation.
3. Make criminals seem heroic and justified.

Revenge in modern times shall not be justified. In lands and ages of less developed civilization and moral principles, revenge may sometimes be presented. This would be the case especially in places where no law exists to cover the crime because of which revenge is committed.

Because of its evil consequences, the drug traffic should not be presented in any form. The existence of the trade should not be brought to the attention of audiences.

The use of liquor should never be excessively presented. In scenes from American life, the necessities of plot and proper characterization alone justify its use. And in this case, it should be shown with moderation.

II. Sex

Out of a regard for the sanctity of marriage and the home, the triangle, that is, the love of a third party for one already married, needs careful handling.

The treatment should not throw sympathy against marriage as an institution.

Scenes of passion must be treated with an honest acknowledgement of human nature and its normal reactions. Many scenes cannot be presented without arousing dangerous emotions on the part of the immature, the young or the criminal classes.

Even within the limits of pure love, certain facts have been universally regarded by lawmakers as outside the limits of safe presentation.

In the case of impure love, the love which society has always regarded as wrong and which has been banned by divine law, the following are important:

1. Impure love must not be presented as attractive and beautiful.

2. It must not be the subject of comedy or farce, or treated as material for laughter.

3. It must not be presented in such a way to arouse passion or morbid curiosity on the part of the audience.

4. It must not be made to seem right and permissible.

5. It general, it must not be detailed in method and manner.

III. Vulgarity; IV. Obscenity; V. Profanity; hardly need further explanation than is contained in the Code.

VI. Costume

General Principles:

1. The effect of nudity or semi-nudity upon the normal man or woman, and much more upon the young and upon immature persons, has been honestly recognized by all lawmakers and moralists.

2. Hence the fact that the nude or semi-nude body may be beautiful does not make its use in the films moral. For, in addition to its beauty, the effect of the nude or semi-nude body on the normal individual must be taken into consideration.

3. Nudity or semi-nudity used simply to put a "punch" into a picture comes under the head of immoral actions. It is immoral in its effect on the average audience.

4. Nudity can never be permitted as being necessary for the plot.

Semi-nudity must not result in undue or indecent exposures.

5. Transparent or translucent materials and silhouette are frequently more suggestive than actual exposure.

VII. Dances

Dancing in general is recognized as an art and as a beautiful form of expressing human emotions.

But dances which suggest or represent sexual actions, whether performed solo or with two or more; dances intended to excite the emotional reaction of an audience; dances with movement of the breasts, excessive body movements while the feet are stationary, violate decency and are wrong.

VIII. Religion

The reason why ministers of religion may not be comic characters or villains is simply because the attitude taken toward them may easily become the attitude taken toward religion in general. Religion is lowered in the minds of the audience because of the lowering of the audience's respect for a minister.

IX. Locations

Certain places are so closely and thoroughly associated with sexual life or with sexual sin that their use must be carefully limited.

X. National Feelings

The just rights, history, and feelings of any nation are entitled to most careful consideration and respectful treatment.

XI. Titles

As the title of a picture is the brand on that particular type of goods, it must conform to the ethical practices of all such honest business.

XII. Repellent Subjects

Such subjects are occasionally necessary for the plot. Their treatment must never offend good taste nor injure the sensibilities of an audience.

Formulated and formally adopted by The Association of Motion Picture Producers, Inc. and The Motion Picture Producers and Distributors of America, Inc. in March 1930.

The Communications Decency Act of 1996

In 1995 the Communications Decency Act (CDA), which later became a section of the Telecommunications Reform Act of 1996, was proposed by Senator James Exon. The most significant effect of this act was that it outlawed all on-line communications that were defined, very broadly, as "indecent" or "patently offensive." Despite intense opposition from organizations dedicated to preserving constitutional liberties on-line, the CDA was passed by Congress and signed by President Clinton. One year later, in a decision known as Reno v. ACLU, *the Supreme Court struck down the Communications Decency Act of 1996 as unconstitutional. The following is the full text of the act.*

Title V—Broadcast Obscenity and Violence

Subtitle A Obscene, Harassing, and Wrongful Utilization of Telecommunications Facilities

Sec. 501. Short Title.

This title may be cited as the "Communications Decency Act of 1995."

Sec. 502. Obscene or Harassing Use of Telecommunications Facilities Under the Communications Act of 1934.

Section 223 (47 U.S.C. 223) is amended—

(1) by striking subsection (a) and inserting in lieu thereof:
"(a) Whoever—
"(1) in interstate or foreign communications—
"(A) by means of a telecommunications device knowingly—
"(i) makes, creates, or solicits, and
"(ii) initiates the transmission of, any comment, request, suggestion, proposal, image, or other communication which is obscene, lewd, lascivious, filthy, or indecent, with intent to annoy, abuse, threaten, or harass an other person;
"(B) by means of a telecommunications device knowingly—
"(i) makes, creates, or solicits, and
"(ii) initiates the transmission of, any comment, request, suggestion, proposal, image, or other communication which is obscene or indecent knowing that the recipient of the communication is under 18 years of age regardless of whether the maker of such communication placed the call or initiated the communication;
"(C) makes a telephone call or utilizes a telecommunications device, whether or not conversation or communication ensues, without disclosing his identity and with intent to annoy, abuse, threaten, or harass any person at the called number or who receives the communication;
"(D) makes or causes the telephone of another repeatedly or continuously to ring, with intent to harass a person at the called number; or
"(E) makes repeated telephone calls or repeatedly initiates communication with a telecommunications device, during which conversation or communication ensues, solely to harass any person at the called number or who receives the communication;
"(2) knowingly permits a telecommunications facility under his control to be used for any activity prohibited by paragraph (1) with the intent that it be used for such activity, shall be fined under title 18, United States Code, or imprisoned not more than two years, or both."; and

(2) by adding at the end the following new sub sections:
"(d) Whoever—
"(1) in interstate or foreign communications knowingly—
"(A) uses an interactive computer service to send to a specific person or persons under 18 years of age, or
"(B) uses any interactive computer service to display in a manner available to a person under 18 years of age, any comment, request suggestion, proposal, image, or other communication that, in context, depicts or describes, in terms patently offensive as measured by contemporary community standards, sexual or excretory activities or organs, regardless of whether the user of such service placed the call or initiated the communication; or
"(2) knowingly permits any telecommunications facility under such person's control to be used for an activity prohibited by paragraph (1) with the intent that it be used for such activity, shall be fined under title 18, United States Code, or imprisoned not more than two years, or both.
"(e) In addition to any other defenses available by law:
"(1) No person shall be held to have violated subsection (a) or (d) solely for providing access or connection to or from a facility, system, or network not under that person's control, including transmission, downloading, intermediate storage, access software, or other related capabilities that are incidental to providing such access or connection that does not include the creation of the content of the communication.
"(2) The defenses provided by paragraph (1) of this subsection shall not be applicable to a person who is a conspirator with an entity actively involved in the creation or knowing distribution of communications that violate this section, or who knowingly advertises the availability of such communications.
"(3) The defenses provided in paragraph (1) of this subsection shall not be applicable to a person who provides access or connection to a facility, system, or network engaged in the violation of this section that is owned or controlled by such person.
"(4) No employer shall be held liable under this section for the actions of an employee or agent unless the employee's or agent's conduct is within the scope of his employment or agency and the employer (A) having knowledge of such conduct, authorizes or ratifies such conduct, or (B) recklessly disregards such conduct.
"(5) It is a defense to a prosecution under sub section (a) or (d) that a person—

"(A) has taken in good faith, reasonable, effective, and appropriate actions under the circumstances to restrict or prevent access by minors to a communication specified in such subsections, which may involve any appropriate measures to restrict minors from such communications, including any method which is feasible under available technology; or

"(B) has restricted access to such communication by requiring use of a verified credit card, debit account, adult access code, or adult personal identification number.

"(6) The Commission may describe measures which are reasonable, effective, and appropriate to restrict access to prohibited communications under subsection (d). Nothing in this section authorizes the Commission to enforce, or is intended to provide the Commission with the authority to approve, sanction, or permit, the use of such measures. The Commission has no enforcement authority over the failure to utilize such measures. The Commission shall not endorse specific products relating to such measures. The use of such measures shall be admitted as evidence of good faith efforts for purposes of this paragraph in any action arising under subsection (d). Nothing in this section shall be construed to treat interactive computer services as common carriers or telecommunications carriers.

"(f)(1) No cause of action may be brought in any court or administrative agency against any person on account of any activity that is not in violation of any law punishable by criminal or civil penalty, and that the person has taken in good faith to implement a defense authorized under this section or otherwise to restrict or prevent the transmission of, or access to, a communication specified in this section.

"(2) No State or local government may impose any liability for commercial activities or actions by commercial entities, nonprofit libraries, or institutions of higher education in connection with an activity or action described in subsection (a)(2) or (d) that is inconsistent with the treatment of those activities or actions under this section: Provided, however, that nothing herein shall preclude any State or local government from enacting and enforcing complementary oversight, liability, and regulatory systems, procedures, and requirements, so long as such systems, procedures, and requirements govern only intrastate services and do not result in the imposition of inconsistent rights, duties or obligations on the provision of interstate services. Nothing in this subsection shall preclude any State or local government from governing conduct not covered by this section.

"(g) nothing in subsection (a), (d), (e), or (f) or in the defenses to prosecution under (a) or (d) shall be construed to affect or limit the application or enforcement of any other Federal law.

"(h) For purposes of this section

"(1) The use of the term 'telecommunications device' in this section

"(A) shall not impose new obligations on broadcasting station licensees and cable operators covered by obscenity and indecency provisions elsewhere in this Act; and

"(B) does not include the use of an interactive computer service.

"(2) The term 'interactive computer service' has the meaning provided in section 230(f)(2).

"(3) The term 'access software' means software (including client or server software) or enabling tools that do not create or provide the content of the communication but that allow a user to do any one or more of the following:

"(A) filter, screen, allow, or disallow content;

"(B) pick, choose, analyze, or digest content; or

"(C) transmit, receive, display, forward, cache, search, subset, organize, reorganize, or translate content.

"(4) The term 'institution of higher education' has the meaning provided in section 1201 of the Higher Education Act of 1965 (20 U.S.C. 1141).

"(5) The term 'library' means a library eligible for participation in State-based plans for funds under title III of the Library Services and Construction Act (20 U.S.C. 355e et seq.)."

Sec. 503. Obscene Programming on Cable Television

Section 639 (47 U.S.C. 559) is amended by striking "not more than $10,000" and inserting "under title 18, United States Code."

Sec. 504. Scrambling of Cable Channels for Nonsubscribers

Part IV of title VI (47 U.S.C. 551 et seq.) is amended by adding at the end the following:

Sec. 640. Scrambling of, Cable Channels for Nonsubscribers

"(a) Subscriber Request. Upon request by a cable service subscriber, a cable operator shall, without charge, fully scramble or otherwise fully block the audio and video portion of each channel carrying such programming so that one not a subscriber does not receive it.

"(b) Definition. As used in this section, the term 'scramble' means to rearrange the content of the signal of the programming so that the program cannot be viewed or heard in an understandable manner."

Sec. 505. Scrambling of Sexually Explicit Adult Video Service Programming.

(a) Requirement. Part IV of title I (47 U.S.C. 551 et seq.), as amended by this Act, is further amended by adding at the end the following:

Sec. 641. Scrambling of Sexually Explicit Adult Video Service Programming

"(a) Requirement. In providing sexually explicit adult programming or other programming that is indecent on any channel of its service primarily dedicated to sexually-oriented programming, a multichannel video programming distributor shall fully scramble or otherwise fully block the video and audio portion of such channel so that one not a subscriber to such channel or programming does not receive it.

"(b) Implementation. Until a multichannel video programming distributor complies with the requirement set forth in subsection (a), the distributor shall limit the access of children to the programming referred to in that subsection by not providing such program during the hours of the day (as determined by the Commission) when a significant number of children are likely to view it.

"(c) Definition. As used in this section, the term 'scramble' means to rearrange the content of the signal of the programming so that the programming cannot be viewed or heard in an understandable manner."

"(b) Effective Date. The amendment made by subsection (a) shall take effect 30 days after the date of the enactment of this Act."

Sec. 606. Cable Operator Refusal to Carry Certain Programs

(a) Public, Education, and Governmental Channels. Section 611(e) (47 U.S.C. 531(e)) is amended by inserting before the period the following: "except a cable operator may refuse to transmit any public access program or portion of a public access program which contains obscenity, indecency, or nudity."

(b) Cable Channels for Commercial Use. Section 612(c)(2) (47 U.S.C. 532(c)(2)) is amended by striking "an operator" and inserting "a cable operator may refuse to transmit any leased access program or portion of a leased access program which contains obscenity, indecency, or nudity."

Sec. 507. Clarification of Current Laws Regarding Communication of Obscene Materials through the Use of Computers

(a) Importation or Transportation. Section 1462 of title 18, United States Code, is amended

(1) in the first undesignated paragraph, by inserting "or interactive computer service (as defined in section 230(f)(2) of the Communications Act of 1934)" after "carrier"; and

(2) in the second undesignated paragraph

(A) by inserting "or receives," after "takes";

(B) by inserting "or interactive computer service (as defined in section 230(f)(2) of the Communications Act of 1934)" after "common carrier"; and

(C) by inserting "or importation" after "carriage."

(b) Transportation for Purposes of Sale or Distribution. The first undesignated paragraph of section 1465 of title 18, United States Code, is amended—

(1) by striking "transports in" and inserting "transports or travels in, or uses a facility or means of,";

(2) by inserting "or an interactive computer service (as defined in section 230(f)(2) of the Communications Act of 1934) in or affecting such commerce" after "foreign commerce" the first place it appears;

(3) by striking ", or knowingly travels in" and all that follows through "obscene material in inter state or foreign commerce," and inserting "of."

(c) INTERPRETATION. The amendments made by this section are clarifying and shall not be interpreted to limit or repeal any prohibition contained in sections 1462 and 1465 of title 18, United States Code, before such amendment, under the rule established in United States v. Alpers, 338 U.S. 680 (1950).

Sec. 508. Coercion and Enticement of Minors

Section 2422 of title 18, United States Code, is amended

(1) by inserting "(a)" before "Whoever knowingly"; and

(2) by adding at the end the following

"(b) Whoever, using any facility or means of inter state or

foreign commerce, including the mail, or within the special maritime and territorial jurisdiction of the United States, knowingly persuades, induces, entices, or coerces any individual who has not attained the age of 18 years to engage in prostitution or any sexual act for which person may be criminally prosecuted, or attempts to do so shall be fined under this title or imprisoned not more than 10 years, or both."

Sec. 509. Online Family Empowerment

Title II of the Communications Act of 1934 (47 U.S.C. 201 et seq.) is amended by adding at the end the following new section:

Sec. 230. Protection for Private Blocking and Screening of Offensive Material

"(a) Findings. The Congress finds the following:

"(1) The rapidly developing array of Internet and other interactive computer services available to individual Americans represent an extraordinary advance in the availability of educational and informational resources to our citizens.

"(2) These services offer users a great degree of control over the information that they receive, as well as the potential for even greater control in the future as technology develops.

"(3) The Internet and other interactive computer services offer a forum for a true diversity of political discourse, unique opportunities for cultural development, and myriad avenues for intellectual activity.

"(4) The Internet and other interactive computer services have flourished, to the benefit of all Americans, with a minimum of government regulation.

"(5) Increasingly Americans are relying on interactive media for a variety of political, educational, cultural, and entertainment services.

"(b) POLICY. It is the policy of the United States

"(1) to promote the continued development of the Internet and other interactive computer services and other interactive media;

"(2) to preserve the vibrant and competitive free market that presently exists for the Internet and other interactive computer services, unfettered by Federal or State regulation;

"(3) to encourage the development of technologies which maximize user control over what in formation is received by individuals, families, and schools who use the Internet and other interactive computer services;

"(4) to remove disincentives for the development and utilization of blocking and filtering technologies that empower parents to restrict their children's access to objectionable or inappropriate online material; and

"(5) to ensure vigorous enforcement of Federal criminal laws to deter and punish trafficking in obscenity, stalking, and harassment by means of computer.

"(c) Protection for 'Good Samaritan' Blocking and Screening of Offensive Material.

"(1) Treatment of Publisher or Speaker. No provider or user of an interactive computer service shall be treated as the publisher or speaker of any information provided by another information content provider.

"(2) Civil Liability. No provider or user of an interactive computer service shall be held liable on account of

"(A) any action voluntarily taken in good faith to restrict access to or availability of material that the provider or user considers to be obscene, lewd, lascivious, filthy, excessively violent, harassing, or otherwise objectionable, whether or not such material is constitutionally protected; or

"(B) any action taken to enable or make available to information content providers or others the technical means to restrict access to material described in paragraph (1).

"(d) Effect on Other Laws.

"(1) No Effect on Criminal Law. Nothing in this section shall be construed to impair the enforcement of section 223 of this Act, chapter 71 (relating to obscenity) or 110 (relating to exploitation of children) of title 18, United States Code, or any other Federal criminal statute.

"(2) No Effect on Intellectual Property Law. Nothing in this section shall be construed to limit or expand any law pertaining to intellectual property.

"(3) State Law. Nothing in this section shall be construed to prevent any State from enforcing any State law that is consistent with this section. No cause of action may be brought and no liability may be imposed under any State or local law that is inconsistent with this section.

"(4) No Effect on Communications Privacy Law. Nothing in this section shall be construed to limit the application of the Electronic Communications Privacy Act of 1986 or any of the amendments made by such Act, or any similar State law.

"(f) Definitions. As used in this section:

"(1) Internet. The term 'Internet' means the international

computer network of both Federal and non-Federal interoperable packet switched data networks.

"(2) Interactive Computer Service. The term 'interactive computer service' means an information service, system, or access software provider that provides or enables computer access by multiple users to a computer server, including specifically a service or system that provides access to the Internet and such systems operated or services offered by libraries or educational institutions.

"(3) Information Content Provider. The term 'information content provider' means any person or entity that is responsible, in whole or in part, for the creation or development of information provided through the Internet or any other interactive computer service.

"(4) Access Software Provider. The term 'access software provider' means a provider of software (including client or server software), or enabling tools that do any one or more of the following:

"(A) filter, screen, allow, or disallow content;

"(B) pick, choose, analyze, or digest content; or

"(C) transmit, receive, display, forward, cache, search, subset, organize, reorganize, or translate content."

Electronic Privacy Information Center's *Faulty Filters: How Content Filters Block Access to Kid-Friendly Information on the Internet*

The Electronic Privacy Information Center (EPIC) is a public-interest research organization based in Washington, D.C. EPIC's mission is to promote privacy and First Amendment freedoms on-line, and it views filtering as a violation of these goals. In 1997 EPIC released the following report on Internet filtering software, which found that filtering programs tended to block out a host of innocuous information. Though the efficacy of filters is a subject hotly debated by groups supporting and opposing their use, this report argues that filters are blocking more than just pornography. The text of this report is available at EPIC's web site, http://www.epic.org, and is reprinted here with permission.

Summary

In order to determine the impact of software filters on the open exchange of information on the Internet, the Electronic Privacy Information Center conducted 100 searches using a traditional search engine and then conducted the same 100 searches using a new search engine that is advertised as the "world's first family-friendly Internet search site." We tried to locate information about 25 schools; 25 charitable and political organizations; 25 educational, artistic, and cultural institutions; and 25 concepts that might be of interest to young people. Our search terms included such phrases as the "American Red Cross," the "San Diego Zoo," and the "Smithsonian Institution," as well as such concepts as "Christianity," the "Bill of Rights," and "eating disorders." In every case in our sample, we found that the family-friendly search engine prevented us from obtaining access to almost 90 percent of the materials on the Internet containing the relevant search terms. We further found that in many cases, the search service denied access to 99 percent of material that would otherwise be available without the filters. We concluded that the filtering mechanism prevented children from obtaining a great deal of useful and appropriate information that is currently available on the Internet.

Introduction

The subject of whether to promote techniques to limit access to information available on the Internet grows out of the litigation against the Communications Decency Act. In that case, the Supreme Court ruled that the First Amendment protected the right to publish information on the Internet. The Court also found that "the interest in encouraging freedom of expression in a democratic society outweighs any theoretical but unproven benefit of censorship."

Shortly after the Supreme Court issued its decision, the White House convened a meeting to discuss the need to develop content filters for the Internet. The Administration unveiled a "Strategy for a Family Friendly Internet." According to the White House proposal, a key component would be the promotion of labeling and screening systems designed to shield children from inappropriate Internet content.

President Clinton said that he thought it was necessary to develop search engines specifically designed to screen out objectionable material. He said that it "must be our objective" to ensure that the labeling of Internet content "will become standard practice." Vice President Gore said, "Our challenge is to make these blocking technologies and the accompanying rating systems as common as the computers themselves."

In a statement released during the White House meeting, five Internet companies—CNET, Excite, Infoseek, Lycos and Yahoo!—expressed their support of the "White House proposal for the Internet industry to adopt a self-regulated rating system for content on the Web."

Following the White House summit, several companies announced that they would develop products and services for content filtering. On October 6, Net Shepherd and AltaVista launched Family Search. They described the product as "the world's first family-friendly Internet search site." Family Search is the first product to incorporate two of the goals identified at the July White House meeting—content rating and filtered search engines.

The Family Search Service

Net Shepherd Family Search is a web-based search engine located on the Internet at http://family.netshepherd.com. According to the "Frequently Asked Questions" (FAQ) file available at the site, Family Search "is designed to make the Internet a friendlier, more productive place for families. This is achieved though filtering out web sites judged by an independent panel of demographically appropriate Internet users, to be inappropriate and/or objectionable to average user families."

The Family Search service operates as follows: A user submits a search request, such as "American Red Cross." That request is then directed to the AltaVista search engine. The AltaVista results are then filtered through Net Shepherd's ratings data base, and the filtered results are presented to the user. For this reason, conducting a search using the AltaVista search engine, and then conducting the same search using the Net Shepherd search engine, shows exactly how much information is removed by the Net Shepherd filter.

Net Shepherd claims that it has completed the most comprehensive rating of material on the World Wide Web. According to the company (as reported in the FAQ), in March of 1997 it had rated "97% of the English language sites on the Web."

For this survey, it is particularly important to emphasize two claims made by Net Shepherd about its family-friendly search engine. First, Net Shepherd states that the filtering criterion is whether a web site is "inappropriate and/or objectionable to average user families." Second, Net Shepherd states that its review of material available on the Web is comprehensive—"97% of the English language sites."

Survey Methodology

We set out to determine the actual effect of the filtering process—to quantify the amount of information that was actually blocked by a filtered search engine. Family Search's use of AltaVista results enabled us to conduct a straightforward comparison of a filtered and an unfiltered search. We first entered our search criteria into the AltaVista search engine [http://altavista.digital.com] and recorded the number of documents produced in response to our request. This number appeared at the top of search results returned by AltaVista.

We then duplicated our search request with Family Search and recorded the number of documents located through that search engine. Unlike AltaVista, Family Search does not report the number of matching documents. We had to read each page of the search results and manually count the number of documents retrieved.

All of our searches that contained more than one word in the search were submitted in quotation marks.

Family Search allows the user to designate a desired "quality" level for its search results. In conducting our searches, we used the default of "no preference." This is the most comprehensive setting and allowed us to retrieve all of the documents that Family Search would provide.

All of our searches were conducted between November 17 and November 26, 1997. We conducted 100 searches for key phrases using the unfiltered and the filtered search engines. We divided the 100 searches into four groups:

Elementary, middle and high schools
Charitable and political organizations
Educational, artistic and cultural institutions
Miscellaneous concepts and entities

We were particularly interested in the topics that would interest young people. For this reason we selected search phrases for organizations and ideas that we thought would be or should be of interest to children ages 18 and below. We are aware that not all families would agree that all of the phrases we selected would be appropriate for their children, but by and large we thought the 100 phrases we selected would likely be the types of searches that children who are using the Internet for non-objectionable purposes would conduct and that their parents would probably encourage.

Our findings are contained in the attached table. The results are summarized below:

Survey of Elementary, Middle, and High Schools

With the growth of the Internet, many schools are today taking advantage of new communications technology. Not only are students able to access information around the world from a computer terminal in their classroom, they are also able to set up web sites. Many of these sites contain practical information—how to contact teachers, homework assignments, and cancellation policies. Many sites also include school projects. Although the content of the sites is as different as are the schools, one thing seems clear—the web sites in this category are web sites created for young people and often by young people. Thus when we tried locating these sites through the family-friendly search engine, we were surprised by the outcome.

The Arbor Heights Elementary School in Seattle, Washington, maintains a highly regarded web site at http://www.halcyon.com/arborhts/arborhts.html. More than 70,000 people have visited the web site in the last two years. The school also publishes a magazine specifically for kids aged 7 through 12 called "Cool Writers Magazine" that is available at the web site.

If you go to the AltaVista search engine and search for "Arbor Heights Elementary," you will get back 824 hits. But if you use the Net Shepherd family-friendly search engine, only three documents are returned. In other words, Net Shepherd blocks access to more than 99 percent of the material that would otherwise be available on AltaVista containing the search phrase "Arbor Heights Elementary."

We found similar results with other searches. More than 96 percent of the material referring to "Providence School" is blocked by Family Search. Over 98 percent of the material referring to "Ralph Bunche School" is also blocked.

This seemed extraordinary to us. The blocking criteria deployed by Net Shepherd is, according to the company, whether a site is "inappropriate and/or objectionable to average user families." We looked at several of the pages that were returned with the unfiltered search engine but not with the filtered search engine. We could not find anything that an average user family would consider to be inappropriate or objectionable.

We also noticed that as the web sites became more popular, that is to say as more documents were returned, the percentage of materials available dropped. In our survey of school web sites, the range of materials blocked went from 86 percent to 99 percent, but once more than 250 documents were available from an AltaVista search, at least 94 percent of the material would always be blocked by Family Search. Once more than 500 documents were available from an AltaVista search, that number rose to 98 percent.

Survey of Charitable and Political Organizations

We selected 25 organizations representing national charities and groups across the political spectrum. Many of these organizations were established to provide services and assistance to children and parents. All have made important use of the Internet to provide timely and useful information on-line at little or no cost to families across the country.

The American Red Cross site (http://www.crossnet.org/), for example, provides an extraordinary collection of information about public health and medical resources. The American Red Cross has a special interest in families. It designated November "Child Safety and Protection Month." If you go to this web page [http://www.crossnet.org/healthtips/firstaid.html] you will find a special section devoted to "Health and Safety Tips: How to Protect Your Family with First Aid Training."

These resources and other similar materials are available if you conduct an AltaVista search for "American Red Cross." Almost 40,000 documents were returned with the search. But a search with Family Search for the same phrase produced only 77 hits. The search engine filter had blocked access to 99.8 percent of the documents concerning the "American Red Cross" that would otherwise be available on the Internet.

Similar results were found when we conducted searches for the "Child Welfare League of America," "UNICEF," and "United Way."

Political organizations are also subject to extensive filtering. More than 4,000 documents about the NAACP can be found by means of AltaVista, but Family Search seems to believe that only 15 documents on the Internet concerning the NAACP are appropriate for young people.

Again we found that as search phrases became more popular, that is to say that as more documents were returned in response to an unfiltered search request, Family Search was more likely to block a higher percentage of materials. In this category, the amount of blocked material ranged from 90 percent to 99 percent, but once more than a thousand documents would be available with the unfiltered search, we found that 99 percent of the material would be blocked by Family Search.

Survey of Educational, Artistic, and Cultural Institutions

Many organizations use the Internet today to provide all types of valuable information for young people. We conducted searches for many well known kids' activities, such as "Disneyland," "National Zoo," and the "Boy Scouts of America."

The National Aquarium in Baltimore is one of top attractions for young people in the mid-Atlantic region. The Aquarium has created an extensive web site [http://www.aqua.org/], filled with a lot of neat stuff. If you go to Think Tank, you can try to answer a daily question about aquatic life. In the Education section of the web site, titled "Wonder Leads to Understanding," you will learn more about special programs at the National Aquarium for young people. The Aquarium's resources are widely found across the Internet. An AltaVista search produced 2,134 responses. But the family-friendly search engine produced only 63 responses.

Intrigued by the tremendous discrepancy, we decided to visit every one of the first 200 web pages returned by Alta Vista to see how it could be that, on average, 97 percent of the material would be considered objectionable to the average user family. We did find several speeches and papers that mentioned the National Aquarium as well as several events that were held at the National Aquarium. We also learned that the United States does not have the only National Aquarium. Others can be found in Australia and the Philippines. We learned that a few people take family pictures when they go to the National Aquarium and that people who work at the Aquarium mention it on their resumes. But we couldn't find any objectionable or inappropriate material.

Again, we found that as the sites became more popular, it was more difficult to find information through Family Search. For searches of information on the Internet on many of the most popular educational institutions in the United States for kids, Family Search routinely blocked 99 percent of the documents. "Yellowstone National Park" produced a blocking rate of 99.8 percent. The blocking rate for the "San Diego Zoo" was 99.6 percent.

One of the most peculiar results in the entire survey concerned our search for the "National Basketball Association." A straightforward search on AltaVista produced 18,018 hits. But when we tried Family Search, only two documents were provided. We have no idea what is in the remaining 18,016 documents that Family Search considers to be objectionable for the average family using the Internet.

Survey of Miscellaneous Concepts and Entities

For this last category, we considered the topics that students might be interested in learning more about as part of a school research paper or similar project. We tried to select concepts and entities from a range of areas appropriate for young people—science, history, geography, government, religion as well as famous people.

Consider, for example, a young student who is writing a research paper on Thomas Edison, one of the greatest inventors of all time. If the student undertakes a search with AltaVista, 11,522 documents are returned. But if the student uses the Family Search site, only nine documents are produced. Similar results will be found with such search phrases as "Betsy Ross," "Islam," "Emily Dickinson," and "United States Supreme Court."

We recognize that young people also have concerns about sensitive topics such as eating disorders, puberty, and teen pregnancy. Parents' views on how best to handle such issues vary considerably from family to family. Not surprisingly, most of the documents available on the Internet about these topics are extensively blocked by Family Search. But what was surprising to us is that the blocking of these sensitive matters was not any greater than with such topics as "photosynthesis" (99.5 percent), "astronomy" (99.9 percent) or "Wolfgang Amadeus Mozart" (99.9 percent). In other words, it is just as difficult to get information about the "Constitution of the United States"—actually, somewhat more so—as it is to get information about "puberty" using a family-friendly search engine.

Even Dr. Seuss fares poorly with this family-friendly search engine. Only eight of the 2,638 references on the Internet relating to Dr. Seuss are made available by Family Search. And one of the eight documents that was produced by the search engine turned out to be a parody of a Dr. Seuss story using details from the murder of Nicole Brown Simpson.

Limitations of Survey

We recognized in the course of the survey a number of limitations on our survey method. First, the figures that we provide regarding how much material the search engine blocks actually represent a percentage of the information blocked that would otherwise be available by means of the AltaVista search engine. There is material available on the Internet that is not located by AltaVista, but could be found by other locator services such as

Yahoo! or Hotbot. If this factor were taken into account, the percentage of materials blocked by Family Search, expressed as a percentage of all the material available on the Internet containing the relevant search phrases, would necessarily increase.

We also recognize that there is some ambiguity in search terms and that context is often necessary to establish meaning. We tried where possible to select search terms that would reduce the risk of ambiguity.

We did not attempt to review all of the filtering products currently available. For the reasons described above, and particularly the emphasis that filter proponents have placed on search engines that can perform this task, we believed it was appropriate to limit our study to the one search engine specifically designed to block access to "inappropriate material."

Conclusion

Our research showed that a family-friendly search engine, of the kind recommended by proponents of Internet rating schemes at the White House summit in July 1997, typically blocked access to 95–99 percent of the material available on the Internet that might be of interest to young people. We also found that as information on popular topics became more widely available on the Internet, the search engine was likely to block an even higher percentage. We further found that the search engine did not seem to restrict sensitive topics for young people any more than it restricted matters of general interest. Even with the very severe blocking criteria employed, we noted that some material which parents might consider to be objectionable was still provided by the family-friendly service.

Our review led us to conclude that proponents of filters and rating systems should think more carefully about whether this is a sensible approach. In the end, "family-friendly" filtering does not seem very friendly.

Recommendations

While it is true that there is material available on the Internet that some will find legitimately objectionable, it is also clear that in some cases the proposed solutions may be worse than the actual problem. Filtering programs that deny children access to a wide range of useful and appropriate materials ultimately diminish the educational value of the Internet.

The White House should reconsider its support for the Internet filtering effort, and particularly for the idea of filter-based search engines. This approach is flawed and these programs make it more difficult for young people to find useful and appropriate information.

Vendors of filtering and tagging products need to be much more forthcoming about the actual effect of their programs and services. It is deceptive and fraudulent to say that a program blocks "objectionable content" when it also blocks a great deal of information that is useful and valuable for young people.

Alternatives to software filters and tagging should be explored. The European Union has recently proposed a range of options including codes of conduct, hotlines, and warnings.

Parents should learn more about the benefits of the Internet for their children and families. In the ongoing debate about the availability of objectionable materials, one key point has been lost—the Internet is a wonderful resource for young people.

Parents should continue to take a strong interest in their children's use of the Internet. Helping children tell right from wrong is not something that should be left to computer software or search engines.

We hope that additional research will be done on the impact other filtering programs may have on the ability of young people to obtain useful information on the Internet. Without such studies, it is not possible to say whether it is sensible to promote these programs.

Resources

Internet Free Expression Alliance [http://www.ifea.net/]—IFEA was established to protect the free flow of information on the Internet. It includes more than two dozen member organizations. Information is available from the IFEA web site about rating and filtering systems, including the views of the American Civil Liberties Union, the American Library Association, the Computer Professionals for Social Responsibility, the Electronic Frontier Foundation, the Electronic Privacy Information Center, the National Campaign for Free Expression, the National Coalition Against Censorship, and others.

Excerpt from the Freedom of Information Act

Enacted in 1966, the Freedom of Information Act (FOIA) provides citizens with the right of access to government information; it ensures that people remain informed about their government and that the government remains accountable to the people. Under the FOIA, all records possessed by government agencies must be made available to the public unless they are deemed classified or otherwise vital to national security. Following is an excerpt from the Freedom of Information Act.

5 U.S.C. Sec. 552, As Amended by Public Law No. 104–231, 110 Stat. 2422

Sec. 552. Public information; agency rules, opinions, orders, records, and proceedings

(a) Each agency shall make available to the public information as follows:

(1) Each agency shall separately state and currently publish in the Federal Register for the guidance of the public—

(A) descriptions of its central and field organization and the established places at which, the employees (and in the case of a uniformed service, the members) from whom, and the methods whereby, the public may obtain information, make submittals or requests, or obtain decisions;

(B) statements of the general course and method by which its functions are channeled and determined, including the nature and requirements of all formal and informal procedures available;

(C) rules of procedure, descriptions of forms available or the places at which forms may be obtained, and instructions as to the scope and contents of all papers, reports, or examinations;

(D) substantive rules of general applicability adopted as authorized by law, and statements of general policy or interpretations of general applicability formulated and adopted by the agency; and

(E) each amendment, revision, or repeal of the foregoing.

Except to the extent that a person has actual and timely notice of the terms thereof, a person may not in any manner be required to resort to, or be adversely affected by, a matter required to be published in the Federal Register and not so published. For the purpose of this paragraph, matter reasonably available to the class of persons affected thereby is deemed published in the Federal Register when incorporated by reference therein with the approval of the Director of the Federal Register.

(2) Each agency, in accordance with published rules, shall make available for public inspection and copying—

(A) final opinions, including concurring and dissenting opinions, as well as orders, made in the adjudication of cases;

(B) those statements of policy and interpretations which

have been adopted by the agency and are not published in the Federal Register; and

(C) administrative staff manuals and instructions to staff that affect a member of the public;

(D) copies of all records, regardless of form or format, which have been released to any person under paragraph (3) and which, because of the nature of their subject matter, the agency determines have become or are likely to become the subject of subsequent requests for substantially the same records; and

(E) a general index of the records referred to under subparagraph (D); unless the materials are promptly published and copies offered for sale. For records created on or after November 1, 1996, within one year after such date, each agency shall make such records available, including by computer telecommunications or, if computer telecommunications means have not been established by the agency, by other electronic means. To the extent required to prevent a clearly unwarranted invasion of personal privacy, an agency may delete identifying details when it makes available or publishes an opinion, statement of policy, interpretation, or staff manual or instruction, staff manual, instruction, or copies of records referred to in subparagraph (D). However, in each case the justification for the deletion shall be explained fully in writing, and the extent of such deletion shall be indicated on the portion of the record which is made available or published, unless including that indication would harm an interest protected by the exemption in subsection (b) under which the deletion is made. If technically feasible, the extent of the deletion shall be indicated at the place in the record where the deletion was made. Each agency shall also maintain and make available for public inspection and copying current indexes providing identifying information for the public as to any matter issued, adopted, or promulgated after July 4, 1967, and required by this paragraph to be made available or published. Each agency shall promptly publish, quarterly or more frequently, and distribute (by sale or otherwise) copies of each index or supplements thereto unless it determines by order published in the Federal Register that the publication would be unnecessary and impracticable, in which case the agency shall nonetheless provide copies of an index on request at a cost not to exceed the direct cost of duplication. Each agency shall make the index referred to in subparagraph (E) available by computer telecommunications by December 31, 1999. A final order, opinion, statement of policy, interpretation, or staff manual or instruction that affects a member of the public may be relied on, used, or cited as a precedent by an agency against a party other than an agency only if—

(i) it has been indexed and either made available or published as provided by this paragraph; or

(ii) the party has actual and timely notice of the terms thereof.

(3) (A) Except with respect to the records made available under paragraphs (1) and (2) of this subsection, each agency, upon request for records which (A) (i) reasonably describes such records and (ii) is made in accordance with published rules stating the time, place, fees (if any), and procedures to be followed, shall make the records promptly available to any person.

(B) In making any record available to a person under this paragraph, an agency shall provide the record in any form or format requested by the person if the record is readily reproducible by the agency in that form or format. Each agency shall make reasonable efforts to maintain its records in forms or formats that are reproducible for purposes of this section.

(C) In responding under this paragraph to a request for records, an agency shall make reasonable efforts to search for the records in electronic form or format, except when such efforts would significantly interfere with the operation of the agency's automated information system.

(D) For purposes of this paragraph, the term "search" means to review, manually or by automated means, agency records for the purpose of locating those records which are responsive to a request.

(4) (A) (i) In order to carry out the provisions of this section, each agency shall promulgate regulations, pursuant to notice and receipt of public comment, specifying the schedule of fees applicable to the processing of requests under this section and establishing procedures and guidelines for determining when such fees should be waived or reduced. Such schedule shall conform to the guidelines which shall be promulgated, pursuant to notice and receipt of public comment, by the Director of the Office of Management and Budget and which shall provide for a uniform schedule of fees for all agencies.

(ii) Such agency regulations shall provide that—

(I) fees shall be limited to reasonable standard charges for document search, duplication, and review, when records are requested for commercial use;

(II) fees shall be limited to reasonable standard charges for document duplication when records are not sought for commercial use and the request is made by an educational or noncommercial scientific institution, whose purpose is scholarly or scientific research; or a representative of the news media; and

(III) for any request not described in (I) or (II), fees shall be limited to reasonable standard charges for document search and duplication.

(iii) Documents shall be furnished without any charge or at a charge reduced below the fees established under clause (ii) if disclosure of the information is in the public interest because it is likely to contribute significantly to public understanding of the operations or activities of the government and is not primarily in the commercial interest of the requester. . . .

(F) In denying a request for records, in whole or in part, an agency shall make a reasonable effort to estimate the volume of any requested matter the provision of which is denied, and shall provide any such estimate to the person making the request, unless providing such estimate would harm an interest protected by the exemption in subsection

(b) pursuant to which the denial is made.

(b) This section does not apply to matters that are—

(1) (A) specifically authorized under criteria established by an Executive order to be kept secret in the interest of national defense or foreign policy and (B) are in fact properly classified pursuant to such Executive order;

(2) related solely to the internal personnel rules and practices of an agency;

(3) specifically exempted from disclosure by statute (other than section 552b of this title), provided that such statute (A) requires that the matters be withheld from the public in such a manner as to leave no discretion on the issue, or (B) establishes particular criteria for withholding or refers to particular types of matters to be withheld;

(4) trade secrets and commercial or financial information obtained from a person and privileged or confidential;

(5) inter-agency or intra-agency memorandums or letters which would not be available by law to a party other than an agency in litigation with the agency;

(6) personnel and medical files and similar files the disclosure of which would constitute a clearly unwarranted invasion of personal privacy;

(7) records or information compiled for law enforcement

purposes, but only to the extent that the production of such law enforcement records or information that (A) could reasonably be expected to interfere with enforcement proceedings, (B) would deprive a person of a right to a fair trial or an impartial adjudication, (C) could reasonably be expected to constitute an unwarranted invasion of personal privacy, (D) could reasonably be expected to disclose the identity of a confidential source, including a State, local, or foreign agency or authority or any private institution which furnished information on a confidential basis, and, in the case of a record or information compiled by a criminal law enforcement authority in the course of a criminal investigation or by an agency conducting a lawful national security intelligence investigation, information furnished by a confidential source, (E) would disclose techniques and procedures for law enforcement investigations or prosecutions, or would disclose guidelines for law enforcement investigations or prosecutions if such disclosure could reasonably be expected to risk circumvention of the law, or (F) could reasonably be expected to endanger the life or physical safety of any individual;

(8) contained in or related to examination, operating, or condition reports prepared by, on behalf of, or for the use of an agency responsible for the regulation or supervision of financial institutions; or

(9) geological and geophysical information and data, including maps, concerning wells.

Any reasonably segregable portion of a record shall be provided to any person requesting such record after deletion of the portions which are exempt under this subsection. The amount of information deleted shall be indicated on the released portion of the record, unless including that indication would harm an interest protected by the exemption in this subsection under which the deletion is made. If technically feasible, the amount of the information deleted shall be indicated at the place in the record where such deletion is made.

(c) (1) Whenever a request is made which involves access to records described in subsection (b)(7)(A) and—

(A) the investigation or proceeding involves a possible violation of criminal law; and

(B) there is reason to believe that (i) the subject of the investigation or proceeding is not aware of its pendency, and (ii) disclosure of the existence of the records could reasonably be expected to interfere with enforcement proceedings, the agency may, during only such time as that circumstance continues, treat the records as not subject to the requirements of this section.

(2) Whenever informant records maintained by a criminal law enforcement agency under an informant's name or personal identifier are requested by a third party according to the informant's name or personal identifier, the agency may treat the records as not subject to the requirements of this section unless the informant's status as an informant has been officially confirmed.

(3) Whenever a request is made which involves access to records maintained by the Federal Bureau of Investigation pertaining to foreign intelligence or counterintelligence, or international terrorism, and the existence of the records is classified information as provided in subsection (b)(1), the Bureau may, as long as the existence of the records remains classified information, treat the records as not subject to the requirements of this section.

(d) This section does not authorize the withholding of information or limit the availability of records to the public, except as specifically stated in this section.

This section is not authority to withhold information from Congress.

(e) (1) On or before February 1 of each year, each agency shall submit to the Attorney General of the United States a report which shall cover the preceding fiscal year and which shall include—

(A) the number of determinations made by the agency not to comply with requests for records made to such agency under subsection (a) and the reasons for each such determination;

(B) (i) the number of appeals made by persons under subsection (a)(6), the result of

such appeals, and the reason for the action upon each appeal that results in a denial of information; and

(ii) a complete list of all statutes that the agency relies upon to authorize the agency to withhold information under subsection (b)(3), a description of whether a court has upheld the decision of the agency to withhold information under each such statute, and a concise description of the scope of any information withheld;

(C) the number of requests for records pending before the agency as of September 30 of the preceding year, and the median number of days that such requests had been pending before the agency as of that date;

(D) the number of requests for records received by the agency and the number of requests which the agency processed;

(E) the median number of days taken by the agency to process different types of requests;

(F) the total amount of fees collected by the agency for processing requests; and

(G) the number of full-time staff of the agency devoted to processing requests for records under this section, and the total amount expended by the agency for processing such requests.

(2) Each agency shall make each such report available to the public including by computer telecommunications, or if computer telecommunications means have not been established by the agency, by other electronic means.

(3) The Attorney General of the United States shall make each report which has been made available by electronic means available at a single electronic access point. The Attorney General of the United States shall notify the Chairman and ranking minority member of the Committee on Government Reform and Oversight of the House of Representatives and the Chairman and ranking minority member of the Committees on Governmental Affairs and the Judiciary of the Senate, no later than April 1 of the year in which each such report is issued, that such reports are available by electronic means.

(4) The Attorney General of the United States, in consultation with the Director of the Office of Management and Budget, shall develop reporting and performance guidelines in connection with reports required by this subsection by October 1, 1997, and may establish additional requirements for such reports as the Attorney General determines may be useful.

(5) The Attorney General of the United States shall submit an annual report on or before April 1 of each calendar year which shall include for the prior calendar year a listing of the number of cases arising under this section, the exemption involved in each case, the disposition of such case, and the cost, fees, and penalties assessed under subparagraphs (E), (F), and (G) of subsection (a)(4). Such report shall also include a description of the efforts undertaken by the Department of Justice to encourage compliance with this section.

(f) For purposes of this section, the term—

(1) "agency" as defined in section 551(1) of this title includes any executive department, military department, Government corporation, Government controlled corporation, or other establishment in the executive branch of the Government

(including the Executive Office of the President), or any independent regulatory agency; and (2) "record" and any other term used in this section in reference to information includes any information that would be an agency record subject to the requirements of this section when maintained by an agency in any format, including an electronic format.

(g) The head of each agency shall prepare and make publicly available upon request, reference material or a guide for requesting records or information from the agency, subject to the exemptions in subsection (b), including—

(1) an index of all major information systems of the agency;

(2) a description of major information and record locator systems maintained by the agency; and

(3) a handbook for obtaining various types and categories of public information from the agency pursuant to chapter 35 of title 44, and under this section.

Selected Quotations

This section includes quotations from writers, political and historical figures, judges, and others on censorship and the issues it has raised in our society.

Censorship and Humanity

"Congress shall make no law respecting an establishment of religion, or prohibiting the free exercise thereof; or abridging the freedom of speech, or of the press; or the right of the people peaceably to assemble, and to petition the government for a redress of grievances."
—Amendment I, United States Constitution

"Is uniformity attainable? Millions of innocent men, women, and children, since the introduction of Christianity, have been burnt, tortured, fined, imprisoned; yet we have not advanced one inch toward uniformity. What has been the effect of coercion? To make one half of the world fools, and the other half hypocrites."
—Thomas Jefferson, quoted in *What Johnny Shouldn't Read*, 1992

"[T]he struggle between expression and authority is unending. The instinct to suppress discomforting ideas is rooted deep

in human nature. It is rooted above all in profound human propensities to faith and fear."
—Arthur Schlesinger Jr., in *Censorship: 500 Years of Conflict*, 1984

"A nation that is afraid to let its people judge the truth and falsehood of ideas in an open market is a nation that is afraid of its people."
—John F. Kennedy

"They that can give up essential liberty to obtain a little temporary safety deserve neither liberty or safety."
—Benjamin Franklin

"If we ban whatever offends any group, we will soon have no art, no culture, no humor, no satire."
—Erica Jong

"Each challenge to the freedom of artistic expression sends a powerful and devastating message to Americans, and particularly to our children: that the way to address 'disagreeable' speech is to squelch it—demand its removal, deny its funding, cover it up, or make it inaccessible. That message is plainly at odds with a founding principle of this nation, namely that freedom of expression is a value to be cherished and respected both because it is an inalienable right and because its preservation protects our democratic form of government."
—People for the American Way, *Artistic Freedom Under Attack*, Vol. 4, 1996

"Free speech is life itself."
—Salmon Rushdie

"Of all the tyrannies, a tyranny exercised for the good of its victims may be the most oppressive. It may be better to live under robber barons than under some omnipotent moral busybodies. The robber baron's cruelty may sometimes sleep, his cupidity may at some point be satiated; but those who torment us for our own good will torment us without end, for they do so with the approval of their consciences."
—C. S. Lewis

"Censorship reflects a society's lack of confidence in itself."
—Potter Stewart

Censorship and Literature

"Censorship ends in logical completeness when nobody is allowed to read any books except the books nobody can read."
—George Bernard Shaw

"So long as the possession of these writings was attended by danger, they were eagerly sought and read; when there was no longer any difficulty in securing them, they fell into oblivion."
—Tacitus

"Saint Paul says that all that is written is written for our learning, assuredly. So take the grain and let the chaff be still."
—Geoffrey Chaucer, *Canterbury Tales*

"Our first business will be to supervise the making of fables and legends, rejecting all which are unsatisfactory; and we shall induce nurses and mothers to tell their children only those which we have approved."
—Plato, *The Republic*

"It is not fitting that all people should know these stories. Those who are subject, the people, will be spoiled and the land will be twisted."
—Tlacaelel, advisor to Aztec Emperor Montezuma I

"As good almost [to] kill a man as kill a good book; who kills a reasonable creature, God's image; but he who destroys a good book kills reason itself."
—John Milton, *Areopagitica*

"There is more than one way to burn a book. And the world is full of people running about with lit matches. Every minority . . . feels it has the will, the right, the duty to douse the kerosene, light the fuse."
—Ray Bradbury, *Fahrenheit 451*

The Public Funding of Art

"I would rather have as my patron a host of anonymous citizens digging into their pockets for the price of a book or a

magazine, than a small body of enlightened and responsible men administering public funds."
—John Updike

"The NEA . . . [has] no faith in the judgement of anonymous citizens. They see American art shriveling up unless taxpayers are forced to subsidize arts organizations anointed by the government. It never seems to register with them that American art blossomed long before there was an NEA. Somehow Fitzgerald wrote *The Great Gatsby* without a government check. Somehow Homer painted 'The Veteran in a New Field.' Somehow Copland composed 'Appalachian Spring.' Graham's dances, Whitman's poems, Parker's jazz, Williams's plays—somehow they all came about without Big Brother's help."
—Jeff Jacoby, *Boston Globe* columnist

"In our free country, artists have a right to produce whatever works they wish. They have no right to produce it at the taxpayer's expense."
—James Kilpatrick

"Beauty will not come at the call of the legislature. . . . It will come, as always, unannounced, and spring up between the feet of brave and earnest men."
—Ralph Waldo Emerson

Censorship and the Internet

"As a matter of constitutional tradition, in the absence of evidence to the contrary, we presume that governmental regulation of the content of speech is more likely to interfere with the free exchange of ideas than to encourage it. The interest in encouraging freedom of expression in a democratic society outweighs any theoretical but unproven benefit of censorship."
—Justice John Paul Stevens, in *Reno v. ACLU*

Censorship and the Library

"Libraries should challenge censorship in the fulfillment of their responsibility to provide information and enlightenment."
—Library Bill of Rights

Directory of Organizations

The organizations and associations described in this chapter represent different opinions on the issues surrounding censorship and free expression, and each has helped to shape the public debate on these issues. Some of the organizations are media watchdogs, working to safeguard a free press and ensure balanced media coverage; others are concerned with protecting children from media violence and sexual explicitness. Each of the organizations listed here can provide the reader with information and resources that will be helpful in developing a greater understanding of the issue of censorship.

Accuracy in Media (AIM)
4455 Connecticut Avenue NW, Suite 330
Washington, DC 20008
(202) 364–4401
Fax: (202) 364–4098
E-mail: info@aim.org
Web site: http://www.aim.org

Accuracy in Media is a nonprofit media watchdog organization that criticizes media imbalance and works to inform people about slanted news coverage. AIM encourages its members to contact the media when they feel coverage of a particular story is biased or inaccurate. The goal of AIM is that members of the media report the news fairly, without bias or partisanship. In addition to a daily web report, Media Monitor, AIM writes a syndicated newspaper column.

Publications: AIM Report, bimonthly

American Arts Alliance
805 15th Street NW, Suite 500
Washington, DC 20005
(202) 289–1776
Fax: (202) 371–6601
Web site: http://www.artswire.org

The American Arts Alliance is an advocate for professional nonprofit arts organizations in the United States. It works to represent arts interests before Congress and other branches of the federal government. The alliance seeks to keep policy makers informed about the important role that the arts play in American society, and it encourages the development of national policies that contribute to the flourishing of the arts.

American Booksellers Association (ABA)
828 South Broadway
Tarrytown, NY 10591–5112
(800) 637–0037
Fax: (914) 591–2720
E-mail: info@members.bookweb.org
Web site: http://www.bookweb.org

The American Bookseller's Association, founded in 1900, is a nonprofit trade organization of independently owned bookstores that actively supports free speech, literacy, and programs that encourage children to read. The ABA is one of the sponsors of Banned Books Week each year, a program designed to raise awareness about censorship in the United States.

Publication: Free Expression newsletter, which is archived on the ABA web site and is available to both members and nonmembers.

**American Booksellers Foundation
for Free Expression (ABFFE)**
139 Fulton Street, Suite 302
New York, NY 10038
(212) 587–4025

Fax: (212) 587–2436
E-mail: abffe@bookweb.org
Web site: http://www.bookweb.org

The American Bookseller's Foundation for Free Expression defends the First Amendment rights of booksellers and their customers. Founded in 1990 by the American Booksellers Association, ABFFE is a leading voice for the book industry in First Amendment legislative and legal battles across the country. ABFFE is a key source of information about free expression issues for booksellers and the general public. Each September ABFFE cosponsors Banned Books Week with the American Library Association.

American Civil Liberties Union (ACLU)
132 West 43rd Street
New York, NY 10036–6599
(212) 549–2500
Web site: http://www.aclu.org

Founded in 1920, the American Civil Liberties Union is a nonprofit, nonpartisan public interest organization with over 275,000 members. The ACLU promotes First Amendment rights and works to protect individual liberties from the expansion of government authority. The ACLU provides legal support and assistance to those whose constitutional liberties have been violated. To educate the public about constitutional liberties, the ACLU also provides resource materials and briefing papers.

Publication: Civil Liberties, a quarterly newsletter.

American Family Association, Inc. (AFA)
P.O. Drawer 2440
Tupelo, MS 38803
(601) 844–5036
Fax: (601) 844–9176
Web site: http://www.afa.net

The American Family Association was founded in 1977 by the Reverend Donald Wildmon. The AFA is concerned with the influence of television and pornography on our society and seeks to combat this influence by lobbying the entertainment industry to promote wholesome family values and discourage the glorification of violence and premarital sex. The AFA led successful boycotts against national advertisers who sponsored television programs containing sex, violence, and profanity, causing several major corporations to change their advertising policies. The AFA has also lobbied stores to remove pornographic magazines from their shelves.

Publication: American Family Association journal.

American Library Association (ALA)
50 East Huron Street
Chicago, IL 60611–2795
(800) 545–2433
Fax: (312) 440–9374
E-mail: ala@ala.org
Web site: http://www.ala.org

The American Library Association provides leadership for the development, promotion, and improvement of library and information services and the profession of librarianship in order to enhance learning and ensure access to information to all. Of the ALA's many offices, the Office for Intellectual Freedom implements ALA policy on intellectual freedom and aims to educate librarians and the public about the importance of intellectual freedom in libraries. The OIF distributes resource materials, including the *Banned Books Week Resource Book*, the *Intellectual Freedom Manual*, and *Censorship and Selection: Issues and Answers for Schools*. The OIF also offers counseling and support to assist in intellectual freedom problems. In 1969 the ALA formed the Freedom to Read Foundation as an independent organization dedicated to the legal and financial defense of intellectual freedom in libraries. The Freedom to Read Foundation promotes and defends reading, supports libraries in choosing their books, and fosters First Amendment freedoms.

Publications: Newsletter on Intellectual Freedom, Intellectual Freedom Action News, Freedom to Read Foundation News.

Center for Democracy and Technology (CDT)
1634 Eye Street NW, Suite 1100
Washington, DC 20006
(202) 637–9800
Fax: (202) 637–0968
Web site: http://www.cdt.org

The Center for Democracy and Technology is a nonprofit public interest organization whose mission is to develop and advocate public policies that advance constitutional civil liberties and democratic values in new computer and communications technologies.

Publications: Policy Posts, published on an as-needed basis. *Policy Posts* contain up-to-date information on public policy issues affecting civil liberties on-line, providing a resource for the press, students, and policy makers.

Christian Action Network (CAN)
P.O. Box 606
Forest, VA 24551
(800) 835–5795
Fax: (804) 525–0243
E-mail: info@canetwork.com
Web site: http://www.canetwork.com

Founded in 1990 by Martin Mawyer, former editor of the *Moral Majority Report* and author of *Defending the American Family: The Pro-Family Contract with America*, the Christian Action Network defends the American family and promotes traditional American principles of religious liberty, public virtue, and good government. CAN has waged campaigns against the National Endowment for the Arts for its promotion of indecent art with taxpayers' money. In 1993, CAN arranged a display called "A Graphic Picture Is Worth a Thousand Votes," which contained the images of NEA-funded artists like Andres Serrano and Robert Mapplethorpe. The display was banned from the Capitol, where CAN had sought to install it.

Publication: Family Alert newsletter.

Christian Coalition
1801-L Sara Drive
Chesapeake, VA 23320
(757) 424–2630
Fax: (757) 424–9068
E-mail: coalition@cc.org
Web site: http://www.cc.org

The Christian Coalition was founded by Pat Robertson in 1989 to give Christians a voice in government. Approximately 2 million members strong, the Christian Coalition has chapters in every U.S. state. Dedicated to political, social, and community action, the goals outlined by the Christian Coalition include strengthening the family unit, protecting innocent human life, returning education to local and parental control, easing the tax burden on families, punishing criminals and defending victims' rights, protecting communities from pornography, defending the institution of marriage, and protecting religious freedom.

Publications: Religious Rights Watch newsletter and the *Christian American* newsletter.

Citizens for Community Values (CCV)
11175 Reading Road, Suite 103
Cincinnati, OH 45241
(513) 733–5775
Web site: http://www.ccv.org

Citizens for Community Values is a grassroots Ohio-based organization dedicated to fighting pornography, obscenity, promiscuity, and sexual abuse. CCV's members and volunteers encourage the media to support Judeo-Christian values and to maintain a high standard for decency. CCV works to remove pornographic material from stores and encourages the criminal justice system to enforce obscenity laws and to punish sex offenders. CCV provides educational materials to schools and communities so they can help prevent sexual abuse, teenage sex, and the proliferation of pornography.

Publication: Citizens Courier, a quarterly newsletter.

Citizens for Excellence in Education (CEE)
National Association of Christian Educators (NACE)
P.O. Box 3200
Costa Mesa, CA 92628
(949) 251–9333
E-mail: info@nace-cee.org
Web site: http://www.nace-cee.org

Citizens for Excellence in Education, in partnership with the National Association of Christian Educators, works with Christians and conservatives to help parents and public school teachers restore traditional moral values and academic excellence to the nation's public schools. CEE helps education leaders, policy makers, and other Christian organizations network, with the goal of creating legislation that has a positive impact on the education of the nation's youth.

Publications: Education Newsline.

Committee to Protect Journalists (CPJ)
330 Seventh Avenue, 12th Floor
New York, NY 10001

(212) 465–1004
Fax: (212) 465–9568
E-mail: infor@cpj.org
Web site: http://www.cpj.org

CPJ was founded by U.S. foreign correspondents who wanted to protect their colleagues, who are often endangered by authoritarian governments and other groups who oppose independent journalism. Relying on private donations, CPJ responds to emergencies in which foreign correspondents are compromised.

Publications: Dangerous Assignments, a quarterly newsletter; *Attacks on the Press,* a comprehensive annual report on attacks on the press around the world; and numerous safety guides and reports on international regions.

Computer Professionals for Social Responsibility (CPSR)
P.O. Box 717
Palo Alto, CA 94302
(650) 322–3778
Fax: (650) 322–4748
E-mail: webmaster@cpsr.org
Web site: http://www.cpsr.org

Computer Professionals for Social Responsibility is a public-interest alliance of computer scientists and others who are concerned about the impact of computer technology on society. CPSR works to influence decisions regarding the development and use of computers because of the widespread impact those decisions may have, and because such decisions reflect our priorities and basic values. CPSR seeks to focus public attention on how decisions concerning the applications of computing may affect society.

Publication: CPSR Newsletter Quarterly.

Eagle Forum
Operations Center:
P.O. Box 618
Alton, IL 62002
(618) 462–5415
Fax: (618) 462–8909
E-mail: eagle@eagleforum.org
Web site: http://www.eagleforum.org
Washington, D.C., Eagle Forum Office:
316 Pennsylvania Avenue, Suite 203
Washington, DC 20003

(202) 544–0353
Fax: (202) 547–6996

The Eagle Forum is a pro-family organization headed by Phyllis Schlafly. It encourages conservative men and women to become involved in government in order to preserve the American traditions of individual liberty, private enterprise, public and private virtue, and respect for family. The Eagle Forum opposes forces it perceives to be antireligious, antimoral, antichildren, and antilife. The Eagle Forum also opposes taxation that hurts families.

Publications: Phyllis Schlafly Report and *Education Reporter,* both monthlies.

Electronic Frontier Foundation (EFF)
1550 Bryant Street, Suite 725
San Francisco, CA 94130–4832
(415) 436–9333
Fax: (415) 436–9993
Web site: http://www.eff.org

The Electronic Frontier Foundation is a nonprofit civil liberties organization working to protect privacy, freedom of expression, and public access to on-line resources and information. EFF opposes efforts to impose restrictions on cyberspace and founded the Blue Ribbon Campaign for free expression on-line.

Publication: EFFector Online, a biweekly electronic newsletter.

Electronic Privacy Information Center (EPIC)
666 Pennsylvania Avenue SE, Suite 301
Washington, DC 20003
(202) 544–9240
Fax: (202) 547–5482
E-mail: info@epic.org
Web site: http://www.epic.org

The Electronic Privacy Information Center, established in 1994, is a public-interest research center that focuses public attention on new civil liberties issues and the need to protect First Amendment freedoms, constitutional values, and personal privacy on-line. EPIC has lobbied Congress to reject Internet censorship and to seek high standards for privacy policy on-line.

Publications: EPIC Alert newsletter, numerous reports, and policy papers.

Enough Is Enough
P.O. Box 888
Fairfax, VA 22030
(703) 278–8343
Fax: (703) 278–8510
E-mail: dj@enough.org
Web site: http://www.enough.org

The "Enough Is Enough" campaign was launched in 1992 to restore an environment in which citizens are free to raise their children and conduct their lives without the intrusion of illegal sexual material or predators. Enough Is Enough's mission is to educate the public about the existence and dangers of pornography. Enough Is Enough believes in free speech and reminds citizens that obscenity and child pornography are not protected by the First Amendment, as decided by the Supreme Court in *Miller v. California* (1973) and *New York v. Ferber* (1982). The immediate goal of Enough Is Enough is to make the Internet safe for children, and Enough Is Enough provides educational materials to inform parents and school administrators how to protect children from on-line dangers.

Publications: Fact sheets and other educational materials available upon request.

Fairness & Accuracy in Reporting (FAIR)
130 West 25th Street
New York, NY 10001
(212) 633–6700
Fax: (212) 727–7668
Web site: http://www.fair.org

Fairness & Accuracy in Reporting is a national media watch group working to correct media bias and imbalance. FAIR advocates greater diversity in the press and is especially concerned with corporate ownership of the press, the media's allegiance to official agendas, and media insensitivity to women, labor, and minorities. Relying on the First Amendment, FAIR aims to see alternative voices included in the media. FAIR sponsors "Counterspin," a weekly radio program that exposes censored stories.

Publication: Extra!, a bimonthly magazine of media criticism that examines biased reporting, censored news, and the power of corporate owners.

Family Friendly Libraries (FFL)
7597 Whisperwood Court
Springfield, VA 22153
(703) 440–3654
Fax: (703) 440–8047
Web site: http://www.fflibraries.org

Family Friendly Libraries is a nonprofit organization that encourages libraries to stock materials that support traditional family values and that correspond to community standards and laws rather than federal mandates. Family Friendly Libraries opposes pornography and seeks to protect children and teenagers from harmful and/or age-inappropriate material. FFL believes in parental involvement in children's education, and it encourages all citizens to have a voice in library policy in their town. Family Friendly Libraries has created a charter for family friendly libraries and sponsors Family Friendly Library Books Week to promote balanced library collections that include conservative and pro-family books and to encourage parental input in the selection and display of library materials.

Publication: Family Friendly Libraries News and Views.

Family Research Council (FRC)
801 G Street NW
Washington, DC 20001
(202) 393–2100
Fax: (202) 393–2134
Web site: http://www.frc.org

The Family Research Council, founded in 1983, promotes the traditional family unit and the Judeo-Christian value system. Toward this goal, the FRC seeks to develop legislation that strengthens families, and it encourages the media to promote family values. The council also maintains a database of statistical information on families and their historic and contemporary importance to society.

Publications: Washington Watch, Ideas and Energy, Drug Facts, and Legislative Hotline.

Feminists for Free Expression (FFE)
2525 Times Square Station
New York, NY 10108–2525
(212) 702–6292

Fax: (212) 702–6277
Web site: http://www.well.com/user/freedom/

Feminists for Free Expression is a nonprofit organization that was founded in 1992 in response to attempts to solve societal problems through censorship. FFE's members are a diverse group of feminist women working to preserve the individual's right and responsibility to view and produce materials of his or her choice, without the intervention of the state. The organization believes free expression is essential to women's rights, as censorship has traditionally been used to silence women and suppress feminist social change. FFE assists artists, challenges censorship laws, and maintains a roster of women lecturers. FFE's web site offers links to current legislation related to censorship and has a library of FFE publications as well as links to books on feminism, censorship, and free speech.

Publications: FFE publishes an annual report of their accomplishments; also, the *Feminism and Free Speech* pamphlet series, which addresses arts censorship, the Internet, sexual harassment, and pornography.

Filtering Facts
210 S. State Street #7
Lake Oswego, OR 97034
(503) 635–7048
Fax: (503) 635–7048
Web site: http://www.filteringfacts.org

Filtering Facts is a nonprofit organization that promotes the use of filtering software in libraries as a means of protecting children from the harmful effects of pornography via the Internet. Filtering Facts provides information about Internet software filters to parents, librarians, and activists and educates the public and the media about filters in order to counter misconceptions about the inefficacy of filtering programs. Filtering Facts maintains a web site that includes an archive of newspaper articles on filtering, quotes from library administrators, and legal information on pornography.

First Amendment Center
Vanderbilt University
1207 18th Avenue South
Nashville, TN 37212
(615) 321–9588

Fax: (615) 321–9599
Web site: http://www.freedomforum.org

The First Amendment Center, created by the Freedom Forum, a nonpartisan international foundation dedicated to free press and free speech, aims to create a greater public understanding and appreciation for First Amendment rights. The First Amendment Center is located on the Vanderbilt University campus and pursues its agenda through educational programs, broadcasting, publishing, on-line services, partnerships, and fellowships.

Publications: First Amendment News, Forum News, Media Studies Journal, Legal Watch.

Focus on the Family
P.O. Box 35500
Colorado Springs, CO 80995
(719) 531–5181
Web site: http://www.family.org

Focus on the Family, founded in 1977 by Dr. James Dobson, a Christian Fundamentalist family counselor and author of the book *Dare To Discipline,* is dedicated to helping families live Christian lives. An international organization, Focus on the Family offers professional counseling, referrals, and advice, answering as many as 55,000 letters each week. Focus on the Family also addresses public policy and cultural issues. The organization opposes the NEA's funding of pornographic and antireligious art and supported the Communications Decency Act of 1996 because of its efforts to shield minors from inappropriate material. In 1991, Focus on the Family sponsored and helped pass Colorado's anti-gay Amendment 2.

Publications: Citizen; Teachers in Focus; Brio, a magazine for girls; *Breakaway,* a magazine for boys; *Focus on the Family;* and *Dr. Dobson's Monthly Newsletter.*

Libraries for the Future (LFF)
121 West 27th Street, Suite 1102
New York, NY 10001
(212) 352–2330
Fax: (212) 352–2342
Web site: http://www.lff.org

Libraries for the Future is a nonprofit organization dedicated to preserving and strengthening the free public library system. Recognizing that access to information is increasingly important in a society where economic situations are often tied to education, Libraries for the Future seeks to make libraries accessible to all who wish to use them. LFF advocates free and equal access to information and library services in all communities and encourages public libraries to respond to new technology and to changing communities. LFF publishes reports of its research projects, which include *Government Funding of Public Libraries: Legislative, Administrative, and Judicial Perspectives; Philanthropy and the Public Library;* and *Local Places, Global Connections: Libraries in the Digital Age.* LFF offers products and services to libraries, including action alert updates on library policy information.

Publications: Library Advocate, a quarterly newsletter.

The Media Coalition, Inc.
139 Fulton Street, Suite 302
New York, NY 10038
(212) 587–4025
Fax: (212) 587–2436
Web site: http://www.mediacoalition.org

The Media Coalition is a trade association of booksellers, publishers, librarians, motion picture recording and video game manufacturers, and recording and video retailers that defends the First Amendment rights of all Americans to produce, sell, and have access to the widest possible range of materials offering opinion and entertainment. Founded in 1973, the Media Coalition advises federal, state, and local government officials on legislation affecting material that is protected under the First Amendment. The Media Coalition also files legal challenges to unconstitutional laws and prepares amicus curiae briefs for cases in which the First Amendment rights of the producers and distributors of constitutionally protected works have been infringed.

Publications: Media Coalition research reports, available at their web site.

Morality in Media
475 Riverside Drive, Suite 239
New York, NY 10015
(212) 870–3222
Fax: (212) 870–2765
Web site: http://www.netcom.com/~mimnyc

Morality in Media is a national interfaith antipornography organization providing resource material to public officials and private citizens who seek to combat pornography and obscenity in entertainment media. Morality in Media operates the National Obscenity Law Center, a national clearinghouse for obscenity law. To promote its mission, Morality in Media sponsors two annual campaigns: Turn Off TV Day, on February 14, and the weeklong White Ribbon Against Pornography Campaign, in October.

Publications: Morality in Media newsletter for members, study reports on topics related to indecency and pornography, and booklets such as "How to Win the War in Your Community" (a compilation of articles on how to fight pornography), "Clichés: Debunking Misinformation on Pornography and Obscenity Law," and "TV: The World's Greatest Mindbender."

National Campaign for Freedom of Expression (NCFE)
1918 F Street NW, #609
Washington, DC 20004
(202) 393-ARTS or (800) 477-NCFE
Fax: (202) 347–7376
Web site: http://www.artswire.org/~ncfe

The National Campaign for Freedom of Expression is a network of artists, arts organizations, and concerned citizens who seek to protect and extend freedom of artistic expression and challenge censorship throughout the United States. Focusing on the visual and performing arts, the NCFE assists artists whose work is under attack by helping them to obtain funding that has been vetoed or revoked for political, religious, or moral reasons. The NCFE challenges the "decency" clause established by the NEA's reauthorizing legislation in 1990 and provides legal, financial, and moral support to censored artists. The NCFE assists artists and art organizations by providing the following services: strategic advice; grassroots and national coalition building; effective use of the media, such as letters to the editor and op-ed pieces; legal referrals; letter writing campaigns to alert community members and national coalitions; mediation; and educational materials. The NCFE also produces public service announcements and educational videos.

Publications: The National Campaign for Freedom of Expression Quarterly, a source of news and information for First Amendment and arts advocates that includes a regular "Youth and Freedom of Expression" section detailing the censorship of youth expression;

and the *Artistic Freedom Handbook*, a guide for understanding and responding to attacks on the freedom of artistic expression.

National Coalition against Censorship (NCAC)
275 7th Avenue
New York, NY 10001
(212) 807-6222
Fax: (212) 807-6245
Web site: http://www.ncac.org

Founded in 1974, the National Coalition against Censorship is an alliance of over 40 nonprofit organizations, including religious, educational, professional, artistic, labor, and civil liberties groups, all of whom are dedicated to opposing censorship. The goal of the NCAC is to educate the public about the dangers of censorship and how to oppose it. NCAC has developed a rapid response network and provides strategic advice for dealing with specific types of censorship.

Publications: Censorship News quarterly and numerous educational pamphlets and materials.

The National Coalition to Protect Children and Families (NCPCF)
800 Compton Road, Suite 9224
Cincinnati, OH 45231
(513) 521-6227
Fax: (513) 521-6337
Web site: http://www2.nationalcoalition.org/ncpcf

The National Coalition to Protect Children and Families is an organization devoted to empowering concerned citizens and community leaders to reduce sexual exploitation and violence in the United States by supporting limitations on pornography and increasing public awareness of the dangers of pornography. The NCPCF works to achieve its objectives through educational outreach, legislative strategies, and victim assistance programs. Among the resources available from the coalition are lists of relevant books and studies, community coalition resources packets, audio cassettes, and videos.

National Law Center for Children and Families (NLC)
National Office:
4103 Chain Bridge Road, Suite 410

Fairfax, VA 22030–4105
(703) 691–4626
Fax: (703) 691–4669
E-mail: East@NationalLawCenter.org
Web site: http://www.nationallawcenter.org

West Coast Office:
3000 W. MacArthur Boulevard, Suite 426
Santa Anna, CA 92705
(714) 435–9090
Fax: (714) 435–0019

The NLC is a law enforcement assistance and public education center that maintains a staff of attorneys who provide legal assistance to state and federal prosecutors, police, and legislators. The NLC provides specialized resources to those who enforce obscenity and child exploitation laws. The center is also a clearinghouse for cases involving pornography and the First Amendment.

The National Obscenity Law Center (NOLC)
475 Riverside Drive, Suite 239
New York, NY 10115
(212) 870–3232
Web site: http://www.netcom.com/~nolc

The National Obscenity Law Center is a national clearinghouse in obscenity law operated by Morality in Media, a national interfaith antipornography organization. The NOLC makes information on obscenity and obscenity law available to law enforcement agencies, civic groups, and legislators.

Publications: Obscenity Law Bulletin, a bimonthly periodical; *Obscenity Law Reporter*, a three-volume history of obscenity law cases since 1800; and *The Handbook on the Prosecution of Obscenity Cases*, a guide for law enforcement officials.

PEN American Center
568 Broadway
New York, NY 10012–3225
(212) 334–1660
Fax: (212) 334–2181
E-mail: pen@pen.org
Web site: http://www.pen.org

PEN is a membership association of prominent literary writers and editors that defends the freedom of expression and promotes the reading of contemporary literature. PEN believes literature and ideas should not be inhibited by national borders, political systems, or political ideologies and works to publicize the plight of writers, artists, and others who are being punished for their convictions.

Publication: PEN Newsletter quarterly.

People for the American Way Foundation (PAW)
2000 M Street NW, Suite 400
Washington, DC 20036
(202) 467–4999
Fax: (203) 326–7329
E-mail: pfaw@pfaw.org
Web site: http://www.pfaw.org

People for the American Way Foundation is committed to the American ideals of pluralism and freedom of expression. It conducts research as well as legal and education work and monitors the religious right movement. PAW provides information for policy makers, scholars, and activists nationwide. It opposes groups that attempt to use religion to promote censorship and other antidemocratic values. PAW distributes educational materials and conducts studies on the state of censorship in America today. In 1990 People for the American Way founded the Artsave project to defend artistic expression at both the national and local levels.

Publication: Attacks on the Freedom to Learn, an annual report of censorship incidents and challenges.

Rock Out Censorship
P.O. Box 147
Jewett, OH 43986
(740) 946-2011
Fax: Same
Web site: http://www.theroc.org

Rock Out Censorship is an international grassroots network of music fans and musicians who oppose music censorship. Rock Out Censorship coordinates pro-music freedom campaigns and holds petition drives at rock concerts to protest music censorship. It also monitors instances of censorship in the music industry nationwide.

Publications: The Roc, a periodical devoted to music and fighting censorship.

The Rutherford Institute
P.O. Box 7482
Charlottesville, VA 22906
(804) 978-3888
Fax: (804) 978-1789
Web site: http://www.rutherford.org

Founded in 1982, the Rutherford Institute is an international civil liberties legal and educational organization that draws on its network of affiliate attorneys to defend individuals whose constitutional rights have been violated. The Rutherford Institute provides legal research resources for attorneys involved in constitutional litigation. Areas of interest to the Rutherford Institute include religious liberty, parental rights, and sexual harassment.

Publications: ACTION newsletter, as well as numerous educational pamphlets, papers, and books.

Student Press Law Center (SPLC)
1101 Wilson Boulevard, Suite 1910
Arlington, VA 22209-2248
(703) 807-1904
Web site: http://www.splc.org

The Student Press Law Center is the nation's only legal assistance agency devoted solely to educating high school and college journalists about their First Amendment rights and responsibilities. Run by journalists, journalism educators, and attorneys, the SPLC offers free legal advice and information to students, and it operates an attorney-referral network to help students whose freedom of expression has been infringed. Each year the SPLC receives approximately 2,000 requests for help and information. To educate students on legal topics, the SPLC publishes a variety of materials that it offers to the public at low cost.

Publications: Student Press Law Report.

Selected Print Resources 6

This chapter provides a list of books relevant to the discussion of censorship, violence, pornography, obscenity, freedom of expression in various media, and the issues of democracy and liberty in new media. Also listed are periodicals that may be of specific interest to those studying censorship in various media.

Books

General Books on Censorship and Free Expression

Beahm, George, ed. *War of Words: The Censorship Debate.* Kansas City, Mo.: Andrews and McMeel, 1993. 430 pages. ISBN 0836280156.

A collection of essays, interviews, and articles about censorship and free speech, written by artists, writers, politicians, and others.

Cleary, Edward J. *Beyond the Burning Cross: The First Amendment and the Landmark R.A.V. Case.* New York: Random House, 1994. 314 pages. ISBN 0679424601.

Cleary believed there was a difference between hate crime and hate thought. He tells the story of his attempt to take a controversial case involving a St. Paul hate crime statute all the way to the Supreme Court.

Downs, Robert B., and Ralph E. McCoy, eds. *The First Freedom Today: Critical Issues Relating to Censorship and to Intellectual Freedom.* Chicago: American Library Association, 1984. 341 pages. ISBN 0838904122.

A collection of essays by scholars, librarians, judges, and journalists on the history of censorship and the First Amendment, censorship in schools, and the freedom of the press.

Foerstel, Herbert. *Banned in the Media: A Reference Guide to Censorship in the Press, Motion Pictures, Broadcasting, and the Internet.* Westport, Conn.: Greenwood Press, 1998. 252 pages. ISBN 0313302456.

Foerstel, author of several works on censorship, presents a history of the regulation and censorship of various media, from newspapers and magazines to radio, movies, television, and the Internet. Of particular interest to Foerstel is the extent of corporate control over the media. Also included in this volume are interviews with freedom of expression advocates and victims of censorship.

Foerstel, Herbert. *Free Expression and Censorship in America: An Encyclopedia.* Westport, Conn.: Greenwood Publishing Group, 1997. 260 pages. ISBN 0313292310.

This is an encyclopedia containing entries ranging from the names of organizations involved in the censorship debate, to individuals noted for their contributions to intellectual freedom, to important legislation such as the Freedom of Information Act.

Garry, Patrick. *An American Paradox: Censorship in a Nation of Free Speech.* Westport, Conn.: Praeger, 1993. 157 pages. ISBN 0275945227.

Garry explores the conflict between the American rhetoric of free speech and individual liberty and the reality of censorship. He investigates where and when censorship has occurred in the United States and provides an explanation for its occurrence.

Harer, John B. *Intellectual Freedom: A Reference Handbook.*

Santa Barbara, Calif.: ABC-CLIO, 1992. 315 pages. ISBN 0874366690.

This volume contains an overview on the intellectual freedoms provided by the First Amendment to the Constitution, including freedom of speech, freedom of religion, freedom of the press, and the right to assembly. Important events in the history of intellectual freedom are listed, as are major anticensorship thinkers and activists as well as organizations devoted to intellectual freedom.

Harer, John B., and Steven R. Harris. *Censorship of Expression in the 1980s.* Westport, CT: Greenwood Press, 1994. 181 pages. ISBN 0313287465.

Using data from *Newsletter on Intellectual Freedom, Censorship News, Attacks on the Freedom to Learn,* and *Student Press Law Center Report,* the authors provide a statistical analysis of censorship in various forms of expression during the 1980s, with charts, tables, and graphs depicting the reasons for, the nature of, and the initiators behind censorship activity in the United States.

Hentoff, Nat. *Free Speech for Me But not for Thee: How the American Left and Right Relentlessly Censor Each Other.* New York: Harper Collins, 1993. 416 pages. ISBN 0060995106.

A recognized authority on the First Amendment, journalist Nat Hentoff looks at assaults on free speech that have come from all parts of the political spectrum and examines current challenges to the First Amendment. He discusses how left-wing political thinking, in the form of political correctness, has censored some works of literature on the basis that it is racist or sexist. Hentoff also looks at the way conservative forces such as the religious right have attempted to censor expression for the sake of preserving family values.

Hentoff, Nat. *Living the Bill of Rights: How to Be an Authentic American.* New York: Harper Collins, 1998. 288 pages. ISBN 0060190108.

Hentoff tells the stories of Americans whose lives and work have affirmed the principles embodied in the Constitution's Bill of Rights. Among those cited are Supreme Court justices and lawyers whose commitment to individual rights enabled them to affirm the First Amendment, even if it meant championing an unpopular cause. Among the individuals Hentoff highlights is the African American lawyer Anthony Griffin, who defended the Ku Klux Klan while working as an ACLU volunteer.

Kramnick, Isaac, and R. Laurence Moore. *The Godless Constitution: The Case against Religious Correctness.* New York: Norton, 1996. 191 pages. ISBN 0393039617.

Kramnick and Moore look at the history of the separation of church and state in America, and they refute the claims of those who argue there is a historical basis for the mixing of religion and politics.

Marsh, Dave. *50 Ways to Fight Censorship and Important Facts to Know about Censors.* New York: Thunder's Mouth Press, 1991. 128 pages. ISBN 1560250119.

Marsh is a rock music critic and author of numerous books on rock and roll artists. In this book he explores censorship in music, literature, and the visual arts and lists anticensorship organizations. The book provides the reader with tools to help fight censorship.

Pally, Marcia. *Sex and Sensibility: Reflections on Forbidden Mirrors and the Will to Censor.* Hopewell, N.J.: Ecco Press, 1994. 198 pages. ISBN 0990013648.

Written by the founder of Feminists for Free Expression, a group that champions freedom of speech, this book questions the desire of censors to blame images for the problems of society. It also contains resource materials on sexually explicit and violent material in the mass media, and information on censorship, research, and public policy.

Rauch, Jonathan. *Kindly Inquisitors: The New Attacks on Free Thought.* Chicago: University of Chicago Press, 1993. 178 pages. ISBN 0226705757.

This Cato Institute Book explores the role of liberal science in defending the freedom of speech and thought. It examines the different attacks on freedom of inquiry that have come from fundamentalists, humanitarians, and egalitarians.

Steiner, Rudolf, and the ALA Office for Intellectual Freedom. *Intellectual Freedom Manual.* Chicago: American Library Association, 1996. 393 pages. ISBN 083890677X.

Now in its fourth edition, the American Library Association's *Intellectual Freedom Manual* reviews the official policies of the ALA on intellectual freedom and teaches librarians and others how to resist censorship.

Theoharis, Athan G., ed. *A Culture of Secrecy: The Government Versus the People's Right to Know.* Topeka: University Press of Kansas, 1998. 248 pages. 070060880X.

Essays contributed by lawyers, scholars, and journalists explore how government agencies like the FBI, CIA, National Security Administration, and National Security Council circumvent the Freedom of Information Act and manage to keep information secret. Cases such as the Kennedy assassination, the Nixon tapes, and the FBI practice of maintaining files on prominent individuals are reviewed.

White, Harry. *Anatomy of Censorship: Why Censors Have It Wrong.* Lanham, Md.: University Press of America, 1997. 122 pages. ISBN 0761807012.

White examines the theoretical underpinnings behind censorship activity to understand the motivations of censors. He refutes the arguments of those who censor, explaining why he believes their actions are unjustified.

Zeisel, William, ed. *Censorship: 500 Years of Conflict.* New York: Oxford University Press, 1984. 144 pages. ISBN 0195035291.

Published by the New York Public Library for its 1984 exhibition "Censorship: 500 Years of Conflict," this book provides a history of prohibited books in the United States and abroad, as well as color images of some of the first editions of controversial works. The book also offers nine essays chronicling the history of censorship.

Censorship in Art

Bolton, Richard. *Culture Wars: Documents from the Recent Controversies in the Arts.* New York: New Press, 1992. 363 pages. ISBN 1565840119.

Using documentary evidence in the form of letters, speeches, and articles written by legislators, artists, art critics, and activists, *Culture Wars* illustrates the battle between censors and advocates of free expression. Bolton explores the cultural conflict between conservative pro-family forces and liberal artistic impulses, and he looks at the ways in which the National Endowment for the Arts has become the battleground for these conflicts.

Burt, Richard, ed. *The Administration of Aesthetics: Censorship, Political Criticism, and the Public Sphere.* Minneapolis: University of Minnesota Press, 1994. 381 pages. ISBN 0816623651.

The Administration of Aesthetics explores the philosophical and political issues behind state and federal funding for the arts. It raises the questions of whose art should be funded and whose interests should be taken into account. The book is volume 7 in a University of Minnesota Cultural Politics series.

Dubin, Steven C. *Arresting Images: Impolitic Art and Uncivil Actions.* New York: Routledge, 1994. 374 pages. ISBN 0415904358.

This book explores the battles fought over "subversive" art that depicts taboo images, such as Andres Serrano's *Piss Christ*, Robert Mapplethorpe's homoerotic photographs, and the works of various controversial performance artists. Issues of arts patronage are explored, including the pros and cons of using taxpayers' money to fund the National Endowment for the Arts.

Heins, Marjorie. *Sex, Sin, and Blasphemy: A Guide to America's Censorship Wars.* New York: New Press, 1993. 210 pages. ISBN 1565840623.

Written by the director of the American Civil Liberties Union's Arts Censorship Project, this book explores the importance of artistic freedom as well as the role that sex has played in art. Heins also discusses the legal tactics of those who oppose or support artistic freedom.

Censorship in Cyberspace

Cooper, Jonathan, ed. *Liberating Cyberspace: Civil Liberties, Human Rights, and the Internet.* Chicago: Pluto Press, 1998. 240 pages. ISBN 0745312993.

This book explores the issues raised by new communications media. Cooper discusses the Freedom of Information Act, the right to privacy, and the laws and legislation affecting computers and the Internet and examines the ways in which the Internet can be kept a free and open medium for communication.

Gelman, Robert B. Stanton McCandish, and Esther Dyson. *Protecting Yourself Online: The Definitive Resource on Safety, Freedom, and Privacy in Cyberspace.* New York: Harper Collins, 1998. 198 pages. ISBN 0062515128.

The Electronic Frontier Foundation, an organization that promotes constitutional liberties in cyberspace, presents this book, which deals with issues of security and privacy on-line, as well as a host of other Internet-related issues such as viruses, on-line etiquette, and the protection of material and intellectual property on-line. The book also covers the debate over on-line censorship versus freedom of expression.

Miller, Steven E. *Civilizing Cyberspace: Policy, Power, and the Information Superhighway.* New York: Addison Wesley, 1995. 413 pages. ISBN 0201847604.

A member of Computer Professionals for Social Responsibility's national board of directors, Miller is well equipped to discuss the issues that have emerged as a result of new computer technology. He looks at past inventions that had sweeping applications and altered people's everyday lives, such as the railroad, and investigates how people approached and dealt with that new technology. He then looks at new communications and information technology in the same light, attempting to learn from the lessons of the past.

Wallace, Jonathan, and Mark Mangan. *Sex, Laws, and Cyberspace: Freedom and Censorship on the Frontiers of the Online Revolution.* New York: M and T Books, 1996. 304 pages. ISBN 0805047670.

This book examines the ways in which the growth of the Internet and on-line services has created new legal and ethical debates about whether or not to regulate this new media. Authors Wallace and Mangan look at computer crime and laws and legislation that affect computer users, such as obscenity law. They explore the concept of freedom of speech and look at what is and what is not legal on-line.

Censorship in Film

Black, Gregory D. *Hollywood Censored: Morality Codes, Catholics, and the Movies.* Cambridge: Cambridge University Press, 1994. 336 pages. ISBN 05211452996.

This book looks at the moral and ethical pressures placed on the early motion picture industry by moviegoers, the U.S. government, and the Catholic Church. Black explores the archives of the National Legion of Decency and examines the ways in which conservative scrutiny led to self-censorship in the movie industry.

Bouzereau, Laurent. *The Cutting Room Floor.* New York: Carol Publishing Group, 1994. 243 pages. ISBN 0806514914.

Bouzereau discusses the editing process in the motion picture industry, detailing plots, themes, and censored scenes that never made it to the final production in a number of popular movies such as *Close Encounters of the Third Kind, Basic Instinct,* and *Death Becomes Her.*

Bouzereau, Laurent. *Ultraviolent Movies: From Sam Peckinpah to Quentin Tarantino.* Seacacus, N.J.: Carol Publishing Group, 1998 (revised edition). 244 pages. ISBN 0806520450.

This book explores violence in motion pictures from westerns to horror films. Bouzereau looks at the motivations of those who have directed violent films, including Sam Peckinpah, Oliver Stone, Stanley Kubrick, Martin Scorsese, and Quentin Tarantino. He also discusses the genre of extremely violent films, such as *Pulp Fiction,* which celebrate violence for its own sake without including any moral perspective.

Keough, Peter. *Flesh and Blood: The National Society of Film Critics on Sex, Violence, and Censorship.* San Francisco: Mercury House, 1995. 398 pages. ISBN 1562790765.

Film reviewers from the National Society of Film Critics discuss the role of sex and violence in artistic works and explore the ways in which these controversial themes can be dealt with responsibly, without the need for censorship.

Lyons, Charles. *The New Censors: Movies and the Culture Wars.* Philadelphia: Temple University Press, 1997. 235 pages. ISBN 1566395119.

This book is part of the Culture and Moving Image series published by Temple University Press. Looking back at the past fifteen years of film history, the book explores protests against films and looks at the motivations of those who attempt to censor films. Specific movies that aroused controversy are discussed, as is the cultural conflict between censors and free expression advocates.

Miller, Frank. *Censored Hollywood: Sex, Sin, and Violence on Screen*. Atlanta: Turner Publishers, 1994. 312 pages. ISBN 1570361169.

This book points out the ways each generation expresses its moral bias through film censorship. Miller looks at the Motion Picture Producers and Distributors of America's production code, adopted in 1930. He explores changes in the film industry and provides a background for the contemporary film ratings system.

Petrie, Ruth, ed. *Film and Censorship: The Index Reader.* London: Cassell Academic, 1997. 193 pages. ISBN 0304339369.

This book contains a collection of articles reprinted from *Index on Censorship* magazine. Written by filmmakers, film critics, and film scholars, these articles explore the different impulses behind the censorship of film since its very beginnings.

Walsh, Frank. *Sin and Censorship: The Catholic Church and the Motion Picture Industry.* New Haven, Conn.: Yale University Press, 1996. 394 pages. ISBN 0300063733.

The author examines the influence of the Catholic Church in the early years of the motion picture industry in America. Moral and ethical arguments for the censorship of film are discussed, as are the actions of the National Legion of Decency. Walsh demonstrates the breadth of the Catholic Church's influence on filmmakers, producers, and distributors.

Censorship in Literature

Coetzee, J. M. *Giving Offense: Essays on Censorship.* Chicago: University of Chicago Press, 1996. 289 pages. ISBN 0226111741.

Eight essays by the South African novelist J. M. Coetzee explore the censoring of South African writers and the travails of other writers who have suffered as a result of their beliefs. Coetzee investigates the trials of Soviet writer Alexander Solzhenitsyn and the beliefs and trials of the British writer D. H. Lawrence. He also writes about the American feminist Catharine MacKinnon and his objections to her antipornography campaign.

Vanderham, Paul. *James Joyce and Censorship: The Trials of Ulysses.* New York: New York University Press, 1998. 242 pages. ISBN 0814787908.

Vanderham looks at James Joyce's controversial novel *Ulysses* and traces its history of censorship. He tracks the long process of publishing the novel in the United States, where it was banned for years as "obscene" literature. Following the arguments of the lawyers and literary critics who defended *Ulysses* against claims of obscenity and pornography, Vanderham shows how the novel was eventually allowed into the United States.

Walker, Alice. ***Banned***. San Francisco: Aunt Lute Books, 1996. 105 pages. ISBN 1879960478.

Author Alice Walker examines the decision that led to the removal of two of her short stories from a statewide examination in California in 1994. Parental objections that the stories were "anti-Christian" and "anti-carnivore" contributed to the decision to remove them. Quoting passages from these stories and some of her other works, Walker defends the right to free expression and the freedom to read.

Censorship in Public Schools and Libraries

Bielfield, Arlene, and Lawrence Cheeseman. ***Library Patrons and the Law***. New York: Neal-Schuman Publishers, 1995. 142 pages. ISBN 1555701329.

A resource for librarians and librarian patrons, this book discusses privacy rights, civil rights, legislation affecting libraries in the United States, and censorship in libraries. The rights of library patrons are outlined, and methods for creating library policy that is in line with existing law are also provided.

Burress, Lee. ***Battle of the Books: Literary Censorship in the Public Schools 1950–1985***. Metuchen, N.J.: Scarecrow Press, 1989. 385 pages. ISBN 0810821516.

Covering a 35-year period, this book provides an overview of what is challenged or censored in public schools, who is doing the censoring, and what the objections of the censors are. The book contains an appendix of 800 titles from children's and young adult literature that have been challenged in public schools and libraries.

DelFattore, Joan. ***What Johnny Shouldn't Read: Textbook Censorship in America***. New Haven, Conn.: Yale University Press, 1992. 209 pages. ISBN 0300057091.

Written by an English professor, this book chronicles the major cases of textbook censorship in America, recreating the conflicts. Case studies of specific incidents show how each one began and was resolved. The book also discusses the economics of the textbook publishing industry and the ways in which the industry responds to censors.

Foerstel, Herbert N. *Banned in the U.S.A.: A Reference Guide to Book Censorship in Schools and Public Libraries.* Westport, Conn.: Greenwood Publishing Group, 1994. 231 pages. ISBN 0313285179.

A survey of the most frequently banned books of the past two decades, this guide takes an in-depth look at eight prominent bookbanning incidents in the United States from 1976 to 1992, summarizing each one. Foerstel also interviews three popular but controversial young adult authors—Judy Blume, Robert Cormier, and Katherine Paterson—whose books have been challenged many times in American schools and libraries.

Johnson, Claudia. *Stifled Laughter: One Woman's Story about Fighting Censorship.* Golden, Colo.: Fulcrum Publishers, 1994. 176 pages. ISBN 1555912001.

This is the true story of Claudia Johnson's attempt to restore two classics of children's literature to her Lake City, Florida, school district, where they had been banned. Though she encountered intense local opposition, Johnson never gave up on her effort to fight censorship, and her efforts made her the first recipient of the prestigious PEN/Newman's Own First Amendment Award.

Karolides, Nicholas J., Lee Burress, and John M. Kean, eds. *Censored Books: Critical Viewpoints.* Metuchen, N.J.: Scarecrow Press, 1993. 498 pages. ISBN 0910826674.

A collection of 63 essays written by novelists, poets, playwrights, young adult authors, and teachers, this book examines literature that is frequently challenged or banned in schools and libraries. The book provides a background to censorship in American literature and includes analyses and defenses of books that have been frequently challenged or censored.

Loewen, James W. *Lies My Teacher Told Me: Everything Your American History Textbook Got Wrong.* New York: New Press, 1995. 372 pages. ISBN 156584100X.

Loewen looks at American history textbooks commonly used in schools today and exposes what he sees in them, including errors of fact, ideological biases, omissions, distortions of truth, and a tendency to show only one side of a complex person or issue.

Monks, Merri M., and Donna Reidy Pistolis, eds. *Hit List: Frequently Challenged Books for Young Adults.* Chicago: American Library Association, 1996. 92 pages. ISBN 0838934595.

Compiled by the Intellectual Freedom Committee of the Young Adult Library Services Association and the American Library Association, this reference book provides a list of the most frequently challenged books in public schools and libraries. *Hit List* also offers reasons why these books have been challenged, as well as information on who is doing the challenging.

Moon, Eric, ed. *Book Selection and Censorship in the Sixties.* New York: R. R. Bowker Company, 1969. 421 pages. ISBN 0835202054.

A series of addresses, essays, and lectures, some of them previously published in the *Library Journal,* this book addresses issues of censorship encountered by libraries during the 1960s. Book selection as a subtle form of censorship is addressed, and librarians talk about their methods for choosing books and other materials. The book includes surveys and some statistical data on challenged materials.

Robbins, Louise S. *Censorship and the American Library: The American Library Association's Response to Threats to Intellectual Freedom, 1939–1969.* Westport, Conn.: Greenwood Publishing Group, 1997. 251 pages. ISBN 0313296448.

Relying extensively on primary sources, Robbins traces the development of American librarianship and its gradual embrace of intellectual freedom. From the *Library Bill of Rights* of 1939, to the development of the Freedom to Read Foundation in 1969, to contemporary issues addressed by the American Library Association, the book chronicles the development of an ideology of intellectual freedom.

Censorship in the News Media

Herman, Edward S., and Noam Chomsky, *Manufacturing Consent: The Political Economy of the Mass Media.* New York: Pantheon, 1988. 412 pages. ISBN 0394549260.

In this exploration of world politics, mass media, and public opinion, Herman and Chomsky attempt to show how an elite group structures the news by framing stories in a certain way, as well as how the news is affected by market forces and the publishing industry. *Manufacturing Consent* questions the notion of objectivity in the media and examines the ways in which information is shaped and distributed.

Jenson, Carl. *Twenty Years of Censored News.* New York: Seven Stories Press, 1997. 352 pages. ISBN 1888363517.

Project Censored, founded by Dr. Carl Jensen, tracks censorship in the news media and publishes an annual yearbook of stories that fail to make it into the mainstream media. This book presents 200 stories from a 20-year period and represents a compilation of Project Censored's work since 1976. Censored stories are broken down by category, and the top ten most-censored subjects in the news, including political, corporate, international, and military issues, are listed.

MacArthur, John R. *Second Front: Censorship and Propaganda in the Gulf War.* Berkeley: University of California Press, 1993. 274 pages. ISBN 0520083989.

This book explores the press coverage of the Persian Gulf War of 1991, unique among wars for the way in which the media was able to broadcast information about the conflict to world audiences almost continuously. MacArthur examines how the military managed the media during the war and looks at the ways in which the news media practiced forms of self-censorship.

Books on Censorship for Young Adults

Hentoff, Nat. *The Day They Came to Arrest the Book.* New York: Delacorte, 1982. 169 pages. ISBN 0440020395.

Renowned journalist and First Amendment advocate Nat Hentoff tells a story about censorship in this novel about high school students and teachers who become players in a censorship case involving the book *Huckleberry Finn*.

Hentoff, Nat. *The First Freedom: The Tumultuous History of Free Speech in America.* New York: Delacorte Press, 1980. 340 pages. ISBN 0440038582.

Hentoff presents a history of free speech in America from earliest times to the present. He includes accounts of contemporary and controversial court cases such as *Smith v. Collin,* which involved the right of Nazi party members to march in a community of Holocaust survivors, and *Tinker v. Des Moines,* which addressed the rights of students to express themselves in school.

Sherrow, Victoria. ***Censorship in Schools.*** Issues in Focus Series. Springfield, N.J.: Enslow Publishers, 1996. 128 pages. ISBN 089490728X.

Censorship in Schools examines the censorship of school textbooks and courses and children's and young adult literature, as well as the censorship of students' right to free expression. The book provides a historical perspective on censorship that includes the viewpoints of both censors and anti-censors.

Stay, Byron L., ed. ***Censorship: Opposing Viewpoints.*** San Diego: Greenhaven Press, 1997. 192 pages. ISBN 1565105079.

In an attempt to provide the reader with a background to the censorship conflict, this book presents articles and speeches written by people on both sides of the censorship debate. The result is an objective look at the issue of censorship and a greater understanding of the motivations of both free expression advocates and those who feel the need to protect others from harmful or dangerous information.

Weiss, Ann E. ***Who's to Know?: Information, the Media, and Public Awareness.*** Boston: Houghton Mifflin, 1990. 182 pages. ISBN 0395497027.

This book examines the public's right to know and looks at factors that interfere with that right and limit public knowledge. Citing specific events, the author explains the ways in which the government and the media can manipulate the flow of information. The Freedom of Information Act, the right to privacy, and the role of the mass media in bringing information before the public are discussed.

Zeinert, Karen. ***Free Speech: From Newspapers to Music Lyrics.*** Issues in Focus Series. Springfield, N.J.: Enslow Publishers, 1995. 129 pages. ISBN 0894906348.

This book contains chapters on the issues raised by censorship in various media, such as newspapers, magazines, books, radio, television, movies, and music lyrics. First Amendment rights such as the freedom of speech and the freedom of the press are discussed.

Books on Protecting Children from Violent or Explicit Media

Axelrod, Lauryn. *TV-Proof Your Kids: A Parent's Guide to Safe and Healthy Viewing.* New York: Carol Publishing Group, 1997. 256 pages. ISBN 1559724080.

Written by an educator and media specialist, this book offers parents ways to make TV-watching a healthy experience for kids. Rather than remove television from their lives, Axelrod suggests parents select age-appropriate materials for their children, and she offers advice on how to avoid violence on TV.

Hughes, Donna Rice, and Pamela T. Campbell. *Kids Online: Protecting Your Children in Cyberspace.* Chicago: Fleming H. Revell Company, 1998. 272 pages. ISBN 080075672X.

This book encourages parents to become computer literate and create guidelines for their children's web use; it advocates the use of filtering and blocking software on home, school, and library computers used by children and discusses the benefits of customized Internet access.

Levine, Madeline. *See No Evil: A Guide to Protecting Our Children from Media Violence.* San Francisco: Jossey-Bass Publishers. 304 pages. ISBN 0787943479.

Levine offers practical advice on how to protect your children from exposure to excessive violence on television.

Mack, Dana. *The Assault on Parenthood: How Our Culture Undermines the Family.* New York: Simon and Schuster, 1997. 256 pages. ISBN 0684807742.

The author analyzes government policies, economic pressures, and other factors that have had a negative effect on families and the proliferation of family values. Mack explores the ways in which government programs, public schools, and the court system have usurped the roles of parents, and talks to parents who are trying to reclaim their role from outside institutions that do not always respect their values.

Medved, Michael and Diane. *Saving Childhood: Protecting Our Children from the National Assault on Innocence.* New York: Harper Collins, 1998. 324 pages. ISBN 0060173726.

Parents Michael and Diane Medved explore the ways in which children are exposed to shocking, troubling, or explicit information through television, news, video games, sex education and self-esteem education in schools, peer groups, gangs, and parental absence in their lives. The book teaches parents how to keep their children feeling secure and hopeful by reading to them, spending time with them, and discouraging TV-watching.

Books on Obscenity and Pornography

Hixson, Richard F. *Pornography and the Justices: The Supreme Court and the Intractable Obscenity Problem.* Carbondale, Ill.: Southern Illinois University Press, 1996. 268 pages. ISBN 0809320576.

Hixson provides a historical overview of the Supreme Court's position on pornography, analyzing different cases and the approach of different justices to help readers understand how the Court has grappled with the issues of free speech and pornography over time.

MacKinnon, Catharine A., and Andrea Dworkin. *In Harm's Way: The Pornography Civil Rights Hearings.* Cambridge: Harvard University Press, 1998. 512 pages. ISBN 0674445791.

Testimony from victims of pornography is combined with essays by MacKinnon and Dworkin to present a powerful argument for why pornography is a form of sexual discrimination. The authors explain how pornography is currently protected by constitutional law.

Saunders, Kevin W. *Violence as Obscenity: Limiting the Media's First Amendment Protections.* Constitutional Conflicts Series. Durham, N.C.: Duke University Press, 1996. 246 pages. ISBN 0822317872.

A study of violence in the mass media and of the movement to curb the proliferation of violent images, this book compares violence to obscenity, which is not protected by the First Amendment, and makes a case for enlarging the definition of obscenity.

Periodicals

Extra!
Dept. CN, P.O. Box 170
Congers, NY 10920
(800) 847–3993
Web site: http://www.fair.org
Bimonthly. $19/year

Published by Fairness and Accuracy in Reporting (FAIR), *Extra!* is a magazine of media criticism. Its articles examine biased reporting, censored news stories, and media mergers.

Index on Censorship
Lancaster House
33 Islington High Street
London N1 9LH, UK
(44 171) 278-2313
Web site: http://www.oneworld.org/index
Bimonthly. $52/year; $35/year for students

Published in trade paperback format in 192-page issues and available in bookstores across the United States, *Index on Censorship* provides summaries of censorship incidents occurring around the world and prints works from censored writers. *Index on Censorship* also publishes an on-line version (see electronic journals).

Newsletter on Intellectual Freedom
50 East Huron Street
Chicago, IL, 60611
(312) 944–6780
Web site: http://www.ala.org
Bimonthly. $40/year

Published by the American Library Association, *Newsletter on Intellectual Freedom* reports on censorship and anticensorship activity nationwide, and it provides summaries on First Amendment rulings in U.S. courts.

School Library Media Quarterly (SLMQ)
50 East Huron Street
Chicago, IL 60611
(312) 944–6780

Quarterly. $40/year nonmembers
Web site: http://www.ala.org

School Library Media Quarterly is the official publication of the American Association of School Librarians, a division of the American Library Association. *SLMQ* offers articles of particular interest to school library media specialists and others confronted with censorship challenges. Subscription is free to members of the American Association of School Librarians.

Wired
P.O. Box 55688
Boulder, CO 80323–5688
(800) SO WIRED
Web site: http://www.wired.com
Monthly. $33/year

Wired is a periodical devoted to the computer age and the future. It covers current events and the important issues that shape our society. In addition to award-winning features, *Wired* contains interesting sections such as *Cyber Rights Now!*, devoted to on-line activism for freedom of expression, and *Reality Check*, which interviews technology experts on the latest research and development.

Selected Nonprint Resources 7

This chapter provides a list of nonprint resources that are available on the Internet. Some of the entries denote organizations that have only a "virtual" or on-line presence; other entries refer to documents online or to research projects on censorship that are maintained and continually updated by various individuals, universities, or other organizations. Some of the on-line periodicals require a subscription and password. Also included in this chapter is a listing of videotapes on topics such as censorship, free expression, privacy and freedom on the Internet, and encryption.

Electronic Journals, Magazines, and Newsletters

CDT Policy Posts http://www.cdt.org/publications/pubs.html

The Center for Democracy and Technology (CDT), a self-described "authoritative source for accurate, up-to-date information and detailed analysis of public policy issues affecting civil liberties online," publishes *Policy Posts* to update subscribers on recent events and legislation.

College and Research Libraries News http://www.ala.org/acrl/ c%26rlnew2.html

The on-line version of this newsletter often has articles on the debate surrounding filtering programs and the decisions being made in libraries around the country on how to confront new information technology.

Crypt Newsletter http://www.soci.niu.edu/~crypt

A newsletter of information, satire, and commentary on Internet culture, computer crime, and information warfare.

EFFector Online Newsletter http://www.eff.org/pub/EFF/ Newsletters/EFFector

A newsletter from the Electronic Frontier Foundation, which supports privacy and freedom of speech on-line, offering news and updates on its activism.

Index On Censorship on-line version, http://www.oneworld.org/index_oc

This is the on-line version of the bimonthly magazine for free speech that offers reporting, cartoons, banned literature, and commentary from some of the world's best writers on how free speech affects contemporary political issues; the on-line site also offers an index of back issues.

Telecom Post http://www.cpsr.org/telecom-post/telepost.02.html

The *Telecom Post* is a newsletter affiliated with Computer Professionals for Social Responsibility (CPSR), a nationwide public-interest organization that examines the impact of technology on society. The *Telecom Post* maintains a searchable database of information related to the development and passage of legislation affecting electronic communication.

Wired magazine on-line, http://www.wired.com

The on-line version of *Wired* monthly, featuring news, current events, and the future of technology. Past issues can be accessed or searched from the web site.

Web Sites with Links to Censorship Topics

Banned Books Online
http://www.cs.cmu.edu/People/spok/banned-books.html

This on-line banned books page, maintained by Carnegie Mellon University, features an overview on the history of prohibited books as well as contemporary titles banned in schools and libraries. The site offers links to the texts of many of the books themselves.

Bonfire of Liberties: Censorship of the Humanities
http://www.humanities-interactive.org/bonfireindex.html

An interactive exhibit sponsored by the Texas Humanities Resource Center, this site features a gallery of pictures with corresponding text that leads the viewer through the history of censorship.

The Censorship Pages
http://www.booksatoz.com/censorship

The Censorship Pages offers links to both pro- and anticensorship sites, and it offers links to articles on censorship and book banning.

The Censorware Project
http://www.spectacle.org/cqp

Formed in 1997 by a group of writers and net activists, the Censorware Project is a clearinghouse for the discussion of commercially available filtering and blocking software products and their effectiveness.

Citizens Internet Empowerment Coalition
http://www.ciec.org

The Citizens Internet Empowerment Coalition (CIEC) is a nationwide grassroots network of Internet users, publishers, on-line service providers, and library and civil liberties groups, all of whom advocate freedom of expression in the Information Age. This site contains press releases and news reports related to the CIEC's successful challenge of the Communications Decency Act as well as information on how to take action to protect the future of free expression on the Internet.

Electronic Frontier Foundation's Blue Ribbon Campaign
http://www.eff.org/blueribbon

A grassroots campaign for on-line intellectual freedom sponsored by the Electronic Frontier Foundation (EFF), a nonprofit civil liberties organization working to protect privacy, freedom of expression, and access to public resources and information on-line. The EFF also promotes responsibility in new media. This site offers an archive with a topical annotated index to articles on subjects such as censorship, digital liberty, and encryption.

Electronic Frontier Foundation Quotes Collection
http://www.eff.org/pub/EFF/quotes.eff

This file contains an excellent selection of historic and contemporary quotations described as "the wittiest and stupidest, most sublime and most inane comments ever said or written about free speech, cryptography, privacy, civil liberties, networking, government, communication, society, human nature, reason, optimism and pessimism, progress, and more." Updated frequently, the site welcomes additions.

The File Room
http://www.ncsa.uiuc.edu/SDG/IT94/Proceedings/Arts/brenner/roussos.html

An interactive computer project addressing cultural censorship, the File Room is an illustrated archive of cultural censorship that has occurred throughout history and around the world. The File Room challenges existing definitions of censorship and provides a forum for exploring the issues connected with cultural censorship of the visual arts, music, dance, theater, and literature.

Free Expression Network (FEN)
http://www.freeexpression.org

The Free Expression Network was established to counter attacks on the First Amendment and the right to free expression. FEN is a coalition of writers, artists, filmmakers, librarians, booksellers, publishers, lawyers, and individuals.

Freedom Forum Online
http://www.freedomforum.org

The Freedom Forum is an international nonpartisan foundation devoted to free speech and free press. Freedom Forum operates the world's only interactive news museum and conducts programs in journalism education and press freedom.

Freedom of the Press
http://www.lib.siu.siu.edu/cni/homepage.html

The on-line version of this annotated bibliography by Frank E. McCoy offers over 8,000 entries relevant to censorship and the freedom of expression in all forms of media—including books, pamphlets, periodicals, newspapers, movies, music, radio, television, and theater. The bibliography includes a subject index to major court decisions relevant to censorship and offers a chronology of censorship.

Green Ribbon Campaign for Responsibility in Free Speech
*http://*www.zondervan.com/green

Sponsored by the Zondervan, a Christian publisher, the Green Ribbon Campaign advocates the responsible use of free speech and believes in the principle of self-restraint as a means of preventing the proliferation of vulgar, profane, violent, and insulting speech.

Internet Free Expression Alliance
http://www.ifea.net

The Internet Free Expression Alliance is dedicated to protecting the free flow of information on the Internet and promotes an informed public debate of proposals to rate or filter on-line content.

Peacefire
http://www.peacefire.org

Created in 1996 to represent students' and minors' interests in the debate over free speech on the Internet, Peacefire offers full membership only to people under the age of 21. Primarily student run, Peacefire opposes the use of filtering software because it would deny young people full access to the Internet and because it claims that filtering programs block a host of "clean" sites inadvertently. Peacefire's young members are particularly concerned because they are still of an age where they may be affected by the adoption of filtering software.

Project Censored
http://zippy.sonoma.edu/ProjectCensored

This annual nationwide media research project is in its twenty-second year and is currently administered by Sonoma State University in California. Project Censored publishes *Censored: The News that Didn't Make the News* each year. Project Censored's goal is to publicize the extent of censorship in society by locating significant news stories that the public never gets to hear. Project Censored aims to promote responsible journalism and balanced, unbiased media coverage.

Steven Dunlap's Intellectual Freedom Page
http://internet.ggu.edu/university_library/ifalpha.html

This site is an excellent resource for those interested in censorship issues; it offers A to Z links and listings of organizations and electronic texts that offer information on censorship and intellectual freedom.

Voters Telecommunications Watch (VTW)
http://www.vtw.org

VTW is a New York–based citizens' Internet civil liberties group formed in 1994 to safeguard individual liberty, privacy, and electronic freedom. VTW recommends legislation, actively participates in the democratic process, monitors the voting records and positions of elected officials, informs the public, and helps other grassroots campaigns.

Electronic Texts

"A Legal Definition of Obscenity and Pornography"
http://internet.ggu.edu/university_library.reg/legal_obscene.html

By James S. Tyre, this article offers current legal definitions for obscenity and pornography.

"Faulty Filters: How Content Filters Block Access to Kid-Friendly Information on the Internet"
http://www.epic.org

A 1997 survey of filtered web sites sponsored by the Electronic Privacy Information Center.

"Towards a Conceptual Path of Support for School Library Media Specialists with Material Challenges"
http://www.ala.org/aasl/SLMQ/slmq_toc.html

By Dianne McAfee Hopkins, associate professor, School of Library and Information Studies, University of Wisconsin at Madison. Outlines the resources available to library media specialists who have experienced challenges to the presence or appropriateness of library media center materials.

Videotapes

The following videotapes provide a sampling of the types of recordings available on issues of censorship, intellectual freedom, the Internet, and the First Amendment. Some of these videotapes are available in public libraries, and when applicable, their call numbers are given. Another excellent source for videotapes is the Computer, Freedom, and Privacy (CFP) Video Library Project, which offers an extensive collection of videos about free speech on-line and civil liberties in the new information age. The CFP videos were created during lectures and panel discussions held at annual conferences (1991–present) organized by Computer Professionals for Social Responsibility. The address of the CFP Video Library Project is P.O. Box 912, Topanga, CA 90290; phone, (800) 235–4922; e-mail, cfpvideo@earthlink.net. An on-line catalog is available at http://www.forests.com/cfpvideo.

Videos for Purchase

Censorship and Content Control on the Internet (CFP-609)
Length: 80 minutes
Date: 1996
Cost: $55

This video explores how different societies, both in the United States and abroad, are attempting to deal with controversial material on the Internet. In the United States, the most heated debate centers on whether to limit minors' access to the Internet to protect them from sexually explicit or pornographic content on-line.

Germany has considered whether to extend its restriction on Neo-Nazi hate speech to the Internet. Other countries debate whether to extend freedom of expression to the Internet. Featuring Daniel Weitzner, formerly of the Center for Democracy and Technology; Herbert Burkert, European Commission, Gara LaMarche of Human Rights Watch, and Kate Martin, from the Center for National Security Studies.

The Communications Decency Act of 1996 (CFP-605)
Length: 102 minutes
Date: 1996
Cost: $55

The Communications Decency Act, part of the 1996 Telecommunications Reform Act, made it a criminal offense (punishable by two years in prison and a fine) to transfer any words or pictures that might be considered "indecent" via computer, when it is possible for someone under the age of 18 to access this material. The American Civil Liberties Union and 60,000 Internet users promptly filed suit to challenge the constitutionality of the measure. This panel, taped while the trial was underway, includes speakers on both sides of the issue explaining their viewpoints on the act. Featuring Daniel Weitzner, of the Center for Democracy and Technology; Jill Lesser, with People for the American Way; Barry Steinhardt, representing the ACLU; and Bruce Taylor, from the National Law Center for Families and Children.

*The Constitution in Cyberspace: Law
and Liberty Beyond the Electronic Frontier* (CFP-101)
Length: 75 minutes
Date: 1991
Cost: $55

Harvard Law professor and expert on constitutional law Laurence Tribe speaks on the ways in which he believes the Constitution can apply to new technology. Tribe proposes adding a twenty-seventh constitutional amendment that would extend Bill of Rights protections to the domain of cyberspace.

*Copyright and Freedom of Expression
on the Internet* (CFP-606)
Length: 108 minutes

Date: 1996
Cost: $55

This video asks the question, is copyright obsolete in the digital age? Are the economics of digitally producing and distributing information products so fundamentally different that copyright becomes a barrier to free speech? Or, in the global networked world, will there inevitably be only one law of copyright and free expression? What will it be? Featuring: Pamela Samuelson, professor of Law, Cornell University; David Post, Cyberspace Law Institute; Brent Hugenholtz, Information Law Institute, Amsterdam; and Chris Barlas, Author's Licensing and Collecting Society in London.

Cryptography, Privacy, and National Security (CFP-210)
Length: 77 minutes
Date: 1993
Cost: $55

This video panel explores the topic of cryptography and the legal and security issues surrounding encryption. Should the government be permitted to restrict the use of cryptography, or to restrict export of products that use encryption? Featuring Jim Bidzos, RSA Data Security; David Bellin, Pratt Institute; John Perry Barlow, Electronic Frontier Foundation; John Gilmore, Cygnus Support; and Whitfield Diffie, Sunsoft, Inc. Dorothy Denning of Georgetown University chairs the discussion.

Electronic Speech, Press and Assembly:
An Internet History (CFP-112)
Length: 91 minutes
Date: 1991
Cost $55

Panelists explore civil liberties on-line and discuss the freedoms of speech, the right to assembly, and the freedom to publish on-line. Featuring John McMullen, Newsbytes; George Perry, vice president and general counsel, Prodigy Services Company; Jack Rickard, editor, *Boardwatch* magazine; Lance Rose, an attorney, and David Hughes, Old Colorado City Communications. Eric Lieberman chairs the discussion.

Freedom in Cyberspace (CFP-201)
Length: 50 minutes

Date: 1993
Cost: $55

Freedom Forum's Allen Neuharth, founder of *USA Today*, takes aim at the American Newspaper Publishers' stance on government regulation and the developing world of electronic publishing. He cites differing regulatory constraints on publishers of newspapers, owners of television stations, and the telephone services. The video also makes predictions about the future of newspapers, arguing that the rights to freedom of the press that have protected print media for 200 years must apply equally to evolving telecommunications-based information services.

Law Enforcement and Civil Liberties (CFP-108)
Length: 83 minutes
Date: 1991
Cost: $55

Panelists discuss whether new technology has inhibited law enforcement's ability to define proper procedures against unwarranted search and seizure as well as the application of the Bill of Rights to cyberspace. Featuring Sheldon Zenner, attorney, Katten, Muchin & Zavis; Kenneth Rosenblatt, deputy district attorney, Santa Clara County, California; Mitchell Kapor, president, Electronic Frontier Foundation; Mike Gibbons, supervisory special agent, FBI; Cliff Figallo, executive director, The WELL; Sharon Beckman, attorney, Silverglate & Good; and Mark Rasch, attorney, U.S. Department of Justice. Dorothy Denning chairs the panel.

Law Enforcement Practices and Problems (CFP-107)
Length: 90 minutes
Date: 1991
Cost: $55

In this video the investigators and prosecutors on the front lines of computer crime explain their procedures, including due process and concern about deterring criminal behavior. Details of the notorious Operation Sundevil are discussed, and panelists consider the problems of jurisdiction in cyberspace as well as the need for computer professionals to work with law enforcement agencies to educate officers in new technology. Featuring Robert Snyder, Public Safety Department, Division of Police, Columbus, Ohio; Donald Delaney, senior investigator, New York State Police;

Dale Boll, United States Secret Service, Washington, D.C.; and Don Ingraham, assistant district attorney, Alameda County, California. Glenn Tenney is chair.

Legislation and Regulation (CFP-109)
Length: 82 minutes
Date: 1991
Cost: $55

Panelists discuss the role of the law in protecting privacy and promoting access to information as well as the legal problems created by new computer technology. Panelists include Jerry Berman, director of the Center for Democracy and Technology and former ACLU Information Technology Project Director; Paul Bernstein, attorney with the Electronic Bar Association; and Craig Schiffries, Senate Judiciary Committee.

Limiting Online Speech on Campus (CFP-607)
Length: 90 minutes
Date: 1996
Cost: $55

Universities own the wires for their campus networks, provide equipment, and feel responsible for protecting students as well as their own public image; students value privacy and have a penchant for on-line mischief. This video presents a provocative and often humorous inquiry into conflicts faced by academic communities as administrative concerns clash with student efforts to push the bounds of the on-line world. The video features Arthur Miller, ABC's *Good Morning America* legal editor and Harvard law professor; Greg Jackson, director of Academic Computing, MIT; Declan McCullagh, 1994-1995 student body president of Carnegie Mellon University; Peter Toren, representing the U.S. Department of Justice Computer Crime Unit; Harvey Silverglate, civil liberties defense attorney; and Rikki Klieman, Court TV anchor.

*Privacy & Intellectual Freedom
in the Digital Library* (CFP-208)
Length: 86 minutes
Date: 1993
Cost: $55

How are your privacy rights protected when you seek information? How do libraries protect your right of access to electronic

218 Selected Nonprint Resources

information? How can automation vendors help? How can current library practices to protect intellectual freedom be applied to emerging information networks? These issues are explored by panel members Marc Rotenberg, Computer Professionals for Social Responsibility; Robert A. Walton, CLSI, Inc.; Steve Cisler, Apple Computer, Inc.; and Jean Armour Polly, Liverpool (NY) Public Library.

Where Do We Go from Here? (CFP-115)
Length: 82 minutes
Date: 1991
Cost: $55

Panelists discuss how best to protect personal privacy and fundamental freedoms on-line in the future. Featuring Mary Culnan, associate professor, Georgetown University; David Hughes, Old City Colorado Communications; Donald Ingraham, assistant district attorney, Alameda County, California; Mitch Kapor, president, Electronic Frontier Foundation; Eric Lieberman, Paul Bernstein, and Donn Parker, SRI International; Craig Schiffires, Senate Judiciary Committee; and Robert Veeder, Office of Management and Budget. Jim Warren is chair.

Videos Available in Public Libraries

Books under Fire
Length: 58 minutes
Date: 1983
Library of Congress call number: Z658

Intended for teenagers and adults, this video tracks a censorship case in a Maine school and then widens to include a national perspective on book censorship in U.S. public schools. The video also features commentary from journalist and First Amendment authority Nat Hentoff.

Censorship and the Arts
Length: 29 minutes
Date: 1990
New York Public Library call number: MGZIC 9–3087

Censorship and the Arts was produced by ARC Videodance as part of the television series *Eye on Dance*. Performance artists discuss the National Endowment for the Arts decision to require grant recipients to sign an anti-obscenity clause. Other topics include the role of art in providing social commentary, the importance of grants to artists, and the expression of homosexual themes in art.

Censorship or Selection: Choosing Books for Public Schools
Length: 60 minutes
Date: 1982
Library of Congress Call Number: LB3047

Intended for adult audiences, this video was published by the New York Media and Society Seminar in conjunction with the National School Boards Association Convention. It presents the findings of the 1982 conference of the National School Boards Association and focuses on required reading in the classroom, textbook selection, the removal of school library materials, and the legality of teaching Scientific Creationism.

The Day They Came to Arrest the Book
Length: 47 minutes
Date: 1987
Library of Congress call number: Z657

This is the film version of Nat Hentoff's novel about high school students and teachers who are drawn into in a censorship case involving the book *The Adventures of Huckleberry Finn*.

Glossary

abstinence: The voluntary forgoing of an appetite or craving, such as the practice of abstaining from sex.

bias: Personal, especially unreasonable or distorted, judgment; prejudice.

censor: One who supervises conduct or morals, often examining materials for objectionable content.

challenges: Attacks made on certain books or materials in a public school curriculum or public library because of objections to the content or nature of the material.

Communications Decency Act (CDA): A section of the 1996 telecommunications bill, later overturned by the Supreme Court because it was ruled injurious to free speech on-line, that outlawed the dissemination of pornography on the Internet in situations where anyone under the age of 18 might have access to the material.

comstockery: Term named for censor Anthony Comstock that refers to the strict censorship of materials considered obscene, or any overzealous opposition to supposed immorality.

creationism: The belief or theory that the world, including all matter and life, was created by God out of nothing.

cryptography: The enciphering and deciphering of messages in a secret code or writing, often used to create secure electronic communications.

curriculum: The courses offered by an educational institution.

221

cyberspace: General term used to refer to the realm of the Internet and digital information.

cyberwarfare: Acts of war designed to topple infrastructure and create havoc, involving attacks on computer networks and digital systems.

encryption: The encoding of material so that it cannot be detected by unwanted parties.

evolution: The theory that all life can trace its origin to pre-existing life that has been modified over generations to comprise its present form.

filtering programs: Software blocking programs such as NetNanny or CyberSitter that allow individuals to select and screen out any content they wish to avoid while navigating the Internet.

First Amendment: The First Amendment to the U.S. Constitution, in the Bill of Rights, that protects the freedoms of speech and religion, the right to assembly, and the freedom of the press.

hate speech: Speech that is designed to inflict harm on a person or group, usually because of their gender, sexual orientation, or ethnic or racial background.

Internet: Also known as "the Net," the system of networked computers and databases that allows communication and the exchange of ideas and information between distant people who are linked by computers.

National Endowment for the Arts (NEA): An office of the federal government created to support and foster the arts in the United States.

obscenity: Behavior, language, or material that is repulsive to the senses or to one's morality.

political correctness: A trend that evolved by the early 1990s to stand for a culture of "correct" language and behavior that was tolerant and accepting of diversity and multiculturalism and intolerant of those unwilling to go along with this movement. Sensitivity training workshops, for example, were designed to promote politically correct behavior in the workplace, and speech codes were designed to promote politically correct ways of behavior on college campuses.

pornography: Material such as books or photographs that depict sexual behavior and are designed to cause sexual arousal.

production codes: Standards applied to the film industry in order to maintain a particular level of morality in film.

profanity: Vulgar, irreverent language, such as swear words.

rap: A genre of music that emerged from the African American community in the 1970s when artists began sampling records to create a never-ending dance mix, which is often accompanied by the rhyming talk or commentary of an MC (master of ceremonies).

speech codes: Codes installed by colleges and other institutions designed to prevent hate speech and punish those who use it.

Glossary 223

stereotypes: A mental picture held in common by members of a group and representing an oversimplified assumption or opinion.

v-chip: Technology currently in use in television, and proposed for the Internet, that allows individuals to block out channels whose content they consider inappropriate.

voluntary ratings system: A proposed method of blocking inappropriate or pornographic material on-line that would require all creators of web sites to rate their site according to a set scale, much the way movies are now rated as G, PG, PG-13, R, etc.

voucher system: A plan that would allow parents to use their education tax dollars toward a private or parochial school education for their children.

web site: An address on the Internet, or World Wide Web, that provides information on various topics.

Index

AAA. *See* American Arts Alliance
AASG. *See* American Anti-Slavery Group
ABA. *See* American Booksellers Association
ABFFE. *See* American Booksellers Foundation for Free Expression
Abrams v. United States, 48, 78–79
Abstinence, defined, 221
Accuracy in Media, 171–172
ACLU. *See* American Civil Liberties Union
The Adventures of Huckleberry Finn, 8, 9
Advisory Committee to the Congressional Internet Caucus, 60
"Aeropagitica," 45
AFA. *See* American Family Association
AIDS, 6, 35
AIM. *See* Accuracy in Media
ALA. *See* American Library Association
Albigensian, heretics, 44
America On Line, 30
American Anti-Slavery Group, 29
American Arts Alliance, 26, 172
American Association of University Women, 35
American Booksellers Association, 172
American Booksellers Foundation for Free Expression, 172–173
American Civil Liberties Union, 17–18, 32–33, 34, 48, 49, 55, 57–58, 65–66, 173
Briefing Paper Number 14, 123–129
American Family Association, 13, 20, 22–23, 72, 74–75, 173–174
American Library Association, 5, 8, 13–14, 33, 61–62, 174
Diversity in Collection Development, 113–114
Freedom to Read, 118–123
intellectual freedom policies, 192–193
Library Bill of Rights, 14, 112–113, 169
Office for Intellectual Freedom, 68–69, 104–105
OIF censorship database, 104–105
American Psycho, 53–54
American Union Against Militarism, 58
Analects, 44
Angelou, Maya, 6, 7–8, 10
Angels on Broadway, 21
The Arabian Nights, 47
Are You There God? It's Me Margaret, 60
Aristophanes, 44, 47
Arrested Development, 19
Artistic freedom, 20–24, 38, 167
Arts, 17–26
 books on censorship in, 193–194
Arts funding, 24–26
 quotations, 168–169
Artsave project, 21–22

225

Athie, Mohammed, 29
Aztecs, 44

Baldwin, Roger Nash, 48, 57–58, 65
Banned Books Online (website), 209
"Banned Books Week," 14
Barnes and Noble, 55
Bauer, Gary L., 58–59
Beatles, 51
Beef, 56
Beloved, 8
Berman, Jerry, 59–60
Bias, defined, 221
Bill of Rights, 58, 68, 191–192
Birth of a Nation, 20, 47
Bitol, Solange, 17–18
Black Beauty, 7
Black Boy, 52
Blubber, 60
The Bluest Eye, 8
Blume, Judy, 8, 60–61
Board of Education v. Pico, 52, 95–97
Boccaccio, 47
Bonfire of Liberties (website), 209
"The bonfire of the vanities," 44
Book burning, 44, 45, 49
Books under Fire (video), 218
Bookstores, 71–72
Boston Investigator, 46
Bowdler, Thomas, 46
Bowdlerization, defined, 46
Bradbury, Ray, 168
Briefing Paper Number 14 (ACLU), 123–129
Brown University, 15
Bruce, Lenny, 51
Bryan, William Jennings, 4, 48
Burt, David, 61–62
Butler v. Michigan, 50, 81–82

Campaign for Working Families, 59
CAN. *See* Christian Action Network
Candide, 48
Canterbury Tales, 47
Catch-22, 8
The Catcher in the Rye, 8, 31

Catholic Church, 2, 45, 50, 196, 197
Catholic League for Religious and Civil Rights, 21
CCV. *See* Citizens for Community Values
CDA. *See* Communications Decency Act
CDT. *See* Center for Democracy and Technology
CDT Policy Posts (online periodical), 207
CEE. *See* Citizens for Excellence in Education
Censor, defined, 1, 221
Censorship
  in America, 2–4
  in the arts, 17–26, 193–194
  books on, 189–193, 201–203
  books on young adults and, 201–203
  defined, 1, 5–6
  electronic documents on, 212–213
  electronic journals, magazines, and newsletters on, 207–208
  forms of, 2
  grassroots, 1–2
  Internet, 30–32, 169, 194–195
  in the news media, 27–30, 47, 49, 52, 200–201
  official acts of, 1–2
  periodicals on, 205–206
  in public education, 4–6, 38, 198–200
  quotations, 166–168
  sources of, 12–15
  videos on, 213–219
  web sites on, 209–212
  what constitutes, 1–2
Censorship and Content Control on the Internet (video), 213–214
Censorship and the Arts (video), 218–219
Censorship or Selection (video), 219
The Censorship Pages (website), 209
The Censorware Project (website), 209
Center for Democracy and Technology, 36, 59–60, 174–175

Challenges to books or material,
    5–10, 105, 106f., 107f., 108f.,
    109f., 110f., 213
  defined, 221
Charles V, Emperor, 45
*Charter for a Family Friendly
    Library System*, 14, 114–118
Chaucer, Geoffrey, 47, 168
Child Online Protection Act, 33,
    56
Child Pornography Prevention
    Act, 55
Children, protecting from violent
    or explicit media (books on),
    203–204
The Children's Hour, 21
The Chocolate War, 63
Christian Action Network, 11, 13,
    14, 22–23, 175
Christian Coalition, 20, 175–176
Christianity, 9
Cinderella, 14
Citizens for Community Values,
    176
Citizens for Excellence in
    Education, 13, 14, 176
Citizens Internet Empowerment
    Coalition, 31, 60
  website, 209–210
Civil War, 47
Clinton, Bill, 29, 31, 56
College and Research Libraries News
    (online periodical), 208
The Color Purple, 8
Committee for the Suppression of
    Vice, 62
Committee to Protect Journalists,
    176–177
Communications Decency Act of
    1996, 3–4, 30–32, 54, 55, 60,
    69
  defined, 221
  and *Reno v. ACLU*, 32–33
  text, 140–149
*The Communications Decency Act of
    1996* (video), 214
Communism, 50
Comparative religion, 8–9, 10–11
Computer Professionals for Social
    Responsibility, 177
Computers. *See also* Internet
  encryption software, 37–38, 56

Comstock, Anthony, 47, 62–63,
    221
Comstock Law, 47, 62–63
Comstockery, defined, 221
Confucius, 2, 44
Congressional Black Caucus,
    29
The Constitution in Cyberspace
    (video), 214
"Cop Killer," 19–20, 54
*Copyright and Freedom of
    Expression on the Internet*
    (video), 214–215
Cormier, Robert, 63–64
Corpus Christi, 21, 56
Council on Interracial Books for
    Children, 14
CPJ. *See* Committee to Protect
    Journalists
CPSR. *See* Computer
    Professionals for Social
    Responsibility
Creationism, 4–5, 51, 52
  defined, 221
Crypt Newsletter (online
    periodical), 208
Cryptography, defined, 221
*Cryptography, Privacy, and
    National Security* (video),
    215
Curriculum, defined, 221
Cyberspace, defined, 222
Cyberwarfare, defined, 222

Darrow, Clarence, 4, 48
David, 44
*The Day They Came to Arrest the
    Book* (video), 219
Decameron, 47
Deenie, 8, 60
Deep Throat, 20
Defoe, Daniel, 47
Deliverance, 8
Dennett, Mary Ware, 48
Dickey, James, 8
Diversity in Collection Development,
    113–114
Dobson, James C., 12, 59, 64–65
The Doll's House, 21, 52
Dominic, Saint, 44
Dreiser, Theodore, 62
Dworkin, Andrea, 15

228 Index

Eagle Forum, 177–178
Eastman, Crystal, 58, 65–66
Ed Sullivan Show, 17, 50
Edict of Worms, 45
Education
   books on censorship and, 198–200
   challenges to books or material, 5–10, 105, 106f., 107f., 108f., 109f., 110f., 213
   family orientation, 58–59
   religion and science, 4–5, 38
   sex, 6–8
   textbook controversies, 10–12
EFF. *See* Electronic Frontier Foundation
EFFector Online Newsletter (online periodical), 208
Einstein, Albert, 49
Electronic Communications Privacy Act of 1986, 60
Electronic Frontier Foundation, 31–32, 178
   Blue Ribbon Campaign (website), 210
   Quotes Collection (website), 210
Electronic Privacy Information Center, 33, 178
   Faulty Filters: How Content Filters Block Access to Kid-Friendly Information on the Internet, 149–158
Electronic Speech, Press and Assembly (video), 215
Ellis, Bret Easton, 53–54
Emerson, Ralph Waldo, 169
Encryption software, 37–38, 56
   defined, 222
Engel v. Vitale, 84–86
England, 2, 45–46
Enough Is Enough, 179
EPIC. *See* Electronic Privacy Information Center
Epperson v. Arkansas, 51, 88–89
Espionage Act, 3, 47–48
Esquire magazine, 49
Ethiopia, 52
Evolution, defined, 222

FAIR. *See* Fairness and Accuracy in Reporting

Fairness and Accuracy in Reporting, 28, 179
Family Friendly Libraries, 13–14, 67, 180
   Charter for a Family Friendly Library System, 14, 114–118
Family Research Council, 12, 22–23, 58, 59, 180
The Family Shakespeare, 46
Farrakhan, Louis, 29
"Faulty Filters" (electronic document), 212
Faulty Filters: How Content Filters Block Access to Kid-Friendly Information on the Internet, 149–158
FCC v. Pacifica Foundation, 92–94
Federal Anti-Obscenity Act, 47
Feminists for Free Expression, 180–181
FFE. *See* Feminists for Free Expression
FFL. *See* Family Friendly Libraries
The File Room (website), 210
Films, 50. *See also* Motion Picture Association of America, Motion Picture Producers and Distributors of America
   books on censorship and, 195–197
   ratings, 51, 52, 53
   violence in, 196
Filtering Facts, 61, 181
Filtering programs, defined, 222
Filtering software, 32, 34–36, 56, 61–62
   Faulty Filters: How Content Filters Block Access to Kid-Friendly Information on the Internet, 149–158
First Amendment, 3, 4, 16, 46, 50, 68, 166
   books on, 191
   defined, 222
First Amendment Center, 181–182
Flag Protection Act, 54
Focus on the Family, 5, 9, 11, 12–13, 22–23, 55, 59, 64–65, 70, 182
FOIA. *See* Freedom of Information Act
Forever, 8

Forster, E. M., 9
Fourteenth Amendment, 47
France, 44, 45
Franklin, Benjamin, 167
FRC. *See* Family Research Council
Free Expression Network (website), 210
Free speech, 68
  books on, 189–193
Freedom Forum Online (website), 211
Freedom of Information Act, 190, 193, 194
  excerpt, 158–166
Freedom of the Press (website), 211
Freedom to Read, 118–123
Freedom to Read Foundation, 69
Freedom to Read Foundation News, 69
Friends, 23

George III, King, 46
Gore, Tipper, 17, 66–67
Gounaud, Karen Jo, 67
Green Ribbon Campaign for Responsibility in Free Speech (website), 211
Griswold vs. Connecticut, 51, 87–88
Gutenberg, Johannes, 44

Hamilton, David, 55
Hannegan v. Esquire, 49, 79–80
Hate speech, 15–16, 53, 54
  defined, 222
Hays, Will, 20
Hays Code, 20, 49, 51
  text, 129–140
Hazelwood School District v. Kuhlmeier, 53, 99–100
Heller, Joseph, 8
Helms, Jesse, 24–25, 53, 72
Hemingway, Ernest, 49
Henry VIII, King, 45
Hentoff, Nat, 68
A Hero Ain't Nothing But a Sandwich, 52
Heston, Charlton, 19–20
Holmes, Oliver Wendell, 48
Homosexuality, 13, 22–23
Hughes, Langston, 10

I Am the Cheese, 63, 64
I Know Why the Caged Bird Sings, 6, 7–8
Ibsen, Henrik, 21, 52
Ice-T, 19, 54
In the Night Kitchen, 8
Index librorum prohibitorum, 45
Index of Forbidden Books, 45, 50
Index on Censorship (online periodical), 208
The Indian in the Cupboard, 9–10
Indiana Jones and the Temple of Doom, 52
Inherit the Wind, 21
Intellectual Freedom Action News, 69
International Coalition Against Chattel Slavery, 29
International Gay and Lesbian Human Rights Commission, 34
Internet, 30–32, 39, 169
  books on censorship and, 194–195
  Center for Democracy and Technology, 36, 59–60, 174–175
  and children, 302
  defined, 222
  Faulty Filters: How Content Filters Block Access to Kid-Friendly Information on the Internet, 149–158
  filtering software, 32, 34–36, 56, 61–62
  libraries with acceptable use policy, 105, 110t., 111f.
  and library access, 35–36, 56
  privacy and protection, 195
  V-chip, 33–35
Internet Free Expression Alliance (website), 211
Internet School Filtering Act, 56

Jacobellis v. Ohio, 86–87
Jacoby, Jeff, 169
Jefferson, Thomas, 46, 166
Jensen, Carl, 27
Jong, Erica, 167
Joseph Burstyn, Inc. v. Wilson, 50, 81
Joyce, James, 3, 49, 62, 197–198

Kanawha County (West Virginia) High School, 11–12, 51–52
Kennedy, John F., 167
Khomeini, Ayatollah, 53
Kids Fund, 61
Kilpatrick, James, 169
Kneeland, Abner, 46
Krug, Judith, 68–69
Ku Klux Klan, 20
Kushner, Tony, 21

Lady Chatterly's Lover, 3, 50
The Last Picture Show, 20
The Last Temptation of Christ, 20
Law Enforcement and Civil Liberties (video), 216
Law Enforcement Practices and Problems (video), 216–217
Lawrence, D. H., 50, 62, 197
"A Legal Definition of Obscenity and Pornography" (electronic document), 212
Legislation and Regulation (video), 217
Leo X, Pope, 45
Lewis, C. S., 167
Libraries, 169. *See also* American Library Association
  acceptable use policy, 105, 110t., 111f.
  books on censorship and, 198–200
  challenges to books or material, 105, 106f., 107f., 108f., 109tf, 110f., 213
  and Internet access, 35–36, 56
Libraries for the Future, 182–183
Library Bill of Rights, 14, 112–113, 169
Limiting Online Speech on Campus (video), 217
Literature
  books on censorship and, 197–198
  quotations, 168
Little Black Sambo, 14
Little Red Riding Hood, 7, 14, 53
LLF. *See* Libraries for the Future
Lolita, 3
Loudon vs. Board of Trustees of the Loudon County Library, 56

"Louie Louie," 17
Lovejoy, Elijah, 46
Luther, Martin, 45
Lysistrata, 44, 47

MacKinnon, Catharine, 15, 197
Mad Cow Disease, 56
Manhattan Theater Club, 21, 56
Mann, Sally, 69–71
Mapplethorpe, Robert, 25
Massachusetts, 45, 46
Maurice, 9
MC Lyte, 19
McCain, John, 36, 56
McCarthy, Joseph, 50
McNally, Terrence, 21, 56
The Media Coalition, Inc., 183
The Merchant of Venice, 52
Michelangelo, 44
Michigan, University of, 53
A Midsummer Night's Dream, 24
Military Honor and Decency Act, 55
Miller v. California, 51, 91–92
Million Man March, 29
Milton, John, 45, 168
Moliere, 45
Moll Flanders, 47
Morality in Media, 14, 183–184
Morrison, Toni, 8
Motion Picture Association of America, 20
  ratings, 51, 52, 53
Motion Picture Producers and Distributors of America, 20, 49, 197
Motion Picture Production Code of 1930, 129–140, 197
MPAA. *See* Motion Picture Association of America
MPPDA. *See* Motion Picture Producers and Distributors of America
Multiculturalism, 8–9, 10–11
Music lyrics, 17–20, 53, 54

NAACP. *See* National Association for the Advancement of Colored People
NACE. *See* National Association of Christian Educators
Nasty as They Wanna Be, 19, 54

National Association for the Advancement of Colored People, 14, 20, 29
National Association of Christian Educators, 176
National Campaign for Freedom of Expression, 17, 184–185
National Civil Liberties Bureau, 58, 65
National Coalition to Protect Children and Families, 6, 185
National Committee on Freedom from Censorship, 49
National Endowment for the Arts, 13, 24–26, 53, 194
  defined, 222
National Endowment for the Humanities, 13
National Law Center for Children and Families, 35, 185–186
National Legion of Decency, 196, 197
The National Obscenity Law Center, 186
National Political Congress of Black Women, 19, 73
National Society of Film Critics, 196
Natonal Organization for Women, 34
Nazis, 49
  U.S., 52
NCFE. *See* National Campaign for Freedom of Expression
NCLB. *See* National Civil Liberties Bureau
NCPCF. *See* National Coalition to Protect Children and Families
NEA. *See* National Endowment for the Arts
NEH. *See* National Endowment for the Humanities
New York Society for the Suppression of Vice, 62
New York Times, 51
New York Times v. United States, 90–91
New York v. Ferber, 97–98
New York Weekly Journal, 46
News media, 27–30, 47, 49, 52

books on censorship and, 200–201
Newsletter on Intellectual Freedom, 69
Ninety-Five Theses, 45
NLC. *See* National Law Center for Children and Families
NOLC. *See* The National Obscenity Law Center
North Briton, 46

Obscenity, 3–4, 47, 50, 51
  books on, 204
  defined, 222
Of Mice and Men, 8
Offensive language, 8, 9–10
Operation Rescue, 55
Overton, William R., 52

Palmer, Mitchell, 48
Parents Music Resource Center, 17, 18, 53, 54, 66, 67
Paul, Saint, 168
PAW. *See* People for the American Way Foundation
Peacefire, 34
  website, 211–212
PEN American Center, 186–187
Penal Lexicon, 34
Pennsylvania, University of, 16, 54
Pentagon Papers, 27, 51
People for the American Way Foundation, 5, 6, 105, 187
  Artistic Freedom Under Attack (quotation), 167
  Artsave project, 21–22
Periodicals on censorship, 205–26
Persian Gulf War, 201
Philadelphia, 9
"Piss Christ," 25, 72
Plato, 168
PMRC. *See* Parents Music Resource Center
Political correctness, 15–16, 39, 53, 54
  defined, 222
Pornography, 6, 14–15, 55, 56
  books on, 204
  defined, 222
  Internet, 30, 32, 54, 67
Pornography Victims Compensation Act, 15

Powell, Michael, 71–72
Powell's Bookstore, 71
Presley, Elvis, 17, 50
Privacy & Intellectual Freedom in the Digital Library (video), 217–218
Production codes, defined, 222
Profanity, 8
  defined, 222
Project Censored, 27, 28, 201
  website, 212
Pumsy in Pursuit of Excellence, 9

Queen Latifah, 19

Racism, 9–10, 14, 20, 24
Rap music, 18–20, 54, 74
  defined, 222
Reagan, Ronald, and administration, 59, 65
Religious right, 13–14
Remarque, Erich Maria, 49
Reno v. ACLU, 32–33, 55, 103–104, 169
Rhode Island colony, 45
Rock Out Censorship, 17, 187
Roger Baldwin Medal of Liberty, 58
Roman Empire censor, 43–44
Roth v. United States, 50, 82–84
Rushdie, Salman, 53, 167
The Rutherford Institute, 188

Salinger, J. D., 8
Salt-n-Pepa, 19
Sanger, Margaret, 3, 47, 62–63
Sanger, William, 63
The Satanic Verses, 53
Savonarola, 44
Schlesinger, Arthur Jr., 166–167
School newspapers, 53
School prayer, 53
Schools. *See* Education
Scopes, John T., 48
Scopes trial, 4, 21, 48
Sedition Acts, 3, 46, 47–48, 58
Self-censorship, 23–24
Sendak, Maurice, 8
Separation of church and state, 4
Serrano, Andres, 25, 72–73
Sex, 6–8, 13, 192, 194
Shakespeare, William, 52, 55

Shaw, George Bernard, 63, 168
Shih Huang-ti, 44
Simon and Schuster, 53–54
Simpson, O. J., 24
Sistine Chapel, 49
Slaughter House Five, 8, 52
Slavery, 46
  Sudan, 29–30
Smith v. Collin, 52, 94–95
Socrates, 2, 44
Solzhenitsyn, Alexander, 197
Song of Solomon, 8
Soul on Ice, 52
South Pacific, 23–24
Spanish empire, 44
Speech codes, defined, 222
SPLC. *See* Student Press Law Center
Stamp Act, 45–46
Steinbeck, John, 8
Stereotypes, defined, 222
Steven Dunlap's Intellectual Freedom Page (website), 212
Stevens, John Paul, 55, 169
Stewart, Potter, 168
Student Press Law Center, 188
Sturges, Jock, 55
Sudan, 29–30

Tacitus, 168
Tartuffe, 45
Taylor, Bruce, 25
Telecom Post (online periodical), 208
Telecommunications Reform Act of 1996, 30–31
Ten Commandments Defense Act, 59
Terry, Randall, 55, 70
Textbooks
  books on censorship and, 198–200, 202
  Kanawha County (West Virginia) High School, 11–12, 51–52
  liberal bias, 10–11
Then Again, Maybe I Won't, 8, 60
Thomas, Norman, 58, 65
Time magazine, 24
Time Warner Corporation, 18, 19, 23
The Tin Drum, 20–21, 55

Tinker v. Des Moines School District, 89–90
Tlacaelel, 168
Tolstoy, Leo, 62
"Towards a Conceptual Path of Support for School Library Media Specialists with Material Challenges" (electronic document), 213
TransAfrica, 29
Tropic of Cancer, 3
Tucker, C. Delores, 19, 73–74
Turner Broadcasting, 23
Twain, Mark, 8, 9
Twelfth Night, 55
2 Live Crew, 19
Tyndale, William, 45

Ulysses, 3, 49, 197–198
United States v. Eichman, 54, 100–101
Updike, John, 168–169

V-chip, 33–35
  defined, 222
Venus de Milo, 47
Vietnam War, 27, 51
Vintage Press, 53–54
Voltaire, 48, 62
Voluntary ratings system, defined, 222
Vonnegut, Kurt, 8
Voters Telecommunications Watch (website), 212
Voucher programs, 12–13
  defined, 222

"Wake Up, Little Susie," 17
Walker, Alice, 8
Wallace v. Jaffree, 52–53, 98
Web site, defined, 222
Weitzner, Daniel, 36
Where Do We Go from Here? (video), 218
Wildmon, Donald, 23, 74–75
Wilkes, John, 46
Williams, Roger, 45
Winfrey, Oprah, 56
Wired (online periodical), 208
Wisconsin, University of, 16, 54
Wisconsin v. Mitchell, 54, 101–102
Women's International League for Peace and Freedom, 65
Woolsey, John M., 49
Wright, Richard, 10
Wyatt, Barbara, 18

Young adults and censorship (books on), 201–203

Zappa, Frank, 53
Zenger, John Peter, 2–3, 46

Mary E. Hull is a freelance writer specializing in history and current events. She has authored several books for young adults including *Rosa Parks* (1994), *The Travels of Marco Polo* (1994), *Ethnic Violence* (1996), *Struggle and Love* (1997), *The History of Slavery* (1997), *The Mongol Empire* (1997), and *The Boston Tea Party in American History* (1998).